MICHAEL WITTMANN

AND THE WAFFEN SS
TIGER COMMANDERS OF THE
LEIBSTANDARTE IN WORLD WAR II

VOLUME TWO

Other titles in the Stackpole Military History Series

THE AMERICAN CIVIL WAR

Cavalry Raids of the Civil War
Pickett's Charge
Witness to Gettysburg

WORLD WAR II

Armor Battles of the Waffen-SS, 1943–45
Australian Commandos
The B-24 in China
Beyond the Beachhead
The Brandenburger Commandos
Bringing the Thunder
Coast Watching in World War II
Fist from the Sky
Flying American Combat Aircraft of World War II
Forging the Thunderbolt
Germany's Panzer Arm in World War II
Grenadiers
Infantry Aces
Luftwaffe Aces
Messerschmitts over Sicily
On the Canal
Packs On!
Panzer Aces
Panzer Aces II
Surviving Bataan and Beyond
The 12th SS, Volume One
The 12th SS, Volume Two
Tigers in the Mud

THE COLD WAR / VIETNAM

Flying American Combat Aircraft: The Cold War
Land with No Sun
Street without Joy

WARS OF THE MIDDLE EAST

Never-Ending Conflict

MICHAEL WITTMANN

AND THE WAFFEN SS TIGER COMMANDERS OF THE LEIBSTANDARTE IN WORLD WAR II

VOLUME TWO

Patrick Agte

STACKPOLE
BOOKS

Published in 2006 by
STACKPOLE BOOKS
5067 Ritter Road
Mechanicsburg, PA 17055
www.stackpolebooks.com

www.jjfpub.mb.ca

Printed in the United States of America

10 9 8 7 6 5 4 3 2 1

FIRST EDITION

Library of Congress Cataloging-in-Publication Data

Agte, Patrick.
    [Michael Wittmann, erfolgreichster Panzerkommandant im Zweiten Weltkrieg und die Tiger der Leibstandarte SS Adolf Hitler. English]
    Michael Wittmann and the Waffen SS Tiger commanders of the Leibstandarte in World War II / Patrick Agte.— 1st ed.
        p. cm. — (Stackpole Military history series)
    Originally published in English under the title: Michael Wittmann and the Tiger commanders of the Leibstandarte. 1996.
    Includes index.
    ISBN-13: 978-0-8117-3335-9
    ISBN-10: 0-8117-3335-1
    1. Waffen-SS. SS-Panzer-Division Leibstandarte SS "Adolf Hitler," 1. Tigerkompanie. 2. World War, 1939–1945—Regimental histories—Germany. 3. World War, 1939–1945—Campaigns—Eastern Front. 4. World War, 1939–1945—Campaigns—France. 5. Wittmann, Michael, 1914–1944. I. Agte, Patrick. Michael Wittmann and the Tiger commanders of the Leibstandarte. II. Title. III. Series.

D757.85.A3413 2006
940.54'1343—dc22
                                        2006008125

Table of Contents

The Allied Landing in Normandy

The 101st SS Panzer Battalion was a corps battalion; accordingly it was always committed wherever the situation at the front was the most critical and where immediate action was the dictate of the moment. To this end it was placed under the command of the units of the Ist SS Panzer Corps, whereby the heavy tanks were supposed to overcome any crises that arose. Consequently the battalion was employed in many sectors of the front, split apart and widely dispersed, as had been the case with the 13th Tiger Company. In reconstructing the actions of the 101st SS Panzer Battalion in Normandy, the author was forced to rely on accounts by individual members of the tank crews, which reflect the event from their point of view. Their experiences are therefore representative of their company and the entire battalion.

THE SITUATION ON THE INVASION FRONT

It is not my intention here to study and analyze the reasons why the Allied invasion succeeded, that subject has been sufficiently explored by other authors. Therefore at this point I will provide only a brief summary of the developing situation in Northern France in 1944.

The Foreign Armies West Department of the Wehrmacht High Command constantly kept track of the Allied divisions assembled in England. These assessments of the enemy situation were used to compile the Situation Report West. However, it must be emphasized that the figures given by Foreign Armies West were greatly exaggerated and in no way accurate. On 6 June 1944, the day of the invasion, the Allied Commander in Chief, General Eisenhower, had at his disposal thirty-seven divisions. In contrast, Foreign Armies West reported seventy divisions, or almost twice the actual number. The wilful falsification of the enemy situation was not the only source of error on the German side in Normandy, however.

An Allied landing in Normandy had been anticipated for a long time; however, there was less certainty as to the precise location of the invasion. The section of Channel Coast from Holland to the mouth of the Loire was a possibility. Generalfeldmarschall Rommel had been given the task of smashing the landings. He saw the beach as the main defensive area, and he had the coastal fortifications strengthened and the artillery positioned accordingly. The panzer divisions were to be positioned near the coast, as Rommel assigned them a major role in defeating the landings.

On the other hand General Freiherr Geyr von Schweppenburg, the Commander in Chief of Panzergruppe West, wanted to hold back the panzer divisions as a strategic reserve; in his opinion the landings could not be prevented. On account of the expected Allied air superiority, he planned to move the armored forces to the front primarily at night. Once the focal point of the enemy landing had been identified he would employ the panzers to fight a mobile battle and attack and destroy the enemy. In addition to landings on the coast, Geyr expected large-scale airborne landings, therefore he wanted to concentrate the panzer divisions in the forests north of Paris. In April 1944 Rommel obtained a decision from Hitler, who declared that the panzer divisions could be committed only with his approval. Generalfeldmarschall von Rundstedt, the Commander in Chief West, had three panzer divisions placed under his command. This was the start of the fragmentation of the German armored forces which was later to prove disastrous.

THE INVASION BEGINS

On 30 April 1944 the corps units and the corps headquarters of the Ist SS Panzer Corps Leibstandarte, which at that time was comprised of the 12th SS Panzer Division Hitlerjugend and the Panzer-Lehr Division, were declared part of the OKW (Armed Forces High Command) reserve. German signals intelligence had discovered that the invasion would take place in the first two weeks of June 1944. The BBC began with the transmission of coded signals to the French resistance groups. These broadcasts consisted of two parts; the first meant that the invasion would begin within the next fourteen days, the second that a landing on the French coast was to be expected within the next forty-eight hours.

The BBC sent the first parts on 1 June 1944; the coded signals did not escape German intelligence and the information was immediately passed on. The Armed Forces High Command forwarded the reports to its Foreign Armies West Department with a note that the invasion was to be expected in the next fourteen days, or by 15 June 1944. This office did nothing, however, nor did the Ic of the Commander in Chief West. What reasons could there have been for not issuing a general alert? Either the report wasn't taken seriously at first, or a certain circle had a personal interest in limiting the impact of these reports.

The second part of the transmissions was received at 2215 hours on 5 June 1944. The appropriate staffs were alerted. The Fifteenth Army took it upon itself to issue an alert. Nevertheless, the Ic (officer responsible for assessing the enemy situation) of the Commander in Chief West, General Staff Oberstleutnant Staubwasser, decided ". . . that an invasion is not very likely at this point in time." Therefore the Seventh Army and the Ist SS Panzer Corps were not alerted. Almost 6,500 ships were under way from England to the French coast on the night of 6 June 1944. The British landings began north of Caen at 0015 hours. Further reports came in; at 1000 hours on 6 June the Armed Forces High Command refused to release the Hitlerjugend Division but approved a move closer to the front. At 1430 hours the Hitlerjugend Division was finally released, followed soon afterward by the Ist SS Panzer Corps and all its corps units.

It was clear to Army Group B that this was the beginning of the Allied invasion, and not a "large-scale enemy operation" as Generalleutnant Speidel, the Chief of Staff, put it. The enemy had landed, not at the Pas de Calais or on either side of the mouth of the Somme, but in the sector mouth of the Dieves—southeast coast of the Cotentin Peninsula to east of Montebourg.

THE 101ST SS PANZER BATTALION ON THE MARCH TO THE INVASION FRONT, 6–12 JUNE, 1944

SS-Sturmmann Herbert Klod of the 101st Corps Escort Company of the Ist SS Panzer Corps Leibstandarte SS Adolf Hitler recalled the 5th of June 1944: "It was the evening before the start of the invasion. We were located in a small village between Paris and Normandy. The Ist Platoon had provided the guard for Obergruppenführer Sepp Dietrich, who had taken up quarters in a large country house. In front of the house was a gardner's shed, where we had set up a radio communications center whose code name was 'classmate.' I had begun the night shift in the center, the air was full of fighter-bombers. The company was quartered in the village. Before midnight an order came from headquarters to strengthen the guards and watch out for enemy paratroops. Afterward it was relatively quiet.

It may have been between 0200 and 0300 hours, when headquarters issued a code word with orders to immediately relay it to Obergruppenführer Dietrich. I called him at once and passed on the code word. He was still quite drowsy. Sepp Dietrich said to me, 'That's good, my boy. Wake the company at once, they know what's to be done.' I first woke our company commander, Hauptsturmführer Schmitz, and then the clerk, who had all the documents in case of emergency. Then the company was placed on alert status. Sepp Dietrich soon left in his armored troop carrier in the direction of Normandy. Beyond Verneuil we were attacked by fighter-bombers for the first time. We saw our first action in the evening . . ."

On that 6th of June 1944, a Tuesday, the Ist SS Panzer Corps, all corps units, the 1st SS Panzer Division Leibstandarte SS Adolf Hitler and the 12th SS Panzer Division Hitlerjugend were placed on alert. After the sounding of the alarm, which many thought was just another one of the many exercises, the 101st SS Panzer Battalion came to operational readiness with feverish haste. It had finally happened, the invasion had begun! SS-Oberscharführer Alfred Lasar, motor transport sergeant in the Headquarters Company, arrived at the battalion that day from Berlin-Spandau with the last of the armored troop carriers. The commander of the 1st Company, SS-Hauptsturmführer Möbius, gave a moving speech to his men. The young tank crews exuded energy and confidence, finally they were going to prove themselves. Before departure several tank crews of the 1st Company loaded wine into their tanks, "for bad times," as the saying went.

The Tiger Battalion set off for the invasion front at between 0200 and 0300 hours on 7 June. The Tigers rolled along the D 316 through Gournay-en-Bray in a southwesterly direction toward the Seine. They drove through the Fôrret de Lyons and the Levrierè Valley and arrived in Morgny on the morning of 7 June. At 1000 hours, the 1st Company was attacked by fighter-bombers near Morgny; the enemy aircraft were driven off by the defensive fire of the quadruple flak and anti-aircraft machine-guns. There were no losses, but the men of the 1st Company had been given a foretaste of what enemy air superiority meant. The battalion subsequently resumed its march and passed through Saussay-la-Champagne and les Andelys. As enemy bombs had rendered the Seine bridge impassable, the battalion had to turn on to National Highway N 14, which led to Paris.

Several members of the Tiger Battalion described the alert and the initial phase of the march to the coast. SS-Rottenführer Walter Lau was loader in Tiger 204 of the headquarters squad leader in Wittmann's 2nd Company, SS-Unterscharführer Seifert: "There were a number of practice alerts in the days before the actual Allied landing. They were always the same: once the alarm was sounded everyone had to get to the tanks, which were parked about 400 to 500 meters away in Château Elbeuls park, as quickly as possible, with his kit and ready to go.

When, on 6 June, the alarm was sounded at approximately 0600, just prior to reveille, Franz Elmer and I—probably acting like an old corporal—tried to be too clever by half. We wrapped our kit in a blanket and threw it under the bed, then calmly walked over to the tank, certain that the usual alert hubbub would be over in a half hour. But we became suspicious when we saw that the Spieß was also taking part in the 'practice alert' and even packed up the orderly room. Then, taking a look over the high wall around the château park, we saw that the surrounding roads were filled with march columns. As well, several radio operators had learned by listening to Radio Calais that the Tommies had landed in Normandy. The corporals now double-timed back to the kit they had left behind and just reached the tanks, which were beginning to roll out of the château park.

It was a pleasant march at first, for a panzer man always felt best in a moving tank. Spirits rose when it was announced that we would be driving through Paris. At the time we didn't know whether this drive through Paris was serving propaganda purposes or if it had been so arranged because the Seine bridges could not support our sixty-tonne tanks, there were conflicting rumors. In any case, as we were to learn in the coming night, the Royal Air Force was wise to our march. First, however, there was an imposing drive through the suburbs of Paris, then the city itself. Leading the way in a Schwimmwagen was Michael Wittmann in his leather jacket, and behind him in smart march order his fourteen Tigers, exactly by the numbers, as in the table of organization. It was early in the afternoon. I was glad to be loader. During the entire drive through Paris I stood in the loader's hatch, from where I had a magnificent view. Although we knew that we were heading toward a difficult action, these impressions of Paris were unforgettable.

We first drove for some kilometers through fashionable suburbs. We halted a number of times, on the one hand because Wittmann wanted to keep the company together as we drove through the city, he kept leaving the march column behind in his Schwimmwagen. On the other we had to repeatedly check the tracks, for the hard pavement and the steel road wheels wrecked the cotter pins and bolts in the running gear. (On the Eastern Front we had rubber tires on the road wheels.) We were anxious as to whether we would see the Champs d'Elysées and the Arc de Triomphe. Then suddenly we were there. Wittmann stood in his Schwimmwagen at an intersection and directed the tanks. We rolled about a kilometer down the boulevard with a view of the triumphal arch. There were many people standing at the side of the street, apparently the sixty-tonne giants made quite an impression. We stopped right at the triumphal arch, fifty meters to one side of the structure. We climbed out and had a chat as well as we could 'parlez vous français.' After fifteen or twenty minutes we set off again in the direction of Versailles. We drove past Versailles Castle in awe, and I imagine everyone recalled his history lesson from school on the founding of the Reich on 18 January 1871 and the shameful Treaty of Versailles.

We took shelter for the night a few hundred meters from the castle grounds, at the edge of an allotment colony. After refuelling and checking the tracks, we crawled unsuspectingly beneath the tanks. It happened sometime about midnight. As we later learned, members of the resistance had placed light signals near our bivouac, and a frightful bombing attack followed. We lay pressed flat under the tanks, and it seemed as if the tank would be lifted up. Although it was a considerable strain on our nerves, nothing happened to the company. All the bombs fell beside us in the allotment colony. In the light of the parachute flares the Tommies probably identified the huts as tanks and did a good job on them. Michael Wittmann quickly took charge of the situation. We were told to drive one at a time to the next appointed meeting place in the middle of a large forest, with lengthy intervals between vehicles. Hours later all vehicles reached the appointed meeting place and there we caught up on our interrupted night's rest. As far as I recall, there were no losses or damage of any sort. The next day, however, we heard over the so-called Soldiers' Radio Calais, which was in British hands, that 'the bloodhound Wittmann and his Tiger tanks had been destroyed near Versailles'."

SS-Sturmmann Ernst Kufner, the radio operator in Tiger 305 of company commander SS-Obersturmführer Hanno Raasch, described the 3rd Company's march: "To my knowledge, the company learned of the Allied landing in the morning hours of 6 June 1944. Preparations for departure were made at once. By the evening of 6 June the 3rd Company was ready and it left Soissons that night at 2300 hours. Before we departed, Obersturmführer Raasch told us briefly of the Allied landing and the transfer of the 101st SS Panzer Battalion to the front. The companies of the battalion were quartered in different villages. It was not until 7 June that all the companies were brought together and the actual departure of the battalion took place. At that time I was the replacement radio operator in the tank of Obersturmführer Raasch. Then the march began.

Our driver was overtired after having been on watch all night and then the long wait. Luckily the gunner was also a trained driver and was able to fill in. He took over the tank in the morning hours of 7 June. In a small city outside Paris the road dipped and veered sharply to the right. Due to his lack of experience the gunner lost control of the tank on the downhill grade. The tank left the road on a sharp right turn and drove into a building which had a shop window. We reacted immediately and closed our hatches. Nothing happened, apart from a few bricks that fell on the tank. Our regular driver took over the tank again and drove it down N 14 to Paris. The company reached Paris toward evening. The battalion's route led through the inner city. We drove down a broad street to the triumphal arch and from there into the grounds of Versailles Castle. There the battalion halted. The battalion was bombed during the night. To my knowledge the workshop company suffered the first casualty.

The next day, 8 June, we drove back to Paris. The tanks were parked for several hours on the road, near the Eiffel Tower, beside the Seine. We

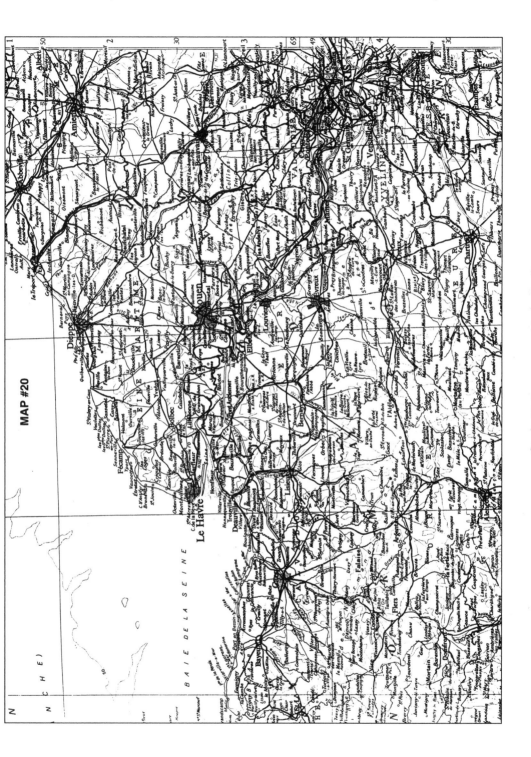

MAP #20

went down to the bank of the Seine and were finally able to have a wash after two days on the march. The French civilians were especially interested in the heavy Tiger tanks. As I recall, our crew were even given sweets by the population. I don't know the reason for the drive back to Paris. Perhaps they intentionally wanted to show our heavy Tiger tanks to the French population or else they were still uncertain whether the real invasion had taken place in Normandy."

SS-Rottenführer Wilhelm Weishaupt added: "When our tanks were sitting near the Eiffel Tower, the city commandant expressed his concern over the presence of our tanks in the city. He feared that the city would be bombed. He repeated this several times to the company commander."

The commander of Tiger 333, SS-Unterscharführer Waldemar Warnecke, described an episode that occurred during the night of 8 June: "During a refuelling stop just outside Paris, water was poured into the fuel tanks of Rolf von Westernhagen's Tiger. The crew poured a few canisters of water into the tank even though the water canisters had two large white crosses on each side. But after all it was night, and they overlooked the markings in the darkness. After the march was resumed Rolf von Westernhagen's Tiger suddenly stopped. Sepp Hafner of the Workshop Company was quickly on the scene. Diagnosis: water in the fuel tank! It was necessary to drain all the fuel and fill the tank again. Then suddenly our commanding officer, Sturmbannführer Heinz von Westernhagen, showed up asked the reason for the halt. Sepp Hafner related what had happened and the commander and his brother stepped aside a few paces. Judging by the loudness of the commander's voice, Rolf seemed to have caught an earful.

Then Sturmbannführer von Westernhagen came to me and said, "I'm letting the 3rd Company drive on. As soon as my brother's Tiger has been refuelled, you take command and follow. You'll have no trouble as you know Paris very well." Then I was given the exact march route. Our route through Paris led us over the Champs d'Elysées and the Place de l'Etoile past the triumphal arch. There I turned off the Place de l'Etoile into Avenue Hoche. After driving several hundred meters I called a halt in front of the Hotel Royal Monceau and invited both crews to take a break. I was good friends with the manager, Erich Guème. My friend greeted us as we walked into the hotel. He spontaneously invited us to a lavish supper at the hotel's expense. A guard armed with a loaded submachine-gun was left in each Tiger; the men took turns standing watch. We resumed our journey after about one and a half hours. On the far side of Paris vehicles from our battalion approached us and told us that the unit had been carpet-bombed. As a result of the two stops, the water episode and supper, we escaped the bombing." Only the 3rd Company returned to Paris; the remaining companies resumed the march toward Normandy on the morning of 8 June.

SS-Rottenführer Lau of the 2nd Company continues his account: "On we went in the direction of Dreux and then via Verneuil and Argentan to Falaise. I found the part of the route to Caen extraordinarily interesting, because the Leibstandarte had been based in that area from August 1942 to January 1943 when it was reorganized as a panzer division. As a rifleman in one of the Leibstandarte's supply companies, on several occasions I had to escort shipments of munitions by truck and by rail in this area. I therefore knew many of the villages and sections of track in the Norman landscape, where soon much blood was to flow, including my own.

The war began again for us in Dreux. We were hit by fighter-bombers at the far exit from the village in the direction of Argentan, and Unterscharführer Kleber became the first member of our company to be killed on the Normandy Front. He was posthumously promoted to Oberscharführer by SS-Obersturmführer Michael Wittmann, as he had proved himself in the east as a capable tank commander. We called him 'Quax the hard-luck pilot.' From then on the fighter-bombers never let us out of their sight. The commanders had removed their turret machine-guns and mounted them on the commander's cupola. I still remember that Bobby Warmbrunn fired at the fighter-bombers like a madman whenever one dove on us at right angles to the road."

SS-Unterscharführer Bobby Warmbrunn of the 2nd Company recalled the hard road to the front: "In Versailles forest the tanks were showered by a carpet of bombs. Like all the other tank crews I lay beneath my tank and lived through the hellish inferno. When we had regained our composure we drove on in the direction of the front and approximately thirty fighter-bombers harried us with bombs and machine-gun fire. I shot one down with the anti-aircraft machine-gun. Once again we had to check for damage and make repairs."

The 2nd Company was attacked by fighter-bombers in Argentan on that 10th of June 1944, after which it continued on in the direction of Falaise. A short time later—the Tigers were just two kilometers north of Occagnes heading in a northerly direction—another group of fighter-bombers suddenly dove out of the clouds. There was a frightful din as cannon shells and machine-gun bullets ricocheted off the pavement, struck the tanks and bounced off. The Tigers widened their march interval in order to offer the fighter-bombers a smaller target. The fighter-bombers made repeated firing passes at the Tigers. In spite of the danger, the three commanders of Obersturmführer Wessel's Ist Platoon—SS-Unterscharführer Woll, SS-Hauptscharführer Höflinger and SS-Unterscharführer

Warmbrunn—and the leader of 2nd Company's headquarters squad, SS-Unterscharführer Seifert, stood in the commander's cupolas of their Tigers and took aim at the approaching fighter-bombers with their machine-guns on anti-aircraft mounts. As a result of their energetic, nonstop fire, one of the fighter-bombers was hit and began to smoke heavily. Moments later it crashed nearby. This obviously impressed the pilots of the other fighter-bombers, which made off. There were shouts of joy and relief from the 2nd Company. They had finally been able to show the enemy that they weren't completely defenseless against the fighter-bomber plague. (The downed aircraft is the one mentioned in Warmbrunn's account.) Fighter-bombers also attacked the battalion's quadruple flak platoon, which shot down one of the enemy aircraft. The platoon commander, SS-Unterscharführer Kurt Fickert, and ten men were wounded in the attack. SS-Sturmmann Dörr was killed and SS-Sturmmann Jagschas wounded.

Walter Lau described the rest of the day: "On the march, not far from Falaise, we met the 1st Company during a halt. I recall that we greeted Staudegger as he was shaving in a fruit grove. His jacket and Knight's Cross hung on a tree; I was interested in his rank, then I saw that he was a Standartenjunker.

The 2nd Company repeatedly had to dodge onto side roads by platoon and we carried out the subsequent march down the Falaise-Caen road with an interval of several hundred meters between tanks. It was dark before we reached Falaise. We met the first units of the Hitlerjugend Division abeam Grimbosq. Something the like of which I had never seen in the east was the Hitlerjugend Division's medical column, whose troop carriers were marked with large red crosses. The medics also wore red cross emblems on their chest and back as well as on both arms and were all unarmed. Such rules meant nothing to the enemy in the east."

The 3rd Company followed the 2nd Company. Ernst Kufner: "After Paris the entire 101st Panzer Battalion was split up. The troops in the vehicles and tanks were now entirely on their own. We drove to the front singly, with lengthy intervals between vehicles. While driving by day we were constantly harassed by the fighter-bombers. At night we rested. The tanks weren't attacked while on the move, danger threatened if they stopped without camouflaging themselves. Beside the road lay burnt-out combat vehicles which had fallen prey to the fighter-bombers. On 13 June I was relieved as radio operator in Falaise by a man back from leave."

The battalion had suffered casualties by the time it reached the front. Three soldiers of the Workshop Company were killed on the Beauvais-Creil road on 7 June, a member of the 1st Company was wounded in Beauvais and a soldier of the Headquarters Company in Versailles. On 8 June an

Unterscharführer and three Sturmmänner of the 2nd Company were killed in the midnight bombing raid on the forest of Versailles. Untersturmführer Bartel of the Headquarters Company and a man from the 1st Company were wounded. On 10 June 1944 the 2nd Company was attacked by fighter-bombers in Argentan and was lucky to escape with only two men wounded. Earlier, however, Unterscharführer Kleber had been fatally hit in the turret of his Tiger. Two more men were wounded near Hilairi. The 1st Company reported one man wounded near Conches, west of Evreux. The Headquarters Company was also hit by fighter-bombers; two NCOs and seven men were wounded in Falaise, one man was killed. Total casualties from the 7th to the 10th of June 1944 were twenty-seven, including nine killed.

Date	Company	Killed			Wounded		
		Officers	NCOs	Men	Officers	NCOs	Men
7/6/1944	1st	-	-	-	-	-	1
7/6/1944	HQ	-	-	-	-	-	1
7/6/1944	Workshop	-	-	3	-	-	-
8/6/1944	1st	-	-	-	-	-	1
8/6/1944	2nd	-	1	3	-	-	-
8/6/1944	HQ	-	-	-	1	-	-
10/6/1944	1st	-	-	-	-	-	1
10/6/1944	2nd	-	1	-	-	-	4
10/6/1944	HQ	-	-	1	-	3	6

THE 1ST SS PANZER CORPS ON THE DAY OF THE LANDING

The alert was sounded for the units of the Ist SS Panzer Corps on 6 June 1944 between 0200 and 0300 hours. The 1st SS Panzer Division Leibstandarte SS Adolf Hitler, which was in the Turnhout area of Belgium for reorganization, was brought to march readiness. Because of the expected second landing in the Pas de Calais, the Leibstandarte was moved into the area east of Brugge during the night of 10 June in order to prevent landings at the mouth of the Schelde. Tied down there unnecessarily, it was late June before it began to move into the invasion area. Not until 28 June were elements of the 1st SS Panzer-Grenadier Regiment in position in Venoix, near Caen. Due to wrecked railway stations and constant fighter-bomber attacks, the entire division was not assembled in the invasion area until 6 July 1944.

The units of the Ist Panzer Corps stationed in France, the corps units and the 12th SS Panzer Division Hitlerjugend, were not sent to the coast immediately after the alarm was sounded, instead they remained where they were as the OKW reserve. Only after repeated inquiries and urgings by the Commander in Chief West was the Hitlerjugend Division released from the OKW reserve at 1430 hours on 6 June, followed by the Ist SS Panzer Corps at 1507 hours. The corps assumed command of the Hitlerjugend and Panzer-Lehr Divisions.

The Panzer-Lehr Division was also held back for an inexplicably long time, and it wasn't until 1700 hours that it was permitted to set out for the invasion front. While under way it was attacked by fighter-bombers and suffered losses. This magnificently-equipped, fully armored army division was 150 kilometers from the coast.

At 1700 hours on 6 June 1944, the Chief of Staff of Army Group B, Generalleutnant Speidel, was still advising the Wehrmacht High Command that he expected a second landing operation. Speidel characterized the first one as a "large-scale enemy operation," not as an invasion. That day Speidel sent the 116th Panzer Division into the Rouen area. The 2nd Panzer Division—the third of the army group reserve—was also north of the Somme and thus was also not on the threatened invasion front, where every man was desperately needed. General Pickert's IIIrd Flak Corps was likewise at the Somme and wasn't even informed of what was taking place.

This list of astonishing failures could be continued. They certainly cannot be interpreted as coincidences and were clearly part of a conscious effort to prevent the massing of the available panzer divisions and their employment under a unified command. By the second day of the invasion, 7 June 1944, the English had succeeded in taking Bayeux, placing the focal point of the enemy attack in the sector held by the 12th SS Panzer Division Hitlerjugend and the Panzer-Lehr Division.

The SS Panzer Division Hitlerjugend attacked the enemy landing forces constantly from the 7th to the 10th of June and its energetic advance prevented the loss of Caen and Carpiquet airport. Had the panzer divisions which the 1st SS Panzer Corps had at its disposal attacked in concert, and in particular if they had been ordered to march at the right time, chances were good that they could have advanced to the coast on a broad front and there split up and destroyed the British-American beachheads.

Rommel's plan to destroy the enemy in his most vulnerable phase, during or immediately after the landing, was frustrated by the intentionally-caused delays described above, and by the piecemeal and belated advance by the German armored forces. It was then that powerful, energetic and concentrated tank attacks could have driven the enemy back into the sea.

Caen was a corner post in the German front. The ancient Norman city near the coast was struck by a devastating bombing raid on 6 June 1944.

Thousands of French civilians died in the hail of bombs. The Allies flew a total of 14,674 sorties on D-Day, losing 113 aircraft to the German defenses. By the evening of 9 June it was apparent that the focal point of the British attacks was Tilly-sur-Seulles. Since General Montgomery had been unable to take Caen, he planned to advance on Tilly from the Bayeux area, take Villers-Bocage and then turn toward Caen again.

The 10th of June saw the English units of the XXXth Army Corps launch futile assaults against the German defenders. Especially in the area east of Tilly, the "desert rats" of the 7th Armoured Division were given a bloody nose by the determined defense mounted by the Panzer-Lehr Division. The English spearhead that advanced the farthest managed to reach the outskirts of Tilly but was wiped out there. Breville, Ranville and other villages were recaptured. In the west, however, a gap in the front posed a threat, and the Panzer-Lehr Division was unable to plug it effectively.

The commanding general of the XXXth British Corps, General Bucknall, saw on 11 June that he had no chance of taking Tilly. The gap in the front west of the Panzer-Lehr's front had not escaped the attention of the English command. An advance there offered a better chance of success than further costly frontal attacks. General Bucknall conceived a daring plan.

At noon on 12 July the British 2nd Army ordered the exploitation of the gap between the Panzer-Lehr Division and the 352nd Infantry Division. A report by the 22nd Armoured Brigade of the English 7th Armoured Division said: "On account of the difficult terrain and the resulting slow advance, it was decided that the 7th Armoured Division should outflank the left flank of the Panzer-Lehr Division left of the American sector. The Americans are directly north of Caumont and chances are good of exploiting this success in the direction of Villers-Bocage and possibly occupying Reference Point 213 (2.5 kilometers northeast of Villers-Bocage, the author)."

The 7th Armoured Division was one of the best and most experienced English armored divisions; it had already fought the Germans in Africa and Italy. During reorganization in England it became the only British division to be equipped with the potent Cromwell and Sherman Firefly tanks.

On 12 June 1944, following the failure of attacks by the 49th and 50th British Infantry Divisions and elements of the 7th Armoured Division, a brigade of the 50th Infantry Division supported by tanks took Verrières. Had they reached Lingèvres they would have surrounded the 902nd Panzer-Grenadier-Lehr Regiment. However, two panzer companies of the Panzer-Lehr Division (6th and 7th Companies, Panzer-Lehr Regiment) intervened effectively and destroyed the enemy force that had broken through. Frontal attacks on Tilly by the British 50th Infantry Division nevertheless kept the Panzer-Lehr Division bound to the front.

The 7th Armoured Division's moment had now come. It disengaged from the 50th Infantry Division's front and then described an arc to the southwest. The 22nd Armoured Brigade reached Livry at approximately 2200 hours and stopped there to rest for the night. The "desert rats" were conscious of their mission: the next day they were to drive farther into this gap in the German front, veer east slowly, take Villers-Bocage, and then advance down National Highway N 175 in the direction of Caen.

Thus on the evening of 12 June 1944 enemy forces were deep in the open flank of the Panzer-Lehr Division, which now found itself in great peril. If the British plan of a further advance to the east, toward Caen, succeeded, a determined advance by the enemy would unhinge the 1st SS Panzer Corps' front. The Panzer-Lehr Division would be surrounded and there would be nothing left standing in the way of a rapid enemy advance down the excellent National Highway in the direction of Caen, into the rear of the German front. This plan had strategic significance and had been well thought out and carefully planned. Veteran, well-equipped troops stood ready to carry it out. The English had thought of everything. What they hadn't calculated on was Michael Wittmann, or the "bloodhound" as they called him on the radio.

But at that time neither Wittmann nor a single Tiger of the 101st SS Panzer Battalion was yet available. One of the battalion's officers, SS-Untersturmführer Kalinowsky, came directly to the battalion in Normandy after recovering from wounds. On 10 June 1944 he wrote: "After much searching I finally reached my destination, where I waited for my unit. It was expected to arrive in the course of the coming night, when I would see my old comrades again. At that moment I was quite close to Sepp Dietrich. As far as the fighting there was concerned, it must still have been very fierce. Tommy got nowhere in spite of his air superiority and his weapons, with which he was now still able to bombard us . . ."

The Ist SS Panzer Corps was not unaware of the gap on its western flank. As the panzer divisions in the front line could not detach any reserves, during the night of 12–13 June arriving elements of the 101st SS Panzer Battalion were positioned behind the left flank of the Panzer-Lehr Division. SS-Hauptsturmführer Rolf Möbius and his 1st Company reached the area south of Caen on the evening of 12 June. "My battalion and I arrived in the area of the front held by the Krause Battalion during the night. I visited the battalion immediately to learn the state of things. Our material losses were very high. The drive to the front was pure poison to the heavy tanks. In fact after this march the battalion was due for several days of maintenance." Möbius was briefed on the situation at the command post of SS-Sturmbannführer Krause, the commander of the Ist Battalion, 26th Panzer-Grenadier Regiment Hitlerjugend. The two men knew each other, for from 1941 to 1943 Möbius had served as a battery commander in the Leibstandarte's flak battalion, which was commanded by Krause.

During the night Möbius moved his unit again, this time to a location ten kilometers northeast of Villers-Bocage, directly on the N 175, the national highway which linked Caen with Villers- Bocage. Möbius had eight Tigers at his disposal.

Michael Wittmann's 2nd Company was likewise positioned on the extreme left flank of the Ist SS Panzer Corps on the evening of 12 June. Wittmann had six Tigers, the rest having broken down on the last leg of the long, fighter-bomber-plagued drive with damage to transmissions and running gear. The Tigers had just been parked and hurriedly camouflaged when a devastating artillery bombardment began. Assuming that the company had been spotted by the enemy and was under directed fire, Wittmann ordered an immediate change of position; however, the company also came under fire in its new position, but luckily no serious damage was inflicted.

Wittmann had the Tigers move for a third time that night in an effort to escape the artillery fire; the Tigers took up position on Montbrocq Hill, south of national highway N 175. The 1st Company was now farther to the east of the 2nd Company. There was no rest that night for the men exhausted from their five-day march. A thorough inspection of the tanks, which urgently needed maintenance after their long drive, was promised for the next morning.

SS-Rottenführer Walter Lau of Wittmann's 2nd Company, who was now SS-Unterscharführer Stief's gunner in Tiger 234, described his first hours in the front-line sector in Normandy: "On 12 June 1944, five or six tanks from our company under the command of Obersturmführer Wittmann arrived from Evrecy at the Villers-Bocage-Caen road. We stopped about two kilometers from the outskirts of Villers-Bocage on a sunken road which ran parallel to the national highway about 100 meters away. My tank, which was commanded by Unterscharführer Stief, was the last to drive into the sunken road, as engine trouble had caused us to lag behind. We had to halt every few kilometers as our motor kept overheating. True the sunken road offered good cover, but we could only drive out of it to the front or back as the sides were too high to climb.

After placing someone else in charge of his tanks, when darkness fell Wittmann drove back in a dispatch vehicle (VW Schwimmwagen). His intention was probably to fetch the elements of his company that had been left behind; as well, the forward combat train with its kitchen and rations trucks lay a few kilometers behind us. We spent a very restless night, during which very heavy naval artillery fire passed overhead. We heard each individual report, the ear-splitting howl as the shells passed over us and the loud impacts not far away. One man kept watch in the turret, the remainder tried their best to get some sleep inside the tank."

In concluding this account of the events of 12 June, a quote from Wittmann's brief situation report: "I was instructed to stand by in the Villers area, ready to attack and destroy an eventual enemy attack from the northeast and northwest." So wrote Michael Wittmann on the evening of 12 June. The 3rd Company was still held up farther to the rear.

"But I Knew That It Absolutely Had to Be": The Battle of Villers-Bocage

At 0500 hours on 13 June 1944 the battle group of the British 7th Armoured Division began its advance. It marched in the following order: 8th King's Royal Irish Hussars (reconnaissance battalion), 4th County of London Yeomanry "Sharpshooters" (tank battalion, battle staff of the 22nd Armoured Brigade), 5th RHA (artillery battalion, minus one battery), 1/7 Battalion The Queen's Royal Regiment (infantry battalion), 1st Battalion The Rifle Brigade (armored infantry battalion, minus two companies), 26th Anti-Tank Battery.

On the way to and through Villers-Bocage the English had no contact with the enemy; the only German units in the city were two medical companies of the Panzer-Lehr Division, and these were able to escape to the north at the last minute.

On the morning of that 13 June 1944 the Tigers of the 2nd Company of the 101st SS Panzer Battalion were preparing for action below the national highway after a brief and eventful night. It was 0800 hours. Wittmann had at his disposal the Tigers of SS Untersturmführer Hantusch, SS-Unterscharführer Stief and Sowa, and SS-Oberseharführer Brandt and Lötzsch. The latter had track damage. SS-Obersturmführer Wessel had departed to establish contact with a unit at the front and receive orders.

The same day Michael Wittmann described his experiences on that Tuesday morning: "I was in my command post and had given no thought to the idea that the enemy might appear suddenly. I had sent one of my officers to establish contact with a unit deployed up front and was waiting for him to return with fresh reports. Then a man suddenly came into my command post and declared, 'Obersturmführer, tanks are driving past outside. They're a peculiar round shape and I don't think they're German.' I immediately went outside and saw tanks rolling past about 150 to 200 meters distant. They were English and American types. At the same time I saw that the tanks were accompanied by armored troop carriers."

What Wittmann was seeing was the tanks of the 4th County of London Yeomanry, and from Villers-Bocage came even more tanks and bren gun carriers. Wittmann did not know the situation that morning; he had only a vague idea of the general situation in that sector of the front. Fascinated, he watched the tremendous column of Cromwells and Shermans, which were accompanied by bren gun carriers, roll unhindered down the national highway in the direction of Caen. "It was an entire armored regiment. This armored regiment had taken me by surprise."

That was Wittmann's dispassionate diagnosis of the extremely precarious situation in which he now found himself. It is impossible to say what went on inside him in that period of only a few seconds. What choices did he have? He could stay in cover, report his sighting by radio and request reinforcements. But then Wittmann wouldn't have been Wittmann. Quick action was called for, as he was obviously faced with an enemy breakthrough with dire consequences. He decided to attack, alone, one panzer against an English armored brigade!

Wittmann knew all too well that under normal circumstances he would have no chance against this huge armada of steel; retreat after he had made his attack would be impossible against this overwhelming superiority. By any human measuring and from the point of view of armored tactics he was headed for certain death by attacking now. These thoughts ran through Wittmann's mind in fractions of a second as, from his vantage point approximately 150 meters from Hill 213, he observed the English tanks on the road. "Yes, I must say that the decision was a very, very difficult one. Never before had I been so impressed by the strength of the enemy as I was by those tanks rolling by; but I knew that it absolutely had to be and I decided to strike out into the enemy."

Wittmann knew that this powerful armored formation would meet no German forces of note on the road leading to Caen. He must avert a catastrophe, the collapse of the front. There was no other choice for him, the born lone fighter, he had to throw himself against the enemy tanks and try to make the impossible possible. Wittmann dashed toward his Tigers which sat camouflaged in the sunken road; his men there were still unaware of his discovery and the great danger that faced them all.

In the nearest tank was SS-Rottenführer Lau: "It was almost morning and the naval artillery fire had subsided somewhat. I, the gunner, was standing watch in the open turret hatch. All of a sudden—it was between 5 and 7 A.M.—Obersturmführer Wittmann, who had leapt onto the first of our tanks sitting in the sunken road, grasped me by the shoulder and said something about the Tommies. As he spoke, he gestured with his hand toward the road (Villers-Bocage-Caen), which was almost impossible to see

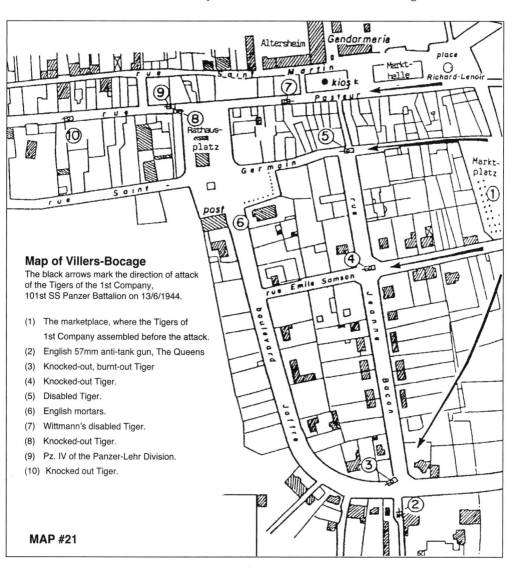

Map of Villers-Bocage

The black arrows mark the direction of attack
of the Tigers of the 1st Company,
101st SS Panzer Battalion on 13/6/1944.

(1) The marketplace, where the Tigers of
     1st Company assembled before the attack.

(2) English 57mm anti-tank gun, The Queens

(3) Knocked-out, burnt-out Tiger

(4) Knocked-out Tiger.

(5) Disabled Tiger.

(6) English mortars.

(7) Wittmann's disabled Tiger.

(8) Knocked-out Tiger.

(9) Pz. IV of the Panzer-Lehr Division.

(10) Knocked out Tiger.

MAP #21

from our position through the bushes. I slid onto the gunner's seat and he
onto the tank commander's seat. The driver had fired up the engine.
Headsets and throat microphones were put on quickly and we backed out
of the defile. Unterscharführer Stief, who had been sleeping at the loader's
position, was instructed by Wittmann to alert and brief the remaining
tanks. Meanwhile we drove toward the main road along a field road. We
had gone about twenty meters by the time the driver and I were able to
explain to Wittmann that our motor was defective. Apparently he had
already deduced this from the sound of the engine. He leapt out of our

tank and climbed aboard the tank of Unterscharführer Sowa, which by then had driven out of the defile."

Michael Wittmann himself now describes his lone attack: "I had no time to assemble my company; instead I had to act quickly, as I had to assume that the enemy had already spotted me and would destroy me where I stood. I set off with one tank and passed the order to the others not to retreat a single step but to hold their ground. Drove up to the column, surprised the English as much as they had me. I first knocked out two tanks from the right of the column, then one from the left, then turned about to the left and attacked the armored troop carrier battalion in the middle of the armored regiment. I drove toward the rear half of the column on the same road, knocking out every tank that came toward me as I went. The enemy was thrown into total confusion. I then drove straight into the town of Villers, got to approximately the center of town where I was hit by an anti-tank gun. My tank was disabled. Without further ado I fired at and destroyed everything around me that I could reach; I had lost radio contact and was unable to summon my company. My tanks were out of sight.

I then decided to abandon the tank. We took all the weapons we could carry, but I didn't destroy the tank as I believed that we could regain possession of it. Made my way to a division, about fifteen kilometers. Had to dodge enemy tanks several times; could have taken them out but had no close-range anti-tank weapons, so with a heavy heart had to leave them be. I reached the division and immediately reported to it and to corps. Subsequent counterattack destroyed the enemy. The bulk of the armored regiment and a rifle battalion were destroyed."

With these succinct, factual words Wittmann described his attack against the English armored brigade, an attack unprecedented in its daring. Wittmann smashed the enemy tanks on the national highway without stopping to fire. In doing so he drove down the same road right beside the English armored column, his lone Tiger passing the English tanks face to face. Never before had one tank commander attacked such a superior force. Wittmann scored a direct hit with every shot from his moving Tiger. Loader Sturmmann Boldt had to work very hard; he had never had to load so fast. The driver, SS-Unterscharführer Walter Müller, skillfully maneuvered the Tiger past the English column. The radio operator was SS-Sturmmann Günther Jonas. All senses taut, Michael Wittmann kept his eye on the enemy armored column, the end of which he could not see. The Tiger fired again and again.

"I simply drove along the column." That sounds rather simple; however, the crews of the English Cromwell tanks were not asleep, instead they tried to knock out the lone Tiger as it came toward them, firing without

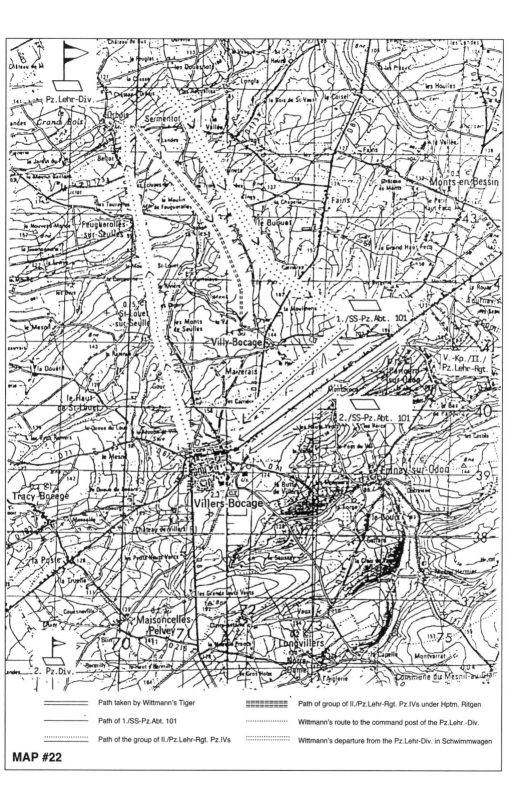

———————— Path taken by Wittmann's Tiger	========= Path of group of II./Pz.Lehr-Rgt. Pz.IVs under Hptm. Ritgen
———————— Path of 1./SS-Pz.Abt. 101	················ Wittmann's route to the command post of the Pz.Lehr.-Div.
·············· Path of the group of II./Pz.Lehr-Rgt. Pz.IVs	···················· Wittmann's departure from the Pz.Lehr.-Div. in Schwimmwagen

MAP #22

pause. They failed to do so, however, because Wittmann was faster then they, more skilled and precise. The well-aimed shots from the Cromwells, fired from extremely close range, bounced off the Tiger's frontal armor. "I was able to take out twenty-one tanks, as well as the armored troop carriers. I don't know how many, that remains to be determined."

The armored troop carriers, in which were sitting the infantry of the Rifle Brigade, found themselves in a hopeless situation and awaited the coming disaster passively. Some of the infantry dove from their carriers and threw themselves into the bushes beside the road. Wittmann: "They never left the road. They were so surprised that they took to flight, but not with their vehicles, instead they jumped out, and I shot up the battalion's vehicles as I drove by."

Tanks, troop carriers, anti-tank guns, Wittmann blasted them all into smoking junk. Then he continued his triumphal march and rolled down the gently-sloping road into Villers-Bocage. In the Rue Georges Clèmenceau Wittmann knocked out two tanks of the regimental headquarters of the 4th County of London Yeomanry, one of which was commanded by Lieutenant-Colonel Lord Cranley. Captain Dyas was able to back his Cromwell tank into the courtyard of the Lemonnier property just in time. A fourth tank also escaped.

Wittmann drove on. Just before the Hotel du Bras d'Or he destroyed the 5th Royal Artillery's lookout tank, a Sherman, and then found himself facing several enemy tanks at the exit from the town, the Jeanne-d'Arc Square. He subsequently turned his Tiger around and drove back down the main street, which at that place was called the Rue Pasteur. As it passed the Huet-Godefroy clothing store, the Tiger was hit by a shell fired by an anti-tank gun, which wrecked one of the drive sprockets.

Wittmann then made his way alone out of the town and headed north to the command post of the Panzer-Lehr Division in Orbois. He quickly informed the la, General Staff Oberstleutnant Kauffmann, of the dangerous situation, telling him that there were powerful enemy units west of Villers-Bocage with no German forces to oppose them. Wittmann also had the Ist SS Panzer Corps informed. Since all the units of the Hitlerjugend Division were committed near Caen, the Panzer-Lehr Division, which was itself heavily engaged once again in Tilly-sur-Seulles, had to release units and send them to Villers-Bocage to eliminate the acute threat in the rear of the front.

Deployed to Villers-Bocage were elements of the land Battalion of the Panzer-Lehr Regiment, which, after the death of Major Prince von Schönburg-Waldenburg on 11 June, was commanded by Hauptmann Ritgen. Ritgen was only able to withdraw parts of the battalion from the front, however; the 6th Company was fighting with the 901st Panzer-Grenadier-Lehr Regiment at Tilly and other panzer companies were engaged as well. He received a total of approximately fifteen Panzer IVs.

Hauptmann Helmut Ritgen recalled this action: "I was ordered by division to barricade the northern exit from Villers-Bocage and prepare for a counterattack against the deep British penetration through Villers-Bocage to the east. The companies deployed with the 901st Panzer-Grenadier-Lehr Regiment were engaged and could not be pulled out. While driving south, in the approximate area of Villy-Bocage I was stopped and briefed by General Bayerlein. From there we drove west in trail, north of the stream, accompanied by the general. To our south stretched the wall of the city of Villers-Bocage; we came under heavy anti-tank gun fire from that direction. Stabsfeldwebel Bobrowski was hit and his tank caught fire. We could not locate the British anti-tank guns. Without supporting panzer-grenadiers and artillery, a further advance through the hedgerow terrain would have been madness. General Bayerlein ordered a withdrawal to Villy-Bocage."

Oberstleutnant Kauffmann hurriedly scraped together forces from the headquarters of the Panzer-Lehr Division and drove from Orbois to the outskirts of Villers-Bocage in order to prevent a breakout by the enemy. Wittmann did not take part in this action, instead he set out in a Schwimmwagen toward the N 175, the Villers-Bocage-Caen road. After Ritgen's panzers made smoke and withdrew, in Parfouru, below National Highway N 175, the damaged tanks of the IInd Battalion of the Panzer-Lehr Regiment were hurriedly made operational, after which they set off toward Villers-Bocage.

In one of the approximately ten Panzer IVs was Gefreiter Leo Enderle of the 6th Panzer-Lehr Company: "When the counterattack started we advanced down the national highway, where knocked-out tanks and transport vehicles lay for kilometers. I also saw dead lying about when I was outside the tank. A dispatch rider emerged from a defile; horrified, he braked suddenly and plunged off the road. The attack on Villers-Bocage was delayed by at least a half hour until the tanks had formed up to the left and right of the attack road. Several tanks went left around the city, others right, in order to intercept stationary or fleeing troops there. We drove into the town. At an intersection sat two Tigers, knocked out by a self-propelled gun which was positioned in the street to the left.

We sent our first two tanks through the intersection at high speed. They made it, and after they had disappeared around a bend in the street were fired on by anti-tank guns. We heard over the radio that the first had been knocked out; the second withdrew and, though warned several times not to recross the intersection, was knocked out there. The shell went in

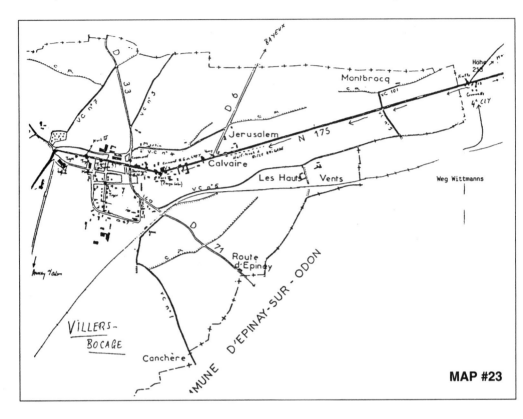

MAP #23

the left side and out the right. We were certain no one would get out, but soon afterward the loader's hatch opened and a man dove out of the tank head-first on to the street and disappeared into a side street where, as we were told later, he bled to death.

I was in the third panzer, still behind the intersection. We were operating as part of a pair; the right tank advanced while the left provided covering fire, then the procedure was reversed. Our tank was on the right side, directly in front of the intersection where the enemy could not get their sights on us. The gunfire from in front rang out clearly, that from the side sounded hollow."

Directly behind was the tank of Unteroffizier Rother of the 5th Panzer-Lehr Company. His gunner Hans Burkhardt wrote: "As we moved up, in front of Villers-Bocage we passed a huge column of wrecked British troop trucks, armored troop carriers and these small, fully-tracked vehicles. The column, which had been shot up by an SS Tiger unit, had been driving east. In front of Villers-Bocage I saw two Tigers to our left sitting at the edge of the forest. One of them had definitely been knocked out. The crew were still there. Several were wounded, unfortunately one dead as well.

After stopping for a short while to observe, we drove slowly into Villers-Bocage. After several hundred meters we came to an intersection. When our first tank drove up to this intersection, it came under anti-tank gun fire from the left. The latter was so far from the intersection that it couldn't be seen until one was fully in the intersection. The tank was put out of action. The same happened to the second tank. The third tank in the line moved off, and we in the fourth panzer had just received our commander's order to close hatches and move forward when we were halted by radio and ordered to drive to the right. Then we were overtaken by a group of two or three Tigers. These Tigers drove toward the intersection and destroyed the anti-tank gun. I think that the leading Tiger was knocked out in the exchange of fire, but I'm not certain. There was talk afterward that a Tiger had run over the enemy anti-tank gun. Everything certainly happened very quickly. It was all over in a few minutes."

The Tigers in question belonged to the 1st Company of the 101st SS Panzer Battalion. In addition to his own tank, company commander SS-Hauptsturmführer Möbius' force of combat-ready Tigers included the tanks of the following commanders: SS-Obersturmführer Philipsen, SS-Untersturmführer Lukasius and Hahn, SS-Oberscharführer Bode, Zahner, Swoboda and Ernst, and SS-Unterscharführer Wendt and Salamon. After the alarm was sounded the Tigers of the 1st Company had set out for Villers-Bocage. The departure was made in great haste; SS-Hauptsturm-führer Möbius recalls the attack:

"Operational order: 'Something must be going on there. Take your company and check it out!' Wittmann came upon Möbius near Hill 213 and briefed him on the situation. Möbius: 'I had deployed two platoons around Villers-Bocage, in order to prevent a breakout by the English to the east in the direction of Caen, and was in the town with one platoon. I really had little idea how strong the English were.'"

What had become of the 2nd Company in the meantime? After Wittmann roared off in SS-Unterscharführer Sowa's Tiger, SS-Rottenführer Lau remained in his Tiger just below Hill 213 at the national highway. He described what happened: "English tanks were already driving past to my right, in the direction of Caen. Then we heard the sound of gunfire from Wittmann on the road. I was standing in the turret of my tank, now with-out a commander, about fifty meters from the highway. Unterscharführer Sowa was also sitting in the middle of open ground where Wittmann had left him. I shouted to him—for with the engine noise and the tank gunfire that was the only way to be heard—, 'Kurt, come here, I have no com-mander.' With Unterscharführer Sowa in command we drove on to the highway.

The left side of the road was one pile of wreckage which was obscured by smoke from burning vehicles. To the right in the direction of Caen we discovered two Cromwell tanks. They began to turn around, but we were able to destroy them both. Terrified Englishmen were running everywhere. We pulled back from the highway in the direction of the sunken road, in order to obtain a better view while standing guard and to shut down the overheated engine. Elements of our combat train now showed up and set about taking the English prisoner.

A Russian Hiwi from the field kitchen distinguished himself in this. He was a member of the crew of a T 34 we had knocked out at Cherkassy. Armed with pistol in one hand and a kitchen knife in the other, he flushed the Tommies from the bushes lining the sides of the highway. Soon there were more than a hundred prisoners in an open barn in front of our tank; our train people searched them for weapons. We had removed the machine-gun and positioned it on top of the tank. Meanwhile, thirty to sixty minutes had passed, when more Tigers rolled past us from the direction of Caen headed for Villers-Bocage. We read off the numbers: 111, 112, 121, 131—the tanks belonged to our 1st Company."

SS-Oberscharführer Jürgen Brandt of the 2nd Company destroyed three Shermans and a number of tankettes by the side of the national highway; he and his crew brought in seventy British prisoners. The other crews succeeded in taking prisoner another 160 British soldiers. Soon afterward the previously mentioned armored group of the Panzer-Lehr Regiment joined the tank crews of the 2nd Company beside the national highway and its commander, an Army Hauptmann, enquired about the situation. Having already described the attack by these tanks, we will now focus on the 1st Company. Wittmann met the advancing Tigers on the national highway and there briefed the commander of the 1st Company on the situation as he saw it.

From Hill 213 the men saw the burning tanks of the 22nd Armoured Brigade. The first four Tigers of the 1st Company then drove into Villers-Bocage, with SS-Obersturmführer Philipsen in the leading tank. Meanwhile the English had gone over to the defensive in Villers-Bocage and a number of Sherman Fireflies and anti-tank guns lurked in the small city. Several of the English tanks tried to break out and ran straight into the Tiger platoon commanded by SS-Obersturmführer Philipsen, which was leading the German attack. SS-Untersturmführer Walter Hahn of the 1st Company described the attack by the Tigers:

"Hannes was able to score a fine success in our very first battle on the invasion front. He led the attack on Villers-Bocage on 13 June, destroyed eight tanks from a group of enemy vehicles attacking from out of the city, and thus brought the attack to a halt. When he then entered bitterly defended Villers-Bocage, his tank was knocked out from very close range. Hannes got out of the burning tank unhurt, immediately climbed into another tank and continued to take part in the battle."

This attack entailed a certain degree of risk, for without infantry support tanks were supposed to avoid the close confines of built-up areas. Part of the 1st Company drove to Villers-Bocage, where there were already several Panzer IVs of the Panzer-Lehr Division.

Now, however, the city became a true witch's cauldron; the constant roar of tank cannon and anti-tank guns reverberated through Villers-Bocage. The Tigers were unable to exploit their advantages to the full in the narrow streets, and the battle withthe English was fought at close quarters. Close-range weapons were fired at the Tigers from niches and cellar windows. SS-Oberscharführer Heinrich Ernst's Tiger was knocked out and Ernst was killed. Both sides fought all out in the city, the bitter battle raged back and forth.

A Panzer IV of the Panzer-Lehr Division was knocked out, as was Tiger 112. An anti-tank gun fired from a side street until a Tiger rammed the corner house in front of it; falling rubble silenced the anti-tank gun. Instead of attacking along the narrow main street, three Tigers drove west along parallel streets to the south. All three were put out of action on the Rue Jeanne Bacon, which led to the main street. The first was knocked out at the intersection with Rue Saint-Germain, the second was fired on in the middle of the intersection with Emile Samson by an anti-tank gun positioned in a garden in front and to the right. The Tiger returned fire but was hit and immobilized. The third Tiger was knocked out by a 57 mm anti-tank gun manned by the Queens even farther south, at the intersection of the Rue Jeanne Bacon and Boulevard Goffre. Though wounded, the tank's commander, SS-Unterscharführer Arno Saloman, was able to free himself from his disabled Tiger. Commanding the other Tigers of the 1st Company fighting in Villers-Bocage were SS-Oberscharführer Hein Bode, SS-Untersturmführer Lukasius and Hahn, and SS-Obersturmführer Philipsen, as well as SS-Oberscharführer Heinrich Ernst and Hans Swoboda, both of whom were killed.

Only the Tigers of 1st Company fought in Villers-Bocage. "There was firing everywhere. We battled anti-tank guns and infantry. To this day I can still see the Tiger of SS-Untersturmführer Lukasius being knocked out by close-range weapons. He got out. His burns were frightful looking. By late in the afternoon the whole nightmare was over." So recalled SS-Unterschar-

führer Wendt, commander of Tiger 132, which remained on guard outside
the city. The battalion medical officer, SS-Hauptsturmführer Dr. Rabe, was
also in action constantly.

A battalion report stated: "On 13 June 1944 battalion medical officer
Rabe accompanied an attack on Villers-Bocage by the Ist Battalion, 101st
SS Heavy Panzer Battalion in a Kfz. 81. After remaining behind the company to treat the wounded, Rabe suddenly found himself confronted by
four English Churchill type tanks with supporting infantry. Acting quickly,
Rabe, accompanied only by his driver, set out against the enemy armed
with just a submachine-gun. He forced the totally-surprised infantry to surrender and the crews of the tanks to bail out and took a total of sixty-two
prisoners. As a result of this act an acute danger in the company's rear was
eliminated. In the same battle Rabe, after making his way back to the company, personally travelled the Villers-Bocage-Caen road, which was in plain
view of the enemy and under heavy artillery fire, four times in his
wounded-laden vehicle."

Members of the 1st Company who fell in Villers-Bocage included:
Oberscharführer Heinrich Ernst and Hans Swoboda, Unterscharführer
Robert Zellmer, Rotteführer Hermani, Sturmmann Hruschka and four
other men. Those wounded were tank commanders Untersturmführer
Lukasius, Unterscharführer Salamon, Langer and seven men. The 2nd
Company's casualties were Rottenführer Eugen Schmidt (KIA), who had
been Wittmann's driver in the winter of 1944, and three men wounded. Six
Tigers were lost in Villers- Bocage. The Panzer-Lehr Division lost at least
two tanks, number 634 was knocked out at the entrance to the town and
another was lost inside. A Tiger was also lost. It may have been the action
which Hans Burkhardt of the Panzer-Lehr Division described.

VILLERS-BOCAGE: AN ENEMY FIASCO

In the following account two members of the British 7th Armoured Divi-
sion describe their experiences at Villers-Bocage. First J.L. Cloudsley-
Thompson, a tank commander with the 4th Country of London Yeomanry:
"We set off at dawn, with A-Squadron, 4th County of London Yeomanry and
A-Company of the 1st Rifle Brigade leading the way. The country was lovely
and there was no resistance, and so we hoped to take the hill beyond
Villers-Bocage before we were noticed by the enemy. Villers-Bocage is a
rather large, rural town. There was no sign of the enemy and so we drove
down the main street through the town. The brigadier and the colonel
were on their way to the head of the column in their scout car and we were
to join them as quickly as possible.

A-Squadron had just passed through the town, as had the regimental staff, which I was leading, when suddenly tanks of A-Squadron went up in flames and the crews bailed out. The staff tank began backing up. One of the shortcomings of the Cromwell tank was that its top speed in reverse gear was only two miles per hour. The brigadier, who had discussed the situation with the colonel, ran across the road, jumped into a car and drove back, followed by another scout car. Suddenly an armor-piercing shell whizzed between my radio operator's head and me and barely missed us. I was half deaf until the next day, even though I had my headset on. I instructed my driver to drive on the left side and we pushed through a hedge between two houses. Pat Dyas, the adjutant, turned his tank beside mine. His forehead was bleeding.

At this point probably all of the tanks in front were burning. Visible through the smoke was the gigantic outline of a Tiger. I was no more than twenty-five yards away from it. Our 75 mm guns fired, but the shells bounced off the massive armor of the Tiger. I fired the 58 mm mortar, but the smoke caused me to miss. The Tiger traversed its big 88 mm gun slightly. Boom! We were hit. I felt a burning sensation between my legs and was astonished that I had been wounded again. A lance of fire swept over the turret and my mouth was full of sand and burnt paint. I shouted 'Get out!' and jumped out of the tank. I saw my crew get out. Suddenly a machine-gun fired at me and 1 threw myself onto the grass. The Tiger rumbled past and Dyas' Cromwell followed it down the street. I took the headset, which was still hanging round my neck, and waved to him with it. Then I heard my name called softly and looked around. It was my crew, who had hidden themselves in a currant bush. Luckily all were unhurt. My troop sergeant had been fortunate. As he had been leaning sideways when our tank was hit, the shell passed over his shoulder and between my legs and struck the motor. A piece of metal had struck him behind the ear. Joe, the driver, was pale and trembling. Once again shells and machine-gun bullets whizzed over our heads, and I quickly threw myself to the ground.

A frightful din could be heard from inside the town. I decided to go back along the back side of the houses beside a wall and try to find B-Squadron. When we set off I saw Dyas some distance away on foot. He had hoped to be able to knock out the Tiger from behind. He hit it after it had destroyed the rest of the regimental staff. The Tiger fired once, killing the co-driver and gunner, but Dyas and his driver were able to get out unhurt. Machine-guns fired at him from the first-floor windows of the houses, but nevertheless he ran to a burning tank whose radio was still working and warned B- and C-Squadrons, which werestill unaware of what had happened. He then ran down the main street until he came to a corner and saw me from a distance. There he came under fire from another machine-gun and was forced to take cover. He later made it to B-Squadron. Undamaged, the Tiger drove on; its commander waved his cap and laughed. Its armor was so strong that none of our Cromwells were in a position to take it out."

Cloudsley-Thompson's tank had been knocked out by Wittmann just beyond Villers-Bocage. Captain Dyas then followed the lone Tiger into the town, but was then himself hit and knocked out. Another member of the "Sharpshooters," Sergeant Bobby Bramwell provided the following account: "We headed out at first light and drove down the road in the direction of Villers-Bocage, with A-Squadron in the point position, then the regimental staff and B-Squadron, and finally C-squadron. It was a beautiful day, at least it began that way, in contrast to the afternoon. Brigade reported that Villers-Bocage was free of the enemy and Brigadier 'Loony' Hinde came and ordered us to drive on at maximum speed. A-Squadron drove through the town to the hill beyond. The staff stopped in the center of town and my B-Squadron even farther west, outside the town. C-Squadron was right in the middle.

It was 1000 hours when we heard the first sounds of fighting from the town, machine-guns and the awful 88 mm cannon. That was the first clue that something wasn't right. A Tiger entered the town. First it destroyed the artillery observation tanks, Shermans, and then made its way through the town to the western exit. There my friend Sergeant Lockwood fired at it with his seventeen-pounder gun. He wasn't able to destroy it but at least he drove it away. Meanwhile other German tanks attacked A-Squadron on the hill beyond Villers-Bocage. They blew up the command tank and the one at the back and then rolled along our rank and shot up the rest. It was one big junk heap. They got the commanding officer and we had no contact with brigade. 'Ibby' Aird assumed command.

We were all still in contact with the regimental radio net, which enabled it to keep us informed. My platoon, the IIIrd Platoon of B-Squadron, received orders to undertake an advance through the southern part of the town in order to help A-Squadron. So we drove off, with my tank leading the way. Lieutenant Bill Cotton was in command. Bill was a short, stocky chap, quite fearless, a good leader.

When we entered the town we found there were firefights everywhere, concentrated mainly around the square near the main street. Soon afterward three German tanks came down the main street. I am sure that the leading tank was a Panzer IV; some said it was a Tiger, but I fired at it and therefore knew that it wasn't. I didn't hit it, however. The range was too small to aim the cannon accurately. Fortunately a six-pounder anti-tank gun of the Queen's was moved into position and was able to knock it out.

The next tank was a Tiger, however. I had pulled back a distance and could see it through the windows of the house on the corner. We traversed our gun and began firing at it through the windows. I don't know how often we fired, but at some point we disabled it. I suspect that it was now about noon. The sound of machine-guns and anti-tank guns firing could be heard everywhere in the city. In the afternoon came news that the Queen's were being attacked from the south by tanks and infantry. Then the third German tank, also a Tiger, came round the corner of the square. I was ready, however, having aimed the seventeen-pounder, not with the telescopic sight, as the range was too short, but by looking through the barrel at a sign on the wall at the other side of the street. When the Tiger covered the sign we fired, and that was it.

It now began to rain heavily. One of the panzers had caught fire, the crew were either dead or had got out, but the Germans would be able to come back and tow the tank away. Bill Cotton therefore took a German gas can and a few wool blankets and we went out to destroy the panzer. Bill opened up an umbrella on account of the rain; we must have been crazy! We went from panzer to panzer, Bill with his open umbrella and the blankets and I with the gas can. We soaked a blanket with gasoline and tossed it inside the turret, followed by a match. Later we learned that the local fire-brigade had come and tried to put out the fire. Probably out of fear that the tank would explode, but I saw nothing of it. During the night we were pulled back to Amayé-sur-Seulles, west of Villers-Bocage. Our regiment had been badly mauled. Its losses included A-Squadron and the regimental staff, as well as Colonel Onslow and a number of other officers."

In the afternoon three Tigers of the 2nd Company under the command of SS-Untersturmführer Hantusch drove several kilometers down the national highway in the direction of Caen, where they took up a security position. There they met the armored troop carriers of the 4th (Light) Company. English prisoners trudged past in the direction of Caen. In the evening Wittmann visited his men there. As the battle went on, the first units of the 2nd Panzer Division arrived from the south in front of Villers-Bocage to close the gap on the left wing of the 1st SS Panzer Corps. The English now gave up for good and withdrew west into the area between Villers-Bocage and Amayè-sur-Seulles.

As a result of his courageous actions, which contradicted all the rules of tactical armored warfare, Michael Wittmann had achieved a sensational success; he destroyed twenty-one English tanks and a much larger number of armored vehicles, anti-tank guns and bren gun carriers. His twenty-minute attack against the British 22nd Armoured Brigade led him to a triumphant victory in his very first action on the invasion front.

This victory had great significance for the left wing of the Ist SS Panzer Corps; without Wittmann's determined attack on the armored column, the British force would have driven unhindered down the dead-straight national highway in the direction of Caen, deep in the rear of the corps, all of whose divisions were engaged in heavy fighting farther north.

That this potential catastrophe was averted, was due solely to Wittmann's potentially sacrificial attack. Finally, the attack by the 1st Company of the 101st SS Panzer Battalion brought about the complete collapse of the advance by the English 7th Armoured Division and inflicted further serious losses on it in the fighting in the town. The 7th Armoured Division lost more than thirty tanks and countless Universal Carriers, anti-tank guns, armored troop carriers and trucks.

In the afternoon Wittmann gave a complete account of his battle at Villers-Bocage to SS-Sturmbannführer von Westernhagen and SS-Obergruppenführer Sepp Dietrich. Both officers were visibly impressed by this act of daring by the young soldier from the Upper Pfalz. The same day Dietrich had his staff write up the application for the award of the Knight's Cross with Oak Leaves and Swords.

Corps Headquarters Ist SS Panzer Corps "Leibstandarte"
Corps C.P., 13 June 1944

On 12/6/44 SS-Obersturmführer Wittmann was ordered to cover the corps' left flank near Villers-Bocage, because it was assumed that English armored forces which had broken through would advance south and southeast. There were no more panzergrenadiers available.

Wittmann arrived at the specified time with 6 Panzerkampfwagen VI. The Wittmann Company was forced to change positions three times during the night of 13/6/1944 on account of very heavy artillery fire and on the morning of 13/6/1944 was positioned near Reference Point 213 northeast of Villers-Bocage with 5 Panzerkampfwagen VI ready for action.

At eight o'clock a lookout reported to SS-Obersturmführer Wittmann that a large column of enemy tanks was advancing on the Caen-Villers-Bocage road.

Wittmann, who was in cover with his Tiger 200 m south of the road, saw an English armored battalion followed by an English armored troop carrier battalion.

The situation called for immediate action. Wittmann was unable to get orders to his men who had moved off, instead he immediately drove into the English column with his tank, firing on the move. This rapid intervention initially split the column. From 80 meters Wittmann destroyed 4 Sherman tanks, positioned his Tiger next to the column and drove, 10 to 30 meters beside it firing in his direction of travel, along the column. He succeeded in knocking out 15 heavy enemy tanks in a very short time. An additional six tanks were hit and their crews forced to bail out. The accompanying battalion in armored troop carriers was almost completely wiped out. The following four tanks of the Wittmann Company took about 230 prisoners. Wittmann drove on, in advance of his company, into Villers-Bocage. His tank was hit and immobilized by a heavy enemy anti-tank gun in the center of the town. Nevertheless, he still destroyed all the enemy vehicles in range and scattered the enemy unit. Wittmann and his crew sub-sequently abandoned their tank and made their way north on foot approximately 15 km to the Panzer-Lehr Division. There he reported to the Ia, turned about with 15 Panzer IVs of the Panzer-Lehr Division and once again headed for Villers-Bocage. His amphibious-Volkswagen having meanwhile found him, he then drove to the 1st Company, which was deployed along the main street of Villers-Bocage and based on his impressions of the battle and the situation committed them against the enemy tanks and anti-tank guns still in the town.

Through his determined action Wittmann and his Tiger tank destroyed the greater part of a powerful enemy offensive column already deep in the rear of our front—the English 22nd Armoured Brigade—and acting solely on his own initiative, and displaying the highest personal bravery, he averted a threat to the entire front of the Ist SS Panzer Corps. At that time there were no reserves available to the corps.

With today's action Wittmann has destroyed 138 enemy tanks and 132 anti-tank guns with his tank.

signed Dietrich
SS-Obergruppenführer
and Panzergeneral der Waffen-SS

Michael Wittmann

Two more photos
of Wittmann.

Brief pause during combat training. *From left:* Lötzch, Warmbrunn, Kleber, Wittmann and Woll.

Wittmann, Warmbrunn (partly concealed) Höflinger, Lötzch, Woll and Kleber.

More shots of
Wittmann.

From left:
SS-Hauptscharführer Hans Höflinger and SS-Oberscharführer Georg Lötzsch, Wittmann, SS-Rottenführer Bobby Warmbrunn and SS-Unterscharführer Bobby Woll. All were tank commanders in Wittmann's 2nd company.

Kurt Kleber, Michael Wittmann and Bobby Woll.

SS-Obersturmführer
Jürgen Wessel.

SS-Untersturmführer
Georg Hantusch.

SS-Rottenführer
Walter Lau (gunner).

SS-Sturmmann Hubert Heil
(radio operator).

SS-Untersturmführer
Heinz Belbe

SS-Sturmmann Rudi Hirschel
(radio operator).

SS-Oberscharführer
Jürgen Brandt.

Michael Wittmann.

SS-Unterscharführer
Kurt Kleber.

SS-Unterscharführer
Bobby Woll.

SS-Unterscharführer
Bobby Warmbrunn, the
youngest Tiger commander.

SS-Rottenführer
Reinhard Wenzel
(Radio Operator).

SS-Hauptscharführer
Hans Höflinger.

SS-Rottenführer
Willi Schenk (Loader).

SS-Oberscharführer
Georg Lötzsch (Commander).

SS-Oberscharführer Jürgen "Captain" Brandt was one of the most experienced tank commanders in Wittmann's 2nd Company.

SS-Unterscharführer Bobby Warmbrunn, another of the 2nd Company's veteran tank commanders.

SS-Oberscharführer Peter Kisters

SS-Rottenführer (FB) Willi Schmidt, Armored Reconnaissance Platoon.

SS-Oberscharführer Peter Kisters, tank commander in the 3rd Company.

SS-Usch. Wolfgang Unruh, HQ Company.

SS-Unterscharführer
Georg Sittek took over the
maintenance echelon of the
3rd Company, 101st SS Panzer
Battalion in Normandy.

SS-Untersturmführer Willi
Iriohn, operations officer, as of
July 1944 platoon commander
in the 3rd company, 101st SS
Panzer Battalion.

SS-Untersturmführer Helmut
W. Dollinger, before the
invasion—battalion adjutant,
afterward—signals officer.

SS-Hauptsturmführer Franz Heurich, Officer in Charge of Motor Vehicles I (here as an SS-Oberscharführer in 1939).

SS-Obersturmführer Wilhelm Spitz, operations officer, as of July 1944 commander of the 4th (Light) Company of the 101st SS Panzer Battalion.

SS-Oberscharführer Johann Schott, Technical Sergeant (Radio) in the Signals Platoon of the 101st SS Panzer Battalion.

A delegation from the Ist SS Panzer Corps Leibstandarte under the command of SS-Obersturmbannführer Max Wünch (left) in the Führer Headquarters in early 1944. Next to Wünch are SS-Untersturmführer Balthasar Woll and SS-Hauptsturmführer Hans Pfeiffer, Hitler's former adjutant and now commander of the 4th Company, 12th SS Panzer Regiment Hitlerjugend. Max Wünch, commander of the 12th SS Panzer Hitlerjugend, shows Hitler photographs of the protoype of the "Wirbelwind" anti-aircraft tank developed by his regiment.

SS-Hauptsturmführer Alfred Veller, administration officer (seen here while still an SS-Scharführer in 1935).

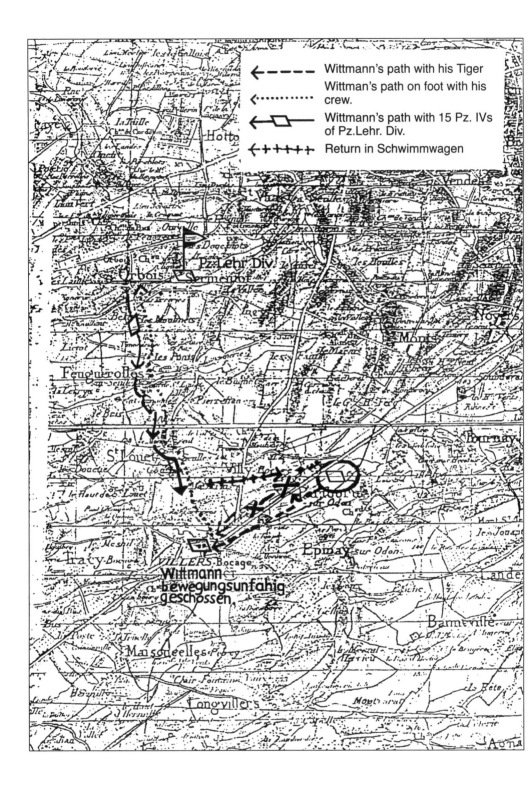

Wittmann's path with his Tiger

Wittman's path on foot with his crew.

Wittmann's path with 15 Pz. IVs of Pz.Lehr. Div.

Return in Schwimmwagen

Pz.Lehr Div.

Wittmann bewegungsunfähig geschossen

Wittmann subsequently sat down in the open with several officers of the corps headquarters staff and talked about his experiences. Dietrich's corps adjutant, SS-Hauptsturmführer Hermann Weiser, produced champagne with which to toast Wittmann's great success. The strain of the battle and the long march to the front were now clearly visible in Wittmann's face, but before he could go he had to answer the questions of a war correspondent and give an account to the German radio network. Then he made his way back to his company. There, too, he was called on to describe his daring raid, this time by his own men. By now Wittmann was dead-tired. After describing his Villers-Bocage experience yet again, he ordered the Tigers dispersed for the night, assigned the guards and then went to bed.

A day of hectic fighting was over. The Tiger battalion's debut had certainly been a dramatic one. Michael Wittmann had demonstrated once again—this time on the Western Front—his unique combination of courage and tactical skill. Considered rationally, his chances of returning from his raid against the English armored brigade were negligible; that he nevertheless did so speaks volumes for him, but also shows that where Wittmann was concerned conventional thinking was taken to its limits. A willingness to risk his own life without hesitation was something Wittmann took for granted.

Michael Wittmann's heroics at Villers-Bocage placed him front and center in the interest of the German war correspondents. Hauptscharführer Dieter Menninger of the Kurt Eggers SS Propaganda Unit recalled his conversation with Wittmann: "We still had to see Michael Wittmann that day. He had done a great deed with his Tiger! We checked over our studio truck once again. My radio technician, Oberscharführer Emil Wunsch, was the personification of dependability. As usual, our Dora tape recorder's batteries were fully charged. Emil was filling in as driver, as our regular driver, Rottenführer Brülls had sustained a grazing wound in the back during a strafing attack a few days earlier. I orientated myself on the map and off we went. We crawled over the summery Norman roads, taking advantage of all the cover offered by the trees, to the Tiger command post where Obersturmführer Michael Wittmann was that afternoon. We were forced to leave our vehicle four to six times—low-flying aircraft.

We arrived in the late afternoon. I reported to the Corps Tiger Battalion of the Ist SS Panzer Corps LAH, while Emil very quickly camouflaged our vehicle, a Steyer. The mood that day was calm and relaxed. I was briefed on the situation and the military action that resulted from Wittmann's bravery. As a war correspondent I wasn't seen as an outsider. I was one of them. The men knew that I had been the commander of an armored car. Several knew me from actions together on the Eastern Front. 'Do you have your magic box with you?' they asked. 'Our old man must think so. I think he'd rather go out in his Tiger again than to speak in your bus.' My radio technician Emil appeared with cables and the capacitor microphone just at the right moment. The joking ceased. We were connected to the studio truck. The front rumbled and roared all the while. An unprecedented war of material was raging near the coast. Obersturmführer Wittmann, slim and quiet in his black panzer uniform, stepped out of his circle of comrades, with whom he had once again been discussing the details of his courageous action, the destruction of twenty-one English tanks and twenty armored troop carriers.

We knew each other from earlier battles and shook hands, offered my congratulations on his extraordinary success. He smiled casually as if he had nothing to do with it, as if it hadn't been his orders and reactions which caused the destruction of the enemy vehicles, his concentrated, quick action which smashed the advance into the rear of the Ist SS Panzer Corps by the English. He made reference to the performance of his gunner and the iron discipline of his crew. I made a suggestion as to the format and content of our taped session for the radio. Wittmann nodded. There was no discussion. 'You're the boss now, and I put myself in your hands,' he said. 'Attention, taping, edit please!' Our conversation began. When it was over we packed up the equipment. The heavy shells from the enemy's naval guns howled over the command post. Michael Wittmann nodded approvingly over his statement. 'Very good.' We had to get back to our war correspondent courier point as quickly as possible. The report would be taken to Paris that night, in order to be sent to Berlin by the Paris transmitter for editing and rerecording. Before we set off into the night with the burning sky, I bade farewell to Michael Wittmann. We agreed that I would soon accompany him into action in his Tiger."

SS War Correspondent Herbert Reinecker met with Michael Wittmann in Baron Park on the evening of 13 June. Memories of this meeting have remained with him over the many years. Reinecker recalled that day: ". . . But I recall very well my visit with him. The day was dull, no light, I think it was even raining softly. Michael Wittmann was not the type of hero one usually imagined, he was almost pale and physically rather frail. He exuded something, a sort of solemnity, as if something was blowing against him, that revealed something of what had recently happened to him—of the event that still affected him, no euphoria, rather deadly seriousness, the victory did not lift the burden from him—how ridiculously great must have been the stress he faced—no one can hide that away. He embodied something: the humility of the victor. I still remember my strong feeling toward him, he was unbelievably likeable for his modesty . . . I will see him in front of me until the end of my life, one of the scenes that stays in the memory—the word hero has since held a different meaning for me."

THE 1ST AND 2ND COMPANIES, 101ST SS PANZER BATTALION, IN ACTION NEAR VILLERS-BOCAGE, 14–16 JUNE 1944

The 1st Company remained south of Villers-Bocage with four Tigers on the evening of 13 June 1944. SS-Unterscharführer Wendt (Tiger 132) guarded Hill 213. The Tigers of the 2nd Company had taken up position 1.5 kilometers east of Villers-Bocage. On 14 June 1944 the 1st Company was involved in minor skirmishes with English units near Villers-Bocage. SS-Unterscharführer Wendt continued to guard Hill 213. When a Sherman tank suddenly emerged from the town, the Tiger prepared to destroy it. Then the crew realized that it had been captured by panzer-grenadiers of the Hitlerjugend Division, who were driving it in an easterly direction. After Wittmann's attack the English had simply abandoned several tanks in the hedgerow- and brush-covered terrain north of the national highway. Wendt's crew examined these intact Cromwells and found, among other things, their complete rations supply, which was a significant and welcome supplement to their own.

Villers-Bocage was entirely in German hands on 14 June. Tigers of the 1st Company also saw combat farther west, in the 2nd Panzer Division's sector. Several months later SS-Untersturmführer Walter Hahn wrote of the action at Cahagnes: "The next day we carried out an attack east of Cahagnes which bogged down in the concentrated artillery fire of the enemy. Hannes' (Philipsen, the author) tank suffered engine damage and the crew had to abandon their vehicle in the midst of the artillery fire. Hannes returned to the tank during the night, repaired the damage in spite of the ongoing, heavy artillery fire, and brought the vehicle back to the company."

The English press nevertheless reported Villers-Bocage free of the enemy that day. According to English sources, that evening there was a German attack against British positions northwest of Villers-Bocage in which numerous Tigers and infantry took part. Objective of the attack was the envelopment of the English from the east and west; the English claimed to have destroyed six Tigers. There is no reference to the attack in the records of the 101st SS Panzer Battalion; additionally the loss lists reveal that six Tigers could not have been lost. Total casualties on 14 June were one NCO and four men wounded, with two of the latter belonging to the 2nd Company. During the night of 15 June 1944 the British 22nd Armoured Brigade, which was stuck west of Villers-Bocage, was supposed to pull back toward Orey, nine kilometers northeast of Caumont. A fighter-bomber attack on Villers-Bocage as dusk was falling was planned, in order to divert attention from the withdrawal, and was to be followed by a heavy bombing raid around midnight. The results of this bombing raid will be described at length elsewhere. On 15 June 1944, four Tigers of the 1st Company took up the pursuit of the enemy forces withdrawing to the northwest, destroying five British tanks and several anti-tank guns.

SS-Unterscharführer Wendt, the commander of Tiger 132, took part in this action. He recalled: "Early in the morning a dispatch rider led me from Hill 213 to the remaining tanks of the 1st Company. Under the command of Philipsen we attacked toward the north. Our four Tigers were supposed to traverse an area of terrain with numerous hedgerows. I was hit while sitting by one of these hedgerows, probably by a so-called hollow-charge projectile, which penetrated the armor and sprayed a jelly-like burning mass inside. The turret was instantly filled with flames. We had to get out, but I was held fast by my headset and throat microphone. I bowed my head and ripped off the cables. In those few seconds my hair was singed. Everyone got out of the burning tank, although my gunner had severe burns on his hands. We were soon able to deliver him to an aid station for treatment, however."

Several Tigers of Wittmann's 2nd Company stood guard at Hill 213. SS-Unterscharführer Stubenrauch and SS-Sturmmann Gaube were killed and one man was wounded. 16 June 1944 once again saw two platoons of the 1st Company in action near Cahagnes. Of that day SS-Untersturmführer Hahn wrote: "Two days later, on 16 June, we carried out the attack near Cahagnes in which Hannes died a hero's death. Our battle group of four tanks, which was under his command, attacked together with grenadiers and made good progress at first. We drove the enemy from a village, but as we exited the village we suddenly cameunder massed anti-tank and artillery fire, the like of which I had never experienced. Hannes' tank was immediately hit twice by anti-tank fire and began to burn. My tank was about twenty meters to the side, and I saw Hannes and a member of his crew get out, apparently uninjured, and try to make their way to the rear. Then a shell landed close by him and I saw Hannes fall and lie still. I immediately got out of my tank to go to his aid, but as I approached I saw that it was already too late. It looked as if he had been killed instantly by several shell fragments. We laid him on my tank and after the engagement was over drove him back to the company."

Philipsen's Tiger was hit by fire from anti-tank guns as it left a sunken road at the exit from the village of Cahagnes. His driver, Unterscharführer

Walter Sturhahn, and the radio operator failed to get out of the burning tank. Under heavy artillery fire, Philipsen, together with his gunner and loader, made his way back through the sunken road. The fatal shell landed about thirty-five meters from the tank; its fragments wounded him fatally in the abdomen. News of the death of the universally-popular SS-Obersturm-führer Philipsen hit the battalion hard. He and his platoon had only been in action three days. Two days later SS-Hauptsturmführer Möbius wrote to Philipsen's father: "SS-Obersturmführer Philipsen was an officer who was liked and respected by everyone in the company; I have lost my best platoon commander. For his accomplishments in the tough fighting of 13-16 June 1944 at Villers-Bocage, battalion commander von Westernhagen recommended him for the Honor Roll Clasp.

In his letter to Philipsen's father the commanding officer wrote: ". . . As to what happened in the action in which Hannes fell, I only know from the combat report that just two platoons had been committed and I thus wasn't present. Herr Philipsen, the heroic death of your son Hannes, as we all called him for short, was not just a great loss to you and yours, it has also hit me personally and the battalion very hard. I can only shake your hand in spirit and salute my fallen comrade Hannes. Hannes was not just an exemplary soldier and SS officer, but the kind of comrade we need today. I became very fond of your son on account of his fine demeanor and the battalion and I proudly mourn Hannes as he was in life . . . After his death I recommended Hannes for inclusion in the honor roll; those named in the honor roll are members of the Waffen-SS or of the armed forces who distinguished themselves several times through acts of bravery. The Honor Roll Pin and a certificate will be awarded, and they will be sent to you."

Sturmmann Hubert Heil, a radio operator serving in the 2nd Company, recalled those first days in Normandy: "The superiority of the enemy's air force and artillery as well as his technically advanced weapons were much more dangerous to us than those on the Eastern Front. The aircraft dived on us like hawks. The best thing we could do by day was to camouflage our tanks and camouflage them again. The Allies offered no heroic resistance on the ground, thus we did not have to reckon with close combat. They placed their main emphasis on carpet bombing and did not go out of their way to spare the civilian population. Our main protection and chance of survival was the woods and trees of the fruit plantations. The delay in launching the main attack on the enemy landing troops, which was ascribable to sabotage, was our undoing. The heavy shells fired by the ships' guns reached deep into the hinterland, as far as our positions.

Date	Company	Killed			Wounded		
		Officers	NCOs	Men	Officers	NCOs	Men
13/6/1944	1st	-	3	6	1	2	7
13/6/1944	2nd	-	-	1	-	-	3
14/6/1944	1st	-	-	-	-	1	2
14/6/1944	2nd	-	-	-	-	-	2
15/6/1944	1st	-	-	-	-	-	-
15/6/1944	2nd	-	1	1	-	-	1
16/6/1944	1st	1	1	2	1	-	3

Sometimes I wished I was at a front whose rear did not have these dangers as in the west in Normandy." None of the tanks of the 3rd Company saw action in the fighting in the Villers-Bocage area.

The 1st Company had thus lost one officer, five NCOs and ten men killed and two officers, three NCOs and eighteen men wounded in its first actions on the invasion front in and near Villers- Bocage during the period 13–16 June 1944. The seriously-wounded SS-Untersturmführer Lukasius was included in the 1st Company's losses. The 2nd Company's casualties were one NCO and two enlisted men killed and six men wounded. The 1st Company lost a total of six Tigers, including five on 13 June in Villers-Bocage.

Seven days after the victory at Villers-Bocage, the men who had taken part in the action received decorations from SS-Sturmbannführer von Westernhagen. SS-Sturmmänner Günter Boldt and Günther Jonas had been awarded the Iron Cross, Second Class for actions in Russia on 15 March 1944, but were not present to receive their decorations as they were in hospital for treatment of wounds. Therefore, on 20 June 1944 both men received the Iron Cross, First Class and the Iron Cross, Second Class. Wittmann's driver, SS-Unterscharführer Walter Müller, received the Iron Cross, First Class. Members of the 2nd Company decorated with the Iron Cross, Second Class were SS-Unterscharführer Herbert Boden and SS-Sturmmänner Julius Luscher, Erich Ditl, Johann Schmidtbauer and Max Schulze.

In the 1st Company SS-Untersturmführer Walter Hahn received the Iron Cross, First Class. The Iron Cross, Second Class was presented to SS-Untersturmführer Lukasius, SS-Oberscharführer Heinrich Bode, SS-Unterscharführer Arno Salamon, Georg Przibylla, SS-Rottenführer Helmut Steinmetz and SS-Sturmmann Adolf Leuschner of the Headquarters Company.

The dominant event of those first days of action in Normandy was Michael Wittmann's feat of 13 June 1944, which gave the battalion security and self-confidence in its own strength. Wittmann's coup de main was the talk of the town. War correspondent SS-Oberscharführer Herbert Reinecker met Wittmann and afterward wrote a major article for The Black Corps. The article's honest observation and portrayal of the combat events and its sensible description of Wittmann the man and soldier made it probably the most accurate of its time. Herbert Reinecker only met with Wittmann that one time; nevertheless his memory of their meeting remains clear after almost forty-nine years.

Concerning this "phenomonal time situation" he wrote that there were "completely inexplicable and fantastic examples of bravery, idealism and spirit of sacrifice—the loftiest human qualities. I name Michael Wittmann to the list of men who are an expression of the highest degree of those virtues. I had only one meeting with him, the one I described. I never saw him again because I was forced to leave the front-line forces. He made a deep impression on me, immediately and quite directly, because he placed the conventional picture of a hero—as was the fashion then—completely into question. His humanity and vulnerability, his sensibility were obvious. The event itself still quivered in him—it was my impression that he had had an unbelievably human experience. He had not just destroyed tanks—he knew too well that there were men in the tanks. What he had done was no mere 'act of heroism,' but took place on a higher plain, something granted to only a few in such scope and depth. I am expressing my personal opinion, my very personal impression—but I believe that what I am saying, what I felt then while conversing with him, is correct.

I received a similar impression from Panzermeyer, who was also on the far side of the border in which military events are classed. Beyond a certain border there reigns a feeling of being bound together in tragedy. It was a lightning meeting, perhaps that is what made it so unforgettable for me."

The Black Corps: Michael Wittmann, the Tank Killer

The original account made by Reinecker after his conversation with Wittmann, which appeared in Black Corps on 3 August 1944: SS-PK. "I saw him for the first time in the Baron park grounds in Normandy. He was running through the rain, shoulders hunched, wearing a black leather vest and blue lightweight fitter's pants. He had his hands in his pockets, for it was cool. Two hours sleep on a field cot somewhere could not take the shadow of exhaustion and a major battle from him, so that the extraordinary was still in him, the aftereffect of a great effort which he had mustered up not only physically, but also with heart and soul.

A few hours ago he destroyed twenty-one English tanks and carried out one of those unbelievable acts, which are like duels with fate and synonymous with the concept of an heroic act. He stood before us, average height, his hair a pale blonde, a face that one would like to call unobtrusive and in which one can read modesty, calm and self-sufficiency, a man with an almost soft voice, frugal in his movements, with a much greater desire to listen than to speak. When he spoke, his words were well-considered, it seems as if he listens to them so as not to make a mistake and to tell a story or give an opinion with the maximum of factuality and truth—we were standing before a man.

Whoever would speak of and with him as a hero will discover that Michael Wittmann will look at him, calmly and deliberately, with mild bewilderment and then with rejection, for he wants nothing to do with such men, and finally walk away because he has no love for the pathetic nor the big words and not the fuss they make of him. And this is not his modesty, of the type that is also pride, rather he is thoroughly aware of what he has done, he knows the value of his success, but he also knows what he had to summon up in moral strength and that the sum of those situations, which place him in the shadow of death and in the midst of great exertions, changes men, creates other measuring sticks, "too much is at stake" to be a hero out of a book.

It must be said once, that he and with him all the others on whom the battle sometimes depends are not created nerveless by nature, that they are not killers, not people who only need appear on the battlefield to triumph, that they are people with desires, passions and hopes, with plans for the future, with entirely bourgeois love for their children and their wives, that one can, for example, talk with Michael Wittmann about good books as well as about tank types, and that his unparalleled success is not the triumph of the heroic but of the human.

I will never forget listening to him tell how he sat alone in the cover of a wood with his lone Tiger and saw the grandiose sight of the passing English armored regiment, vehicle after vehicle, sixty enemy tanks moving at high speed down a road from which he was barely two-hundred meters away. And not only tanks, but troop carriers with a battalion of infantry as well. There stood

Michael Wittmann. Should he give battle? He had never shied away from superior numbers, but this was suicide. When had a single tank ever engaged an entire regiment? It would mean death, Michael Wittmann knew that.

And he thought further: there they go, they will enter Villers, they will burst the front, overrun headquarters, tear open a hole, infantry will follow. Fate allowed Michael Wittmann to see the cards before they were on the table. Then Michael Wittmann took a deep breath; he had made the most difficult decision of his life, he was going to attack, against all the rules, against reason, he was going to approach, fire and fire, and go under, for otherwise it would not end. Was this desperation? A sheer risky gamble, an adventurous and foolhardy testing of fate? Michael Wittmann said: There wasn't anything else I could do. He said it unheroically, he said it quite simply, he placed no weight on the words. And when he then began to move, broke from cover with engine roaring and opened fire, he did not change into a hero with supernatural powers. He was a man, from whom all questions had now dropped away, who now possessed a clarity of purpose that enabled him to act purposely and instinctively.

And that seemed to be the decisive factor in his ability to spring across and leave behind him the boundary between what is human, to, so to speak, free himself from the weight of all questions and normal emotions and act in a mood that was weightless, easy and focused entirely on the battle. It was the mood that is the element of instinct, of independent action by the eyes, hands and heart. And that is how Michael Wittmann fought, and he once said that in those moments death, too, lost its horror, that one simply didn't think about it and that if it ever did come it must be good.

Also part of the mood that surrounded Wittmann's warrior's domain was the total mastery of all the means of warfare, the coolness and the presence of mind as well as the intimate knowledge of his tank and its equipment, a sixth sense in sizing up a situation, which gave his type a unique ability in combat. It is the result of totally focusing all human senses on the process of combat, which takes place beyond the conscious, smells danger, instinctively sizes up a situation and in each case causes the most effective means to be employed. He is thus one of those absolutely martial men who through their career as soldiersbecome artists in the secretive sum of their intuition and in their infinite ability to achieve martial success.

Michael Wittmann was born in Vogelthal near Beilngries in the Upper Pfalz and later resided in Ingolstadt. He was a young farm worker when he joined the Waffen-SS in 1937, and from the day he walked through the guard gate into the domain of the red brick barracks complex in Lichterfelde one can calculate the life of Michael Wittmann, the start of an exceptionally brave career as a soldier. He was an SS-Unterscharführer when war broke out, about twenty-five years old, quiet, conscientious, knew his infantry weapons in his sleep and had a great desire to be allowed to drive tanks.

His love of tanks was love at first sight, and for him there was no more beautiful moment than to finally roll against the enemy standing in an assault gun. But the war still seemed to avoid him. He drove into Greece and it was little more than a vacation trip, no one opposed him. Not until the battle signal rang out in the east was Michael Wittmann summoned. He had nothing left to learn, his first big opportunity displayed the full range of his talents. The advance stopped, a wave of eighteen Soviet tanks was blocking the road with their fire. Michael Wittmann rolled forward in his assault gun, watchful, calm, determined. He measured the terrain, he possessed that concentrating gaze which, as it were, saw the countryside's skeleton of hill lines and bottom lands, hides, low-lying approach routes and level battlefields. Instead of placing himself in the open and firing, he maneuvered his heavy assault gun toward the enemy almost silently, he possessed the great hunter's instinct and now showed what he could do. He knocked out six of the eighteen Soviet tanks, the rest subsequently chose to drive away.

There followed another long wait. He accompanied the Leibstandarte to Rostov, was twice wounded, won both Iron Crosses, but his wish was still to command a heavy tank. Then, at the beginning of 1943, he got his wish. He stood in the turret of a Tiger, its commander and an Untersturmführer. Now the war no longer avoided him, now began the great tank duels, the bitter one-on-one combats, in which Wittmann became an expert practitioner. On the day the great battle began near Belgorod he destroyed eight tanks. In the rapid advance, driving over fields, charging into villages, in unpredictable tank battles, he showed what he could do. He overran batteries, picked out even the most cleverly-camouflaged anti-tank gun nests, overran them, blasted them with his cannon, was cautious when he had to be, aggressive when it paid off, his keen instinct and the luck of the skillful allowed him to drive unscathed through five furious, fire-filled days. Over and over again enemy tanks went up like blazing torches before him, and when Michael Wittmann washed his sweaty, powder-smeared face on the evening of the fifth day, he knew that he had left behind him thirty wrecked T 34s, twenty-eight Soviet anti-tank guns run over and shot up and two batteries of artillery destroyed.

Wittmann continued his success in late autumn. Near Brusilov he ran into a Soviet tank assembly area, taking the enemy by surprise. He was faster, more skilled and braver and blasted ten tanks from the mass of Soviet armor. Three more fell prey to his Tiger later that afternoon . . . He counted every tank, but he rated the anti-tank guns he destroyed twice as high. He hated the concealed nests, those hiding places of death, it was with special satisfaction that he sniffed them out and said that enemy tanks had ceased to be a strain on his nerves, that only the anti-tank guns still made him uncomfortable, lurking in their tails and so much more difficult to spot than tanks.

On 6 December of the same year he defeated a heavy anti-tank front. Once again his skill decided the battle in his favor. He blasted his way through with mighty salvoes, burst through the positions and sat astride the enemy's supply road like a wolf amid the flock. He placed his fiery mark on the road, smashed long columns of vehicles and caused tremendous confusion among the Soviets.

By now Michael Wittmann had become a veteran armored warrior. His instinct, his nose, as one said, told him where something was up. It was told that he could see as well by night as by day, and they said that he did the aiming himself at night until a distant pIIIar of fire unmistakably told the others that a tank must have stood there. Wittmann was now destroying tanks almost every day, almost always several, so that his list of successes grew ever longer. In the Berdichev area he led three Tigers into an assembly of enemy tanks and destroyed ten, raising his total to sixty-five. Now he received the Knight's Cross.

And his pursuit of enemy tanks went on. Now five, now six, now nine, he picked off his victims from masses of tanks as well as from the battle lines. When he blew up his eighty-eighth enemy tank the Führer awarded him the Knight's Cross with Oak Leaves. One could depend on Michael Wittmann. Even in the most difficult hours of the Eastern Campaign, in wintry fields of snow, on icy hills, in the midst of night-shrouded forests, whether on the attack or on the defensive, in cut-off strongpoints, Michael Wittmann

remained calm and businesslike, and God knows they didn't let
him fight, shoot and destroy tanks unhindered.

The Soviets pounded his tank, anti-tank rounds seemed to literally saw pieces from the steel of the Tiger. There were moments
that spared him nothing in danger, difficulty and threats. After his
117th tank kill Obersturmführer Wittmann changed theaters and
engaged the English and Americans in the west. His arrival
brought the most successful, toughest and most experienced tank
commander onto the battlefield and the English were very soon to
learn what that meant: Michael Wittmann set out against the
English armored regiment commanded by Colonel Payne,
destroyed twenty-one of its tanks, having burst upon them like
death incarnate. Colonel Payne related that he spent the most terrible moments of his life on that road in front of Villers-Bocage
when Wittmann's Tiger set out alone against sixty of the English.

We have no wish to underrate this unmatched success or take it
for granted. Behind it lies a vast sum of difficult experiences, a
high expenditure of mental strength, and a passionate conviction
in the rightness of our martial mission.

After his 138th kill the Führer awarded Michael Wittmann the
Swords and in doing so decorated a man feared by his enemies,
loved by his friends and comrades, and known by the German
people as their finest soldier.

SS War Correspondent Herbert Reinicker.

A Tiger Destroys a Superior Force: The First Swords on the Atlantic Front—SS-Obersturmführer Wittmann Destroys His 138th Enemy Tank

Berlin, 26 June. On 22 June 1944 the Führer awarded the Knight's
Cross of the Iron Cross with Oak Leaves and Swords to SS-Obersturmführer Michael Wittmann, commander of a heavy panzer
company in the SS Panzer Division "Hitler-Jugend", making him
the 71st soldier of the German Armed Forces to be so honored.

On 30 January 1944 he became the 380th soldier of the German
Armed Forces to be decorated with the Knight's Cross of the Iron
Cross with Oak Leaves after raising his total in the east to 114 tanks
destroyed. Since the beginning of the defensive battles in Normandy SS-Obersturmführer Wittmann has once again engaged the
enemy in his tank. On 13 June the SS-Obersturmführer carried out
the act for which he has now received this high decoration from

the Führer. That morning he and his heavy tank company were standing ready in the Caen area. SS- Obersturmführer Wittmann was in cover with his "Tiger", separated from his company, when suddenly an English armored battalion, followed by an English armored troop carrier battalion, was reported. After quickly issuing additional orders to his company, he drove into the English column, firing on the move. From 80 meters Wittmann first destroyed four "General Sherman" tanks. Then he positioned himself beside the column and roared along it, firing in his direction of travel. In this way he destroyed 15 heavy enemy tanks in a very short time. Six tanks were damaged and their crews forced to bail out. The escorting armored troop carrier battalion was almost completely wiped out. The following companies took about 250 prisoners from this battalion.

Even though his tank was disabled by a heavy enemy anti-tank gun, he still destroyed every vehicle within range and scattered the unit. SS-Obersturmführer Wittmann and his crew subsequently abandoned their tank and made their way on foot 15 kilometers to a neighboring division. SS-Obersturmführer Wittmann returned to the scene of the fighting with 15 of that division's tanks and briefed another heavy panzer company from his division, which had arrived in the meantime, on the situation. This company immediately engaged the enemy tanks and anti-tank guns still in the town.

It was due solely to the determined and courageous behavior of SS-Obersturmführer Wittmann that the English 22nd Armoured Brigade, already deep in the rear of our front, was destroyed, thus averting a serious threat to the entire corps. On that day of combat SS-Obersturmführer Wittmann raised his total of victories to 138 enemy tanks and 132 enemy anti-tank guns.

Further newspaper extracts:

The Swords for SS-Obersturmführer Wittmann

Berlin, 26 June 1944. The Führer awards the Oak Leaves with Swords to SS-Obersturmführer Michael Wittmann, company commander of a heavy panzer company in the SS Panzer Division Hitlerjugend as the 71st soldier.

SS-Obersturmführer Wittmann was born on 22 April 1914 in Vogelthal (Upper Pfalz). In 1937 Wittmann voluntarily joined the Leibstandarte SS Adolf Hitler. On 14 January 1944 the Führer awarded him the Knight's Cross and on 30 January the Oak Leaves. Since the beginning of the defensive battle in Normandy SS-Obersturmführer Wittmann has once again faced the enemy in his tank. On 13 June the heavy tank company under his command was on alert in the Caen area. Due to his determined and courageous behavior an English armored brigade already deep in the rear of our front was destroyed, averting a deadly threat to the entire corps. In this one day of combat SS-Obersturmführer Wittmann raised his victory total to 138 enemy tanks and 132 enemy anti-tank guns.

The Oak Leaves with Swords for
SS-Obersturmführer Michael Wittmann

Berlin, 26 June 1944. The Führer awards the Oak Leaves with Swords to SS-Obersturmführer Michael Wittmann, company commander of a heavy panzer company in the SS Panzer Division Hitlerjugend. Wittmann was the 71st soldier of the Wehrmacht to receive this decoration.

On 13 June the SS-Obersturmführer Wittmann and his heavy tank company were standing ready in the Caen area. SS-Obersturmführer Wittmann was in cover with his "Tiger", separated from his company, when suddenly an English armored battalion, followed by an English armored troop carrier battalion, was reported. After quickly issuing additional orders to his company, he drove into the English column, firing on the move. Wittmann first destroyed four tanks. Then he positioned himself beside the column and roared along it, firing in his direction of travel. In this way he destroyed 15 heavy enemy tanks. The escorting armored troop carrier battalion was almost completely wiped out.

Even though his tank was disabled by a heavy enemy anti-tank gun, he still destroyed every vehicle within range and scattered the unit. SS-Obersturmführer Wittmann and his crew subsequently abandoned their tank and made their way on foot to a neighboring division. SS-Obersturmführer Wittmann returned to the scene of the fighting with 15 of that division's tanks.

It was due solely to the determined and courageous behavior of SS-Obersturmführer Wittmann that the English 22nd Armoured Brigade, already deep in the rear of our front, was destroyed. On that day of combat SS-Obersturmführer Wittmann raised his total of victories to 138 enemy tanks and 132 enemy anti-tank guns.

Wittmann was born in Vogelthal (Oberpfalz) as the son of a farmer.

THE 3RD COMPANY OF THE 101ST PANZER BATTALION IN EVRECY, 14–15 JUNE 1944

The 3rd Company was late arriving at the invasion front. It reached Falaise on 13 June 1944, and the next day elements of the company moved up to Evrecy, situated northeast of Villers-Bocage below National Highway 175. SS-Sturmmann Ernst Kufner recalled: "On 14 June elements of the company—three tanks, supply vehicles, and the train—were moved into the Evrecy assembly area (ten kilometers southwest of Caen). The tanks were parked and camouflaged in the gardens at the outskirts of Evrecy to the left of the road, the supply trucks to the right. I myself was with the train, for the day before in Falaise I was relieved as radio operator by a man returning from leave.

Untersturmführer Amselgruber's tank arrived in Evrecy during the evening hours. It lacked a radio operator and loader. Both had been killed by fighter-bombers while outside the tank during a march halt. The senior NCO, Hauptscharführer Hack, ordered me to join the crew as replacement radio operator. At about midnight Untersturmführer Amselgruber assigned me to stand guard. Untersturmführer Günther, a wearer of the Knight's Cross, and his tank were about twenty meters to our left. Several enemy aircraft were in the air at dusk on 14 June, circling constantly over the Evrecy area. Most of the crews of the four Tigers and the men of the supply trucks slept outside, under their vehicles. As ordered, I began my watch at approximately 01.00 hours. It was very quiet. One occasionally heard the rumble of guns in the distance and the droning of aircraft.

All of a sudden the trees, the grass between the tanks, the houses and the church in Evrecy were burning. Aircraft dropped bombs, at first phosphorous bombs. I woke the tank crews sleeping beneath the panzers. We all climbed into the tanks. The company commander was heard to shout, 'Start engines, get the tanks out of here!' Our driver tried to fire up the engine. The starter failed. We had to leave the tank sitting there. We could see everything through the periscopes and were forced to look on as everything beside and in front of us burned. The driver had to watch with the rest of us as Untersturmführer Günther's tank went up in flames. It was twin-engined aircraft that dropped their bombloads on us and the town of Evrecy. The attack was all over in twenty to thirty minutes. It took a combined effort to open the hatches. There was a layer of earth on the tank twenty centimeters deep. In Evrecy the houses were still burning. There was nothing to be seen or heard of our comrades. The starter worked now, and we drove the tank to the war memorial. The engine began to overheat after only several hundred meters. The cooling fans were stopped up by the layer of earth. Around us were huge bomb craters, so big that a Tiger could have fit inside.

We looked for our comrades in the morning twilight. As I recall, the assistant armorer-artificer turned up. His coat was all in tatters. He had taken cover in a bomb crater and had been lucky. Of the other members of the train we saw nothing. The other three Tigers had been put out of action. Untersturmführer Günther's tank took a direct hit and was completely burnt out. All that remained of the crew was charred pieces of clothing, buttons, and fragments of bone. The company commander's tank was hit in the gun barrel. The turret was torn off and lay beside the tank. The three men in the turret went with it and all had burns. The driver and radio operator were dead. The third Tiger drove into open country and after covering about three-hundred meters plunged into a six-to-seven-meter-deep defile. The crew was also killed. Apart from the armorer-artificer assistant, all the men of the supply trucks, who had been sleeping in the open, were killed. I myself was fortunate that I had been allowed to join the crew of Untersturmführer Amselgruber's Tiger in place of the fallen radio operator. I was also lucky that I had been relieved as radio operator in the company commander's tank the day before. His radio operator was also killed."

Another member of SS-Untersturmführer Amselgruber's crew, SS-Sturmmann Leopold Aumüller, lived through the night of the bombs at Evrecy. He was the gunner. The driver was SS-Sturmmann Sippel, radio operator SS-Sturmamm Kufner, the loader probably Ewald Graf. Here is Aumüller's account: "We were in the workshop when the invasion began; our Tiger received a new motor and it wasn't until two days later that we set off. Our tank was bombed once before the terrible bombing attack at Evrecy. We drove into a town and camouflaged our tank beneath fruit trees. Unterscharführer Bofinger of the orderly office was temporarily in command. The panzer battalion's command post was in that village. Unterscharführer Bofinger reported in at once. I instructed the crew to refuel the tank while I went into a house to wash. When I returned, the remaining members of the crew went into the same house to wash. While they were inside a single aircraft came and tried to bomb the tank; but it missed its target and instead hit several houses, including the one my friends were in. They were all killed. The radio operator was Jäsche; the SDG at that time, Rottenführer Scherbath, was also there. (The town was Vieux, the author.)

We received replacements immediately and drove on in the direction of Evrecy. There we were attacked again, this time by several aircraft, but were able to save ourselves by driving into a wood at full throttle. Then we reached Evrecy, where we were assigned another new crew under Untersturmführer Amselgruber. The driver was Sippel, the radio operator Kufner, I can't remember the name of the loader, it could have been Ewald Graf. Then came the night of the bombing attack. We quickly left our places under the tank when the parachute flares (Christmas trees) and the first bombs began falling. I climbed in with the driver as that was the fastest way into he tank. Untersturmführer Amselgruber immediately ordered, 'Start the engine and drive!' He was very nervous. However, we stayed in our well-camouflaged position because the starter failed. We were sitting right under a very large tree, it was impossible for the enemy bombers to see us. Our immobility was our good fortune."

Of the members of the 3rd Company in Evrecy, eighteen had been killed and eleven wounded in the thirty-minute bombing raid during the night of 15 June. The dead included SS-Untersturmführer Alfred Stubenrauch, SS-Sturmmann Sepp Heim (the driver of Günther's tank), radio operators Jäschke and Schinitzki, and the armorer-artificer. SS-Untersturmführer Alfred Günther, a wearer of the Knight's Cross, had fallen, company commander SS-Obersturmführer Hanno Raasch was wounded. The 3rd Company had thus lost its commanding officer, a platoon commander and numerous other men before ever seeing action. The death of eighteen of its number hit the company hard. This was the attack that was intended to cover the withdrawal of the battered British 22nd Armoured Brigade. Radio traffic by the headquarters of the 101st SS Artillery Battalion, which was located in Evrecy for a brief period, may have led to the attack, as the enemy had an efficient radio direction-finding system which was capable of locating radio transmitters very quickly. This theory is supported by the lengthy artillery bombardment of the town that preceded the bombing. The artillery bombardment led the headquarters to move to a farm west of Evrecy, as a result of which it suffered no losses to the bombing. In addition to the dead of the Tiger battalion, the Allied carpet bombing claimed the lives of one-hundred-and-thirty residents of Evrecy, which meant that a third of the total population had been killed. The town was completely destroyed.

For the 3rd Company this shock was the prelude to the invasion battle. From then on the men knew what it meant to be helplessly exposed to the enemy's air force. In the days that followed, the dead were buried in the cemetery in Evrecy near the French memorial to the fallen of the First World War. They were laid to rest only a few-hundred meters from where they had died. The graves had to be dug under artillery fire. No members of the 3rd Company were present for the burials, probably to avoid any possible negative affect on morale for the coming actions. SS-Obersturm-führer Philipsen was also buried there on 18 June, next to Knight's Cross wearer SS-Untersturmführer Alfred Günther. Both had been friends of Wittmann's since 1940. Günther, who had been extremely popular with the men, was promoted to SS-Obersturmführer posthumously.

Also buried in Evrecy were SS-Unterscharführer Robert Bofinger, SS-Rottenführer Gerhard Scherbath, and two SS-Sturmmänner, all of who had been killed in Vieux on 13 June. According to the casualty report, the radio operator mentioned by Aumüller, SS-Sturmmann Gerhard Jäschke of Breslau, was in fact killed in the bombing of Evrecy on 15 June 1944. SS-Untersturmführer Amselgruber took command of the 3rd Company in place of the wounded SS-Obersturmführer Raasch. The Tigers had to constantly be on guard against fighter-bomber attacks. The enemy's air force was undisputed master of the skies.

The Tiger crews spent the following days along the N 175 which led from Villers-Bocage to Caen. The 3rd Company was moved forward into that sector, on the left wing of the Ist SS Panzer Corps.

Thus, without having been in action, the 3rd Company had already lost thirty-seven men, twenty-nine during the bombing of Evrecy alone. The Headquarters and 2nd Companies also suffered casualties at Evrecy. After his victory of 15 June, SS-Unterscharführer Wendt of the 1st Company was instructed to recover the men killed in Villers-Bocage and take them to Evrecy. Together with his driver, SS-Sturmmann Janekzek, Wendt fulfilled this last duty to the fallen. They were buried in the battalion's graveyard in Evrecy.

Date	Company	Killed			Wounded		
		Officers	NCOs	Men	Officers	NCOs	Men
13/6/1944	3rd	-	1	3	-	-	-
15/6/1944	3rd	1	3	14	1	3	7
15/6/1944	2nd	-	-	-	-	2	1
15/6/1944	HQ	-	-	1	-	-	-

Fighting on the
Villers-Bocage-Caen Road

Maximum camouflage was vital to all operations by the German armor. Any movement automatically attracted an artillery spotter aircraft, which immediately transmitted its observations, resulting in an artillery bombardment of the designated position. In open terrain the Tigers were immediately harried by fighter-bombers with bombs and rockets and placed under observed fire by the enemy artillery. German armored tactics had to be adapted to a situation completely different from the one that prevailed in Russia. As the enemy's artillery frequently pinned down and knocked out German anti-tank resources, the tanks came to be of increased importance in dealing with penetrations by the enemy.

However, the Tigers had to be held back far enough so that they could attack the advancing enemy from adequate concealment employing the element of surprise. This was often dependent on terrain conditions. If the hedgerows, bushes or rows of trees typical of Normandy were available, the Tigers moved into concealed positions behind their own infantry line. If these opportunities for cover were absent, the panzers had to seek out ambush positions on a reverse slope to escape the artillery air reconnaissance. The Tigers were therefore concentrated in groups at anticipated hot spots, from where they could be dispatched quickly to the scene of a successful armored penetration by the enemy to counterattack and destroy the enemy armor. Supplying the elements of the Tiger battalion deployed at the front proved extremely difficult given the continuous aerial activity on the part of the enemy. Supplies were usually delivered to the front at night. The drivers of the fuel and munitions transport columns were tireless in their efforts to deliver the desperately-needed supplies to their comrades at the front. They were not just active at night, however; often the men of the Headquarters Company were on the road in their trucks during daylight hours because supplies were desperately needed. At such times they were vulnerable to the Mustangs and Lightnings, which attacked lone trucks, indeed even individual soldiers, with guns, bombs and rockets.

The Headquarters Company's fuel and munitions transport column, which consisted of a total of forty-two vehicles, had already suffered heavy losses to fighter-bomber attack in the first days of operations, losing almost half its vehicles. From then on they moved almost exclusively at night, in order to escape the fighter-bomber plague. But the men behind the steering wheels of the supply trucks also included young drivers who worked their way from cover to cover under fire from the fighter-bombers and thus reached their destinations. Those men and their accomplishments deserve the same recognition as the maintenance echelons of the panzer companies. The Workshop Company was situated in Bretteville Forest, hidden from Allied air reconnaissance. The men of the company recovered the heavy, damaged tanks with their 18-tonne prime movers. The maintenance echelons recovered damaged or immobilized tanks, often under enemy fire, and repaired them or towed them to the rear. In the weapons workshop the Tiger's main gun and all other weapons were checked and restored to serviceable condition.

The medical echelon, commanded by SS-Hauptsturmführer Dr. Rabe, cared for countless casualties; enemy wounded were treated exactly the same as German. Often the wounded had to be taken by ambulance to the corps hospital in Sées. These drives were highly dangerous, for the English and American fighter-bombers were quick to attack even vehicles marked with the Red Cross. Many wounded burned to death in ambulances on the way to hospital. These frequent violations of the rules for the treatment of medical facilities were reported to the International Red Cross, but sadly resulted in no change in the situation. The number of enemy troops ashore and the quantity of their materiel grew each day; the German navy and air force were unable to effectively interfere with the landing of supplies by the Allies. Army Group B strove to relieve the panzer divisions at the front with infantry divisions as soon as possible, in order to once again form a mobile reserve. A German offensive launched on the 20th or 21st of June would have caught the enemy in an extraordinarily weak phase. The opportunity to do so was squandered, however, and the English now prepared to launch Operation "Epsom."

ACTIONS WEST OF CAEN, 17–24 JUNE 1944

SS-Sturmbannführer von Westernhagen's command post was plain and spartan. There were no security units in the area, no quadruple flak in position to defend against air attack. Were it not for a number of signs—white with a red band and bearing the inscription "Hein"—hanging in the trees, the battalion command post could very easily have been overlooked. Nor did the commanding officer make use of the available command bus;

before the invasion he had merely used it to sleep in. Heinz von Westernhagen was the commander the battalion wished for. He radiated a serene composure and level-headedness, which instilled his men with self-assurance and confidence. In conversation his brash manner, so pronounced and endearing, showed up in flashes. Everyone felt understood by him. Outwardly he showed little emotion, although the strain of command undoubtedly left its mark. The commanding officer was universally respected and liked. Carrying out the orders given him proved very difficult; he was not able to lead the entire battalion in action as the companies were committed in diverse sectors of the front under the command of various units. There never was an attack in battalion strength; the closest thing to that was the attack by the 1st and 2nd Companies at Villers-Bocage. In addition to radio and telephone links, though the latter were rarely feasible, provided by the Signals Platoon, von Westernhagen also had at his disposal the headquarters' message service.

Von Westernhagen described his daily routine on the invasion front in a letter: "I am now completely deaf in my left ear, having been caught five times in the most terrific air attacks. We have slowly become specialists in this. Once I was lying beneath one of our tanks; the two-thousand kilogram bombs fell right in front of our noses, landing three meters left, ten meters right, and twelve meters behind—the flash of the explosion almost burned our throats and lungs. They're an unrefined lot those fellows, but we will have our revenge." The battalion medical officer, SS-Hauptsturmführer Dr. Rabe, was always out and about in his Kfz. 81, directing the recovery of the wounded. Often he spent time up front with the tanks and assisted the Tiger crews. The battalion dentist, SS-Untersturmführer Dr. Hausmann, and his men built a bunker out of railway ties in a wood. In those days the 4th Company was officially separated from the Headquarters Company and from then on existed as an independent unit.

Promotions took place on 21 June 1944. Heinz von Westernhagen was promoted to SS-Obersturmführer. 2nd Company: Wittmann to SS-Hauptsturmführer and Oberjunker Belbe to SS-Untersturmführer. 4th Company: Oberjunker Walter Brauer, commander of the Pioneer Platoon, to SS-Untersturmführer. Headquarters and Supply Company: Paul Vogt, company commander, to SS-Obersturmführer, Alfred Veller, Administration Officer, to SS-Hauptsturmführer, Georg Bartel, Technical Officer Motor Vehicles II, to SS Obersturmführer.

The next day the news spread through the battalion like wildfire: Michael Wittmann had won the Swords!

The Führer sent the following telegram: "In honor of your oft-demonstrated heroism, I award you as the 71st soldier of the Wehrmacht the Knight's Cross of the Iron Cross with Oak Leaves and Swords. Adolf Hitler"

The 2nd Company was positioned in Grimbosq Forest. On 16 June 1944 Wittmann informed a group of its personnel, including the crews of Hantusch and Lötzsch, that Hannes Philipsen had been killed. In those days SS-Hauptscharführer Dieter Menninger joined the crew of Wittmann's tank. "I don't remember what day it was. Emil Wunsch installed my tape recorder in his tank. We crawled toward the enemy in the light of dawn. The light from the east fell on the edge of a wood. I tried to see something through the vision slit. All I saw was forest undergrowth. Then a command rang out. The gun turret turned and then came the order to fire. The Tiger shook from the recoil and at the edge of the wood a pillar of smoke rose from a stricken English tank. I don't remember what number the kill was. I merely recall that I was astonished that he had even been able to see the camouflaged English tank at the edge of the forest and admired his reaction. This time I put myself in Michael Wittmann's hands. I felt safe with his crew. We said goodbye under a threatening, flashing Normandy sky. The young faces of the tank crew—19, 20, 21 years old—watched us go. I had turned 23 in May 1944. I never saw our brave, quiet, modest comrade Michael Wittmann again."

Wittmann's gunner that day was Bobby Woll. Woll, who was a beloved comrade and chum to the men of the 2nd Company, had little chance to come to the fore as a tank commander. In those days, when Wittmann was still in command of the company, two tank crews were caught outside their tanks by a sudden artillery barrage. The men found what cover they could as shells fell and exploded all around them. Suddenly Woll got to his feet as if to leave cover. Wittmann just managed to catch him and had to strike him with his fist to calm him down. Woll had flipped out because of his old head wound and the great mentalstrain. Wittmann's knockout blow probably saved his life. Woll was taken to hospital the same day and from there to Germany. Soon afterward Wittmann left his unit to go receive the Swords at Fithrer Headquarters. During his absence the 2nd Company was led by SS-Untersturmführer Hantusch since SS-Obersturmführer Wessel was plagued by health problems, which led to sarcastic comments in the company.

The delivery of important news from the companies to the battalion was the job of the company dispatch rider or—if originating from the battalion—a member of the message group, or in some cases an operations officer. The battalion signals officer was SS-Untersturmführer Helmut Dollinger who, together with the radio technical sergeant, SS-Oberscharführer Schott, often went along on attacks by the tanks. All radio traffic within the combat echelons of the panzer companies was coded, due to the ever-present danger of transmissions being intercepted by the enemy. A new radio direction finding system enabled the enemy to pinpoint a radio transmitter with precision. Location was often soon followed by artillery or naval gun fire on the affected point. In these circumstances the tank radio operators were required to maintain strict radio discipline so as not to betray their position through unnecessary radio traffic. While on standby, the Tigers often maintained radio silence for hours. The radios were set to receive. Radio codes were changed often, especially before new operations, and the same applied to the frequencies used. Among the code-names for the company commander used by Wittmann's company were "Granite", "Bedrock", "Basalt", and "Flint". In radio traffic Wittmann would be, for example, "Granite Leader", the commander of the Ist Platoon "Granite 1". The remaining tank commanders in the platoons were called by name. One of Wittmann's favorite expressions, "carbide, carbide", came to be used as the order to attack in battle. The radio operators also used code words when requesting urgently-needed supplies; for example, "Hammer" was ammunition and"Anvil" was fuel.

Following the catastrophe at Evrecy, the 3rd Company moved forward and joined the 1st and 2nd Companies at the Villers-Bocage-Caen road. On 23 June several of the 3rd Company's Tigers were in ambush positions beside the National Highway. SS-Untersturmführer Amselgruber recognized a developing English armored thrust and destroyed a total of five tanks. Following this painful setback the enemy withdrew to his departure position. However, the Tiger crews in their well-camouflaged hides placed no trust in the deceptive calm; they knew that the English would try again to break through there.

The commander of Tiger 333, SS-Unterscharführer Waldemar Warnecke (gunner SS-Panzerschütze Günter Wagner, driver SS-Unterscharführer Gerhard Noll, radio operator SS-Sturmmann Richard Garber, loader SS-Panzerschütze August-Wilhelm Belbe), described the 3rd Company's battles on National Highway 175: "While driving from the workshop company to the front I was stopped by Panzermeyer. He ordered me to follow him and guard an open spot in the front on the road from Villers-Bocage to Caen. He promised to inform my unit and instructed his adjutant to do so.

We moved into an ambush position in some bushes at the side of the road. It remained quiet the whole day. The following night we heard tank noises from a village about 1.5 kilometers in front of us. The village was situated on a rise and any approach was hindered by an anti-tank barricade covering half the road. It all struck me as so strangely quiet that I decided to find out what was going on in the village. I formed a patrol with my radio operator and arrived at the barricade undetected. Approximately 600 meters away I saw a row of English tanks engaged in refuelling. I ran back to my Tiger as fast as I could then roared back to the anti-tank barricade. My gun just cleared the barricade. My gunner Wagner then scored hits on six tanks, which caught fire immediately. It was like they were sitting on a serving tray.

Then something hit us. The lights went out; my gunner lay slumped over with the turret machine-gun on top of him. We immediately withdrew to our previous firing position. Our Tiger had taken a hit right in the machine-gun hole in the gun mantlet. The shell stuck in the mantlet, but the machine-gun was driven back and struck my loader in the head. Dr. Rabe diagnosed a concussion. Belbe stayed with the tank at his request. Then we discovered that the turret was jammed, so it was off to the Workshop Company.

The day before Amselgruber destroyed five tanks on a side road in the same sector. I saw it myself. For our six kills my gunner Wagner and I received the Iron Cross, Second Class on 27 July 1944."

MICHAEL WITTMANN RECEIVES THE KNIGHT'S CROSS WITH OAK LEAVES AND SWORDS

Michael Wittmann had left the unit to receive the Swords, which had been awarded him on 22 June, from Adolf Hitler. On 25 June he found himself facing the Führer again in the Berghof. He became the 71st member of the German Armed Forces to receive the black case containing the Knight's Cross with Oak Leaves and Swords. Michael Wittmann was now at the zenith of his success; within half a year he had received the Knight's Cross, the Oak Leaves, and now the Swords. In the same period he had been promoted from the rank of Untersturmführer to Obersturmführer and then Hauptsturmführer. With 138 tanks and 132 anti-tank guns destroyed, he was unique in the panzer arm. The Führer and the Reich's most successful tank commander had a lengthy conversation. Hitler asked for Wittmann's impressions of the invasion front and listened intently to his response. It was Hitler's intention not to let Wittmann return to the front; instead he would pass on his wealth of experience in armored warfare to young officer candidates at an armored command school.

MICHAEL WITTMANN'S LIFE STORY FROM 1914 TO 1942

Who was this most successful tank commander? Michael Wittmann was born in the tiny village of Vogelthal, near Beilngries in the Upper Pfalz, on

22 April 1914, the first son of farmer Johann Wittmann and his wife Ursula. Michael came from old-established Bavarian farming stock. Both grandparents were farmers. His father Johann was born in Vogelthal, on 5 October 1889; his future wife, Ursula Lachermayer, who was three years older than Johann, was born in Marschall, near Holzkirchen. They were married on 6 April 1913. Michael's grandparents ran the farm in Vogelthal, No. 3.

Vogelthal was a small village with 120 inhabitants. It was a farm village and outwardly was just like thousands of other villages in the Reich. Michael acquired two siblings in Vogelthal: Johann was born on 1 July 1916, while Franziska, who was also called Marie, came into the world on 22 February 1918. Michael spent his childhood in this village setting in Bavaria. Shortly after his sixth birthday he entered the local elementary school and later attended secondary school until April 1930.

At the beginning of the nineteen-twenties Michael's father sold the farm in Vogelthal and moved his family to Niederwöhr, in the Münchmünster District, near Pfaffenhof on the Ilm. A second daughter, Anni, was born there on 20 April 1921. The father went on to buy and sell several farms, which meant more moves for the family. In this way the Wittmann family later moved to Sausthal, near Ihrlerstein in the Kehlheim District. Theresa was born there on 3 October 1923. There were now five children growing up in the Wittmann household; a sixth child died at the age of eight. Johann Wittmann bought yet another new farm and moved with his family to Rammersberg, near Velburg in the Neumarkt District in the Upper Pfalz and soon afterward to Höhenberg, a village of eighty inhabitants near Neumarkt. There he ran an inn.

Michael completed his ten years of scholastic training in April 1930. Later he wrote of that time: "After I left school I worked at home with my parents." The sixteen-year-old had to work on his parent's farm, which in those years of great economic distress was not unusual in Germany. Michael's parents simply could not afford career training for all their children in those difficult times. Michael learned much about agriculture in those years and later a newspaper described him as a farmer, though he had never listed that as his occupation. On 10 December 1932 the father left his family and went to Ingolstadt. Michael's brother Johann, a baker by trade, followed his father to Ingolstadt in April 1933 and that August he took to the road.

Michael had grown up well. At 1.76 meters tall, he was of average height, slim, and had an open, likeable, slightly round face with pale, clear eyes. The quiet young man made an intelligent, alert and interesting impression. After three years on the family farm, from 1 July to 1 October

1933 Michael worked in a dairy. He subsequently voluntarily joined the
Labor Service, in which he served from 1 February to 1 August 1934. In
that period Wittmann's battalion was employed in Benediktbeuren.

After leaving the Labor Service Wittmann lived in Weidenhüll, a small
village near Velburg with about fifty inhabitants. His siblings Anni and
Hans later moved to their mother's home town of Marschall, near
Holzkirchen. It was at this time, with an economic upswing evident in Germany under the National Socialists, that the twenty-one-year-old Wittmann
joined the Reichswehr, signing up for a two-year stint. Compulsory military
service had not yet been reintroduced at that time. Wittmann spent only a
short time in Weidenhüll after leaving the labor service, as he reported for
military service in Freising, north of Munich, on 30 October 1934.

Wittmann's new home was the Arnulf Barracks in Freising. He was a
member of the 10th Company of the 19th Infantry Regiment. In the following twenty-three months the young Bavarian received extended, careful
training in all types of infantry weapons, an asset he could later build on.
His instructors were mostly senior non-commissioned officers, many of
them veterans of the First World War. A standing army which was comprised exclusively of volunteers, the Reichswehr was a high-quality force
which set very high standards for itself. Wittmann became a good infantry-
man. He earned the Marksmanship Badge 1st Class and took part in range
practice, cross-country marches, combat exercises and maneuvers. After
one year in the service he was promoted to Gefreiter on 1 November 1935.
Compulsory military service was reintroduced that year.

Wittmann's period of service ended on 30 September 1936 and he was
given an honorable discharge from the army. While Michael was still a soldier, his father had advised him to come to Ingolstadt. On 1 October 1936
Wittmann went directly from Freising to Ingolstadt, for his chances of finding a position there were better than in the country and work there was
also considered preferable. At first he lived in the house of the pensioner
Joseph Graf at Spretistraße 7, on the periphery of the inner city, until 30
November 1936. His father found him these lodgings, having lived there
himself from February to May 1934. Since 1932 Johann Wittmann had
given up his original occupation, farmer and goods handler, and had
worked in Ingolstadt as a warehouse and later factory worker in the textile
machine-building operation of the Deutschen Werken. Soon after his
move to Ingolstadt Michael Wittmann also found work. From 17 October
1936 he was employed as a railway construction worker in Reichertshofen,
next door to Ingolstadt.

The twenty-three-year-old Wittmann was impressed by the economic
upswing in Germany and by the reconstruction work going on in all areas

of life, as well as by the social achievements which the new state had made on behalf of the farmers and workers resulting in a standard of living never before thought possible and an elevation of their standing. He therefore decided to take part in the continued positive development of the state. He wrote: "On 1 November 1936 I applied for admission to the SS at SS-Sturm 1/92 in Ingolstadt." Wittmann thus became part of the most elite organization in Germany with the highest acceptance criteria; on 1 November 1936 he joined the 1st Sturm of the 92nd Ingolstadt SS Standarte as an SS candidate. After his confirmation from SS-Anwärter to SS-Mann he was given the SS number 311623. Wittmann served with his Sturm in his scarce free time, participating in sports, recruiting and demonstration functions.

Wittmann moved in the winter of 1936, and from 30 November resided in the house of Anna Meyer, a pensioner's widow, at Schleifmühle 38, and then from 18 March 1937 in the house of watchmaker Josef Artmeier at Harderstraße 27. Both houses were in Ingolstadt's inner city. At that time Wittmann was also employed as a guard at the large Wehrmacht munitions dump near Weichering in the Neuburg-Schrobenhausen District. Wittmann was no longer satisfied with his work, however; he wanted to become a soldier again, but with a new and modern outfit, the SS-Verfügungstruppe. He applied for acceptance into the Leibstandarte, which was probably the best known and most popular unit in the Reich. He met the very strict selection criteria and was accepted. On 3 April 1937 he left Ingolstadt for Berlin. His service with his new unit began on 5 April at the former main cadet school at Finckensteinallee 62 in Berlin-Lichterfelde. He was now a member of the Leibstandarte SS Adolf Hitler. Voluntary service was a significant factor in Wittmann's life—voluntary labor service, Reichswehr and now the SS-Verfügungstruppe. On account of his previous military service Wittmann was taken on by the Leibstandarte not as an SS-Anwärter, but as an SS-Mann. He was assigned to the Leibstandarte's 17th Company, the former armored scout platoon. The platoon had been formed on I October 1936 under SS-Obersturmführer Georg Schönberger and a cadre of twelve NCOs and men. The process of enlarging the platoon into a company began in March 1937. New recruits joined the unit and the expansion of the armored scout platoon into a company was completed on 5 April 1937, the same day Wittmann entered the Leibstandarte.

Company commander was SS-Obersturmführer Schönberger, the three platoons were commanded by SS-Untersturmführer Max Wünsche, Ernst Bahls and Hans Pfeiffer. Wünsche was also responsible for training recruits. Michael Wittmann was one of the first panzer soldiers of the Leibstandarte. He and the men of the 17th Company proudly wore the black panzer uniform—the only troops of the Leibstandarte to do so—and the large, round panzer cap, which had a hard inner liner to protect the head. While serving with the 17th Company of the Leibstandarte SS Adolf. Hitler Wittmann wore the usual blue and yellow bayonet tassel of the NCOs and enlisted men.

All-round infantry and armored duty alternated with guard duty in Berlin. The 17th Company found itself in Munich in September 1937 on the occasion of Mussolini's visit to the city; soon afterward the company provided troops for a security cordon at Heerstraße Station when the Duce arrived in Berlin. Wittmann took part in his first maneuver after six months in the Leibstandarte. A contemporary chronicler of the armored scout company wrote of the year 1937: "We were at the troop training grounds in Groß-Born from 7 October until 30 October. The routine included living in the field, live firing, night exercises, and patrol missions with the armored cars. The company completed its basic infantry training there. When we returned to Berlin we were able to marvel at our new eight-wheeled armored cars, which had arrived during our absence.

'I rest, I rust!' That could have been our company's motto. Scarcely a week had passed when we had to pack our kit bags again for the trip to Munich to take part in the commemoration day of the movement. There the men of the 2nd and 3rd Platoons solemnly pledged their loyalty to the Führer. The company was now a solid, unified block. During the Christmas celebration on 17 December we sensed that our service together and trust in one another had made us into a close-knit community of soldiers and comrades. It was an impressive and beautiful day, a real Christmas celebration among soldiers of the SS. The company subsequently went on leave, and we took all these impressions home with us. A year rich in work and experiences came to an end."

From the 7th to the 10th of November 1937 Wittmann and his comrades were in Munich to be sworn in. The torchlight swearing-in ceremony took place in front of the Feldherrnhalle in Munich on the night of 9 November. That same day Michael Wittmann was promoted to the rank of SS-Staffel-Sturmmann. In March 1938 the armored scout company and the rest of the Leibstandarte took part in the march into Austria, marking its reunification with the German Reich. The events of those days made a deep impression on Wittmann and his comrades, one they would never forget. The 17th Company then returned to the Reich capital. April of that same year saw SS-Untersturmführer Wünsche and Bahls transferred to the Führer's Adjutant Office; SS-Untersturmführer Pfeiffer followed at a later date. SS-Untersturmführer Olboeter and Mauer were transferred to the company to take their place.

"The drivers of the armored scout company took part in numerous orientation drives and automotive events, and the gold and silver medals they won were proof of their success. An excellent weapons course made the men thoroughly familiar with the weapons in their armored cars." One month after the weapons course, in August 1938, the armored scout company was once more reduced to platoon strength. In October 1938 Wittmann took part in the entry into the Sudetenland. The reception they received and the gratitude of the people there made a deep impression on him. The storm of jubilation and the cordiality in Austria and the Sudetenland eclipsed anything seen so far. Michael Wittmann was involved in an accident in 1938 in which he suffered head and back injuries. On 13 March and 1 October of that year he was awarded medals commemorating the reunification of Ostmark (Austria) and the Sudetenland with the German Reich.

The German entry into Bohemia and Moravia took place in March 1939. In Berlin there was a resumption of combat training and guard and ceremonial duties. On 20 April 1939 Michael Wittmann was promoted to SS-Unterscharführer. The armored scout platoon returned to the Groß-Born troop training grounds in May 1939, taking part in joint exercises with the 13th, 14th and 15th Companies, the pioneer platoon, and the 1st and IIIrd Battalions of the Leibstandarte. The armored scout platoon provided a cordon detachment during the state visit to Berlin by Prince-Regent Paul of Yugoslavia. When the war broke out Wittmann was an armored car commander.

The Leibstandarte Motorized Regiment fought in Poland from the first day, 1 September 1939; that day the armored scout platoon drove from Namslau to Gola and fought near Boleslavice. Wittmann was only in Poland for a very short time, for he was given the job of returning a damaged armored car to Berlin. He arrived with the vehicle in Lichterfelde soon afterward and was transferred to the newly-formed 5th Company of the replacement battalion of the Leibstandarte SS Adolf Hitler. The 5th Company was the battalion's armored scout company. Company commander was SS-Hauptsturmführer Harry Jobst, platoon leaders were SS-Obersturmführer Vetter and SS-Untersturmführer Fromme.

SS-Unterscharführer Wittmann was employed as a training NCO and he proved to be an efficient, discreet instructor of young recruits. "Shuffling" was not part of his training plan. Like recruits everywhere, the men on the Lichterfelde barracks square clicked their heels together when ordered to attention. Wittmann had the habit of swinging one leg out a little farther than usual and then smacking both heels together to produce a loud crack. During a parade in that winter of 1939 his supporting leg slipped on the icy surface and he fell flat. The men laughed loudly. This made Wittmann angry and he subsequently gave the men of his squad hell and showed them who would have the last laugh.

With only two four-wheeled armored cars available for training, a simulated armored car was produced by modifying an Opel P 4 which was then armed with an MG 34. However, during live firing practice in Berlin-Dahlem this creation proved incapable of withstanding the vibration produced by the machine-gun. Many of the men who came from the ranks of the 5th (Armored Scout) Replacement Company went on to become officers, men such as Michael Wittmann, Heinz Belbe, Hubert Hartmann, Gerhard Ulbrich, Heinz Goltz, Heinz Fuhrmann, Hans Dressel, Horst Kalisch, Ulrich Jansen, Ulrich Marth and Bernd Stichnoth.

In early 1940 Wittmann, together with several other NCOs and men, were transferred to Juterbog, where the Leibstandarte's armored assault battery—the initial designation of the assault gun battery—was being formed at the troop training grounds there. The remaining elements of the 5th Replacement Company were transferred to Ellwangen; in August 1940 they were merged with the existing armored scout platoon to form the new armored scout company of the Leibstandarte's reconnaissance battalion. Commanding the assault gun battery, which was formed on 25 April 1940, was SS-Hauptsturmführer Schönberger, Wittmann's former superior in the armored scout platoon. Five officer candidates, fresh from the Junkerschule, were transferred to the battery. At that time the assault gun battery was still part of the artillery, its training was run by the army. Wittmann was also an NCO instructor in Jüterbog and he trained his men hard and skillfully. They knew that if SS-Unterscharführer Wittmann was in charge of training there would be no nonsense.

Wittmann, already familiar with handling the cannon of an armored vehicle from his service in the armored scout company, added to his knowledge. The assault guns were armed with the short-barrelled 75 mm gun, which had little in common with the 20 mm cannon carried by the armored cars. The men were soon issued assault gun uniforms, which were cut like the panzer uniform but in field-gray cloth instead of black. Their service color was red, the same as the artillery.

When the training was over the six assault guns were organized into three platoons and crews were picked. Wittmann received the second gun in SS-Hauptscharführer Rettlinger's Ist Platoon. The gun commanders were allowed to select their own crews. Wittmann chose as his gunner SS-Sturmmann Karl Brüggenkamp, who had originally been requested by another gun commander. As driver he took SS-Unterscharführer Philipp Fritz and as loader SS-Sturmmann Hermann Kneusgen.

The battery's platoon commanders were SS-Untersturmführer Emil Wiesemann, SS-Hauptscharführer (officer candidate) Karl Rettlinger, and SS-Oberscharführer (officer candidates) Helmut Thede and Hugo Müller. The munitions echelon was commanded by SS-Oberscharführer (officer candidate) Wilhelm Beck. SS-Oberscharführer Nofz, who had served with Wittmann in the armored scout platoon, was also an assault gun commander. Following the conclusion of training, the Leibstandarte's assault gun battery was sent to France, where it joined the parent unit in Paris-Clarmant on 16 July 1940. Soon afterward the Standarte moved to Metz, where it was billeted in barracks. The Assault Gun Battery was billeted in the "At the German Gate" barracks. On 1 August and 1 September 1940 the platoon commanders were promoted to the rank of SS-Untersturmführer.

Expansions and new formations strengthened the Leibstandarte considerably. The new units formed were a reconnaissance battalion, a pioneer battalion, another artillery battalion, a signals battalion and two anti-tank companies. The Assault Gun Battery was incorporated into the newly-established Vth (Heavy) Battalion as its 4th Company. Wittmann spent Christmas and the end of 1940 in Metz.

In February 1941 the Leibstandarte was transferred to Romania to serve as an instruction unit, and soon afterward to Bulgaria. The Balkans Campaign began on 6 April 1941. The German forces advanced through Yugoslavia to Greece, where, in addition to Greek forces, their opponents included English, New Zealand and Australian troops. Wittmann's assault gun drove through trackless mountains and over narrow roads leading through high passes. The fighting in Greece ended on 30 April 1941. After pausing to rest in Thessalia, in May the Leibstandarte was sent through Yugoslavia—where, during a stopover in Slaw. Brod, it received an enthusiastic welcome from the local Croatian and ethnic German population— into the Brünn-Wischau area of the Protectorate of Bohemia-Moravia. The Assault Gun Battery was quartered in Camp Dieditz near Wischau.

There the Leibstandarte received further reinforcements, including an infantry battalion, which was designated the IVth Battalion, Leibstandarte SS Adolf Hitler. The assault gun battery and the self-propelled 47 mm anti-tank company left the heavy battalion and together they formed the "Schönberger" Battalion. SS-Obersturmführer Wiesemann took command of the assault gun battery; platoon commanders were SS- Untersturmführer Rettlinger, Müller and Beck. Other members of the battery included SS-Untersturmführer Stübing and Kleist, while SS Untersturmführer Gilles was acting shop foreman. Commanding the battalion was SS-Sturmbannführer Schönberger, who had been promoted on 9 May 1941.

The Leibstandarte's war in the Soviet Union began in July 1941. Michael Wittmann faced an attack by eighteen Russian tanks in the battery's first days in action. He succeeded in knocking out six enemy tanks in succession, which put the rest to flight. This was Wittmann's first striking success; the incident provided the first hint of his mastery as commander of an armored vehicle and placed him in the spotlight. In recognition of this feat Wittmann was decorated with the Iron Cross, Second Class on 12 July 1941. His driver, SS-Unterscharführer Fritz, also received the Iron Cross, Second Class. The Leibstandarte's relentless advance continued; it smashed the Soviets and gained further ground toward the east. By the end of July it had reached Kiev and soon afterward the Uman Pocket. Committed by platoon, but more often alone, the assault guns stood beside the Leibstandarte's infantry units and proved an outstanding success in an offensive role, but also as the backbone of the defense when the need arose. Unit commanders were always happy to have an assault gun assigned to their sector.

Combat in Russia placed terrific demands on the assault gun crews. Wittmann and his crew were on their own, and he proved himself to be an individualist and a successful lone fighter. Nevertheless, he remained one of the group. Wittmann's gunner at that time, Otto Schälte, described him aptly: "Michel was a quiet, gifted, friendly NCO with firm goals in front of him." Wittmann was forced to be a lone fighter, for the assault guns were never employed en masse, but instead in ones and twos. His friendships with Helmut Wendorff, Alfred Günther (gunner), Hannes Philipsen (dispatch rider), Thomas Amselgruber (driver), SS-Oberscharführer Hannes Fischer (assault gun commander), SS-Unterscharführer Heinz Belbe and other members of the battery were forged in the hard battles of summer 1941.

Based on the number of prestigious decorations for bravery awarded, the Assault Gun Battery of the Leibstandarte SS Adolf Hitler was the Standarte's most successful unit. From the cadre of men who had been with the battery since early 1940, and who as the war went on served in the assault gun battalion, four were decorated with the Knight's Cross, six with the German Cross in Gold and one with the Honor Roll Clasp. Many of the original members of the battery later joined the Leibstandarte's tank units and of these five were decorated with the Knight's Cross, including one with the Oak Leaves and Swords, four with the German Cross in Gold and two with the Honor Roll Clasp.

The German advance along the Black Sea began the first weeks of August 1941. The Leibstandarte fought near Sasselje and Nowyj Bug from the 10th to the 17th of August and on the 19th it captured Kherson. In the course of the fighting in the port city of Kherson the assault guns commanded by Wittmann and Beck engaged an enemy gunboat and a submarine. The gunboat was sunk, the effects of the fire directed at the submarine are unknown. Wittmann had approximately ten enemy tanks to his credit by this point. After the fighting at Kherson, Wittmann's gunner, nineteen-year-old SS-Sturmmann Karl Bruggenkamp, was sent to the Junkerschule.

Wittmann's crew had been the same since the battery was formed in Juterbog. SS-Unterscharführer Alfred Günther joined Wittmann's crew, replacing Brüggenkamp as gunner. After being wounded in the face and back by shell fragments, on 20 August 1941 Wittmann was awarded the Wound Badge in Black. In August, after the capture of Kherson, the Leibstandarte rested near Bobrinets. The assault gun battery was billeted in the same town. In recognition of his accomplishments to date, on 8 September Michael Wittmann was awarded the Iron Cross, First Class. By then he was already counted as one of the best gun commanders in the battery.

The German advance across the Dniepr and the pursuit of the enemy along the south bank of the Dniepr River to the Black Sea began on 9 September 1941. In October the Leibstandarte fought at the Sea of Azov and near Melitopol and Berdyansk. Melitopol was taken on 8 October. Wittmann became entangled with enemy columns during the surprise capture of the port city; luck was with him, however, and he was able to make his way back to his own lines.

That same day Wittmann was wounded in the right thigh by a shell fragment. SS-Hauptscharführer Ernst Walter was his senior NCO from early 1940 until the summer of 1942; he offers an interesting characterization of Wittmann: "Wittmann was a member of my NCO corps from the beginning until his transfer. He was a rather quiet type, but no pussyfooter. In all respects he was a model to his subordinates, and not just to them. His general conduct in the military sphere as well as in the normal human one was always correct. Seldom have I met such a man, in whom all the good virtues were so markedly combined in one person."

The German advance continued through the Eastern Ukraine; Taganrog was taken on 17 October. Michael Wittmann, who had been wounded a total of three times in 1941, was promoted to the rank of SS-Oberscharführer on 9 November. The Leibstandarte had been bloodied in the constant action of the previous months and the combat strengths of its units had fallen to dangerously low levels. On 17 November 1941 began the attack on Rostov on the Don, which was captured after fierce fighting.

On 21 November Michael Wittmann was awarded the Tank Battle Badge in Silver. In late November 1941 the Leibstandarte moved into the winter position along the Sambek River; the assault gun battery was based in Taganrog. From there the assault guns carried out armed reconnaissance sorties to the east and north; combat was rare, as the Soviets had few tanks there. The battery held an NCO course, with Wittmann responsible for weapons training.

In February 1942 the Leibstandarte's assault gun battery was brought up to battalion strength through additions from Germany and the transfer of a battery from the Wiking Division. The batteries were commanded by Beck, Wiesemann and Rettlinger; as well a headquarters battery was formed under SS-Untersturmführer Stübing. As of February 1942, the assault gun battalion was commanded by SS-Hauptsturmführer Max Wünsche, as Schönberger had gone to Germany for the formation of the Leibstandarte's panzer battalion. Wittmann was a gun commander in the 3rd Battery commanded by SS-Obersturmführer Rettlinger.

His platoon commander, SS-Untersturmführer Hans Siegel, recalled of Wittmann: "Michael Wittmann was a dependable gun commander as an Unterscharführer, like many others. I don't recall any special incidents involving Michael Wittmann. He was always correct and 'never caught one's eye.' That was important to every soldier then, to if at all possible avoid 'catching someone's eye,' especially that of the senior NCO of the company. I had the impression that when he took part he was always wide-awake and enthusiastic. He was also a valuable help as an Unterscharführer."

Wittmann was made an SS officer candidate in early 1942. He left the battalion in June in order to attend the 7th Wartime Reserve Officer Candidate Training Course at the SS-Junkerschule in Bad Tölz, which began on 4 June. During his training at what was probably the most modern officer school of its time, Wittmann learned tactical lessons which he combined with his existing abilities. Wittmann was just as wide-awake at the school as he had been as an assault gun commander; he saw the information imparted to him there as an expansion of his knowledge, which was based on almost seven years of practice in military service and combat experience. Wittmann passed both the interim and final examinations and, after the course ended on 5 September 1942, was transferred to the panzers as an SS-Oberscharführer (FA = Officer Candidate). He joined the SS Panzer Replacement Battalion in Weimar as a platoon commander.

The battalion was commanded by SS-Hauptsturmführer Martin Groß; the twenty-eight-year-old Wittmann served as platoon commander in the 2nd Company. Other platoon commanders were SS-Untersturmführer von Kleist and Renner. In August 1942 Wittmann received the Royal Bulgarian Soldiers Cross of the Order of Bravery 2nd Class and the Eastern Front Medal. Wittmann exchanged his gray assault gun uniform for a black panzer uniform, the same one he had worn from 1937 to 1940. During the formative stage of the Waffen-SS panzer force the SS Panzer Replacement Battalion had few tanks, mostly Panzer IIIs with the short 50 mm gun. Since the tanks were seldom available to his platoon, Wittmann tried to liven up the training by supplementing the theoretical with instruction on the 20 mm anti-aircraft gun, which allowed him to demonstrate to his men how a tank cannon functioned, at least in principle.

A member of Wittmann's platoon, SS-Sturmmann Rolf Schamp, recalled the training period: "In Weimar we had calculated on roughly twenty actual training days on the tank, as well as those hours spent in tank exercises and the aforementioned instruction by me on the 20 mm Flak, an interim measure because we couldn't get access to the very limited number of Panzer IIIs each day. Everyone was supposed to have at least seen the inside of a tank. Wittmann suggested to me that we instruct on the 20 mm flak when there were no tanks available for training, as a way to fill the time. As far as I can recall, we were never able to carry out a platoon-or company-size exercise. Once we were on a firing range near Erfurt; everyone had the chance to fire two or three shots with the short-barrelled 50 mm tank cannon. Michael showed me the hand signals used in the most common tank exercises in his room and then we were able to get cracking."

Michael Wittmann was promoted to SS-Untersturmführer on 21 December 1942. On Christmas Day 1942 he received his transfer to Fallingbostel for the formation of the Leibstandarte's Tiger company. There he began his association with the Tigers of the Leibstandarte. His rapid ascent to the top of the German tank arm began with the German Zitadelle offensive in July 1943 and eventually led to his success at Villers-Bocage in Normandy, which can only be characterized as sensational. After the awarding of the Swords, which he received from the Führer, Wittmann spent his leave with his wife and enjoyed several days of peace and quiet in Erbstorf. In spite of all the decorations and honors, Wittmann remained essentially the same, his fame did not go to his head.

He did not go to a school as an instructor in tactics. Wittmann instead rejoined his battalion at the front. He felt he was needed there, and his deep-rooted sense of duty strengthened him in his decision. Wittmann knew that the war had entered its decisive phase. It was his decision, and he could have made it differently; but for Michael Wittmann this easier path was out of the question. In spite of the material superiority of the enemy, which he had seen and experienced first-hand in Normandy, Wittmann was optimistic as he drove back to the front. He had only been able to spend a very short time with his young wife. On 7 July 1944 it was time; he said goodbye and set out for Normandy.

View through a powerful telescope of the Allied invasion fleet lying off the Calvados Coast.

SS-Obersturmführer Jürgen Wessel on the Champs Elysées in Paris on the afternoon of 7 June 1944.

The morning of
7 June 1944. The 101st
SS Panzer Battalion on
the march to the inva-
sion front in Normandy.
Here a 1st Company
Tiger in front of
Morgny. Standing in the
Schwimmwagen on the
right is SS-Unterschar-
führer Willi Röpstorff.

1st Company on the
march to the front.

Tiger 131 in Morgny on 7 June 1944.

1st Company Tiger Morgny. Commander SS-Unterscharführer Wendt, left from SS-Sturmmann Schrader (radio operator) and on the right SS-Sturmmann Fischer (gunner).

Tiger 334 of the 3rd Company photographed during a maintenance stop in a French town.

Tiger 133 of SS-Oberscharführer Fritz Zahner (with peaked hat).

Wittmann's 2nd Company on the road N 316 just outside of Morgny on 7 June 1944. Wittmann is in the turret of his tank 205. The English fighter-bombers have not yet appeared in the sky.

On the road outside of Morgny.

Tiger 223 of the 2nd Company, commander SS-Oberscharführer Jürgen Brandt.

Tigers on the move.

The 2nd Company, 101st SS Panzer Battalion on the March to the front. SS-Untersturmführer Georg Hantusch in the turret of Tiger 221. On the left the emblem of the Ist SS Panzer Corps, two crossed skeleton keys.

Tiger 223 commanded by SS-Oberscharführer Brandt.

Tigers of the 2nd Company. In the lead SS-Obersturmführer Wessel's 211. The crew have removed the radio operator's machinegun and mounted it on the commander's cupola. The anti-aircraft sight has been flipped it and the gun is ready to use.

Operation "Epsom,"
26–28 June 1944

The enemy attack began at 05.00 hours on 25 June 1944. The English 49th Infantry Division (West Riding Division) had as its objective the capture of Rauray Ridge followed by a breakthrough to Noyers and Aunay-sur-Odon. The 146th Brigade achieved penetration against the Panzer-Lehr Division; this also threatened the left wing of the IIIrd (Armored) Battalion, 26th SS Panzer-Grenadier Regiment Hitlerjugend, as the enemy was now deep in its flank. Furthermore the danger existed that the enemy might attack in the rear of the armored troop carrier battalion and drive farther south toward Noyers and Villers-Bocage.

Ist SS Panzer Corps ordered the Hitlerjugend Division to counterattack and close the gap between itself and the Panzer-Lehr Division. A simultaneous attack was to be made by the Panzer-Lehr Division, with the two thrusts meeting near Juvigny. The attack, carried out by three panzer companies, elements of the reconnaissance battalion, and the armored troop carrier battalion, began in the afternoon under the command of SS-Obersturmbannführer Max Wünsche, the commanding officer of the Hitlerjugend Panzer Regiment.

By late in the evening the battle group was five-hundred meters from the Juvigny-Fontenay road and had established contact with the left wing of the 26th Regiment's IIIrd Battalion but not with the Panzer-Lehr Division. The English had failed to take Rauray and Fontenay. The Ist SS Panzer Corps promised the Hitlerjugend and Panzer-Lehr Divisions reinforcements in the shape of the 101st Tiger Battalion for a joint counterattack on 26 June 1944. However, since the Tigers were unable to form up in the assembly area in time, the corps ordered that the two divisions were to carry out the attack with their own forces.

The objective of the June 26 attack was to reach the line south of St. Martin-Juvigny and clear the Tessel Forest. Assembled for this attack were the 5th and 7th Companies, 12th SS Panzer Regiment Hitlerjugend, the IIIrd (Armored) Battalion, 26th Panzer-Grenadier Regiment Hitlerjugend, the 12th SS Armored Reconnaissance Battalion Hitlerjugend, and the Ist Battalion, 12th SS Panzer Artillery Regiment Hitlerjugend. On 25 June 1944 the Tiger battalion's flak platoon moved to AquevIIIe. The platoon commander, SS-Unterscharführer Fickert, left the medical clearing station on 19 June after having his wounds treated and found his way back to his platoon beyond the Orne.

Following a barrage by the artillery of the Hitlerjugend Division, on the morning of 26 June the tanks of the 12th SS Panzer Regiment Hitlerjugend attacked from the Rauray area. They ran straight into English forces advancing out of the Tessel Forest. Fierce tank-versus-tank fighting developed straight away. In the subsequent fighting the Hitlerjugend's positions were breached from St. Manvieu to east of Fontenay. There was fighting for possession of Cheux, Wünsche's tanks were able to hold Rauray. In this extremely critical situation the 3rd Company of the 101st SS Panzer Battalion was moved to Grainville-sur-Odon, 2.5 kilometers south of Caen. There the company commander, SS-Untersturmführer Amselgruber, and another Tiger engaged the onrushing enemy. The two Tigers guarded the break-in point with no infantry support. Amselgruber knocked out three enemy tanks from an enemy attack and successfully engaged the following infantry. After his heavy losses, the enemy suspended the attack. Tanks of the 1st Company also fought there, and SS-Untersturmführer Stamm was wounded. Farther east, near Mouen, a single Tiger was able to stop an attack by the 227th Infantry Brigade. Several tanks of the 9th Royal Tanks and the 23rd Hussars, which were escorted by the 2nd Gordon Highlanders, were destroyed.

The remaining committed elements of the Tiger battalion joined the tanks of the Hitlerjugend in heavy defensive fighting. The British attacked repeatedly with tanks and infantry supported by artillery and had to be beaten back. Contact was lost with the Tigers. SS-Hauptsturmführer Dr. Rabe, who was once again close to the fighting, volunteered to convey orders. In a display of skill and bravery, the Viennese doctor slipped past the British forces that had broken through and reestablished contact with the Tiger company fighting at the front. During the hours-long battle the Tigers destroyed a number of enemy tanks. Nevertheless, there was no hope of recapturing the old main line of resistance with the Tigers and the IInd Battalion of the 12th SS Panzer Regiment Hitlerjugend.

Also in action at that location was the 1st Company under SS-Hauptsturmführer Möbius. Difficult hedgerow terrain often prevented the Tigers from exploiting their longer-ranging guns. The shortage of infantry made it more difficult for the panzers to carry out their mission; as well command of the panzer-grenadiers was hindered by frequent breaks in communications. On the left of the Hitlerjugend Division's sector a determined German defense halted the British armor west of Tessel-Bretteville. The Panthers of the Ist Battalion, 12th SS Panzer Regiment Hitlerjugend were also able to hold near Le Manoir.

With the approval of the corps, the Hitlerjugend Division and the Tigers of the 101st SS Panzer Battalion occupied a new position on the line Marcelet—hill southeast of Cheux-Rauray—Vendes. As darkness fell the enemy attacks abated and it began to rain.

A crisis-filled day came to an end. At least fifty enemy tanks had been destroyed by the Hitlerjugend Division. A situation report submitted by the Hitlerjugend Division stated: "The panzer-grenadiers, pioneers and elements of the artillery fought to their own total destruction at the break-in point."

During the night the surrounded elements of the Hitlerjugend were able to fight their way through to the new main line of resistance. The division had suffered heavy losses that day, and there was still a gap in the front southeast of Cheux. Failing the timely arrival of reserves, the next day the enemy would surely enlarge the penetration on both sides of Cheux. The German line lacked depth, and the backbone of the young panzer-grenadiers of the Hitlerjugend Divisions was provided by the thirty Panzer IVs and seventeen Panthers of the Hitlerjugend Panzer Regiment and several assault guns of the 21st Panzer Division. The current strength of SS-Obersturmbannführer von Westernhagen's Tiger battalion was eighteen serviceable tanks, which were fighting in small groups in the entire corps sector. About six Tigers fought in the area of Grainville and Verson.

Only minor reinforcements arrived on 27 June, including a Panther company of the 2nd Panzer Division which launched an unsuccessful attack near Cheux and lost four tanks. SS-Hauptsturmführer Siegel and the tanks of his 8th Company, SS Panzer Regiment Hitlerjugend repulsed several enemy assaults at the same location, destroying a number of tanks. The day brought further strong attacks by the English, who sought to widen the penetration rather than deepen it. There was a gap between Verson and Carpiquet airfield, but all the defenders could do was send patrols to keep it under observation.

SS-Hauptsturmführer Möbius of the 1st Company of the Tiger Battalion recalled those days of constant action: "It was impossible to employ the Tigers in concentration, the demands from all sides were too great. We were in action constantly; I was forever en route from the Hitlerjugend Division to the Panzer-Lehr or later to the 2nd Panzer Division. Between the 25th and 30th of June I was ordered with all the battalion's Tigers—I had eighteen serviceable tanks—to the command post of the Hitlerjugend Division for a briefing.

The division headquarters had just been moved and I set off at my discretion. I had no major combat orders, but the situation was clear: the enemy could not be allowed on the main road (Caen-Villers-Bocage, the author). My tanks and I had been in action between the fronts for three days. I lost one tank after another to enemy action and had three left, one of which had its barrel shot away. I myself stopped an advance by the English through a defile by destroying six tanks. I then attacked an armored column with another tank (Ustuf. Amselgruber) and knocked out three tanks; my gun jammed and I was shot up by ten tanks. I bailed out; Amselgruber had already done so."

SS-Untersturmführer Belbe of the 2nd Company was wounded near Verson. In Verson was the command post of the Hitlerjugend Division, which was later moved to Louvigny. Manning defensive positions ready to prevent a further breakthrough in the direction of Verson and Grainville were elements of the 2nd and 3rd Companies of the Tiger Battalion, together with a handful of tanks belonging to the 7th Company, 12th SS Panzer Regiment, a company of Panthers, a Panzer IV company from the 21st Panzer Division, grenadiers from the regimental units of the 26th SS Panzer-Grenadier Regiment Hitlerjugend, and the 15th Company, 26th Regiment. The English successfully crossed the National Highway from Caen to Villers-Bocage and reached Baron.

The Tigers were constantly in action, attempting to stop enemy attacks, bringing relief to the hard-fighting panzer-grenadiers, and launching counterattacks to eliminate incursions by the enemy.

SS-Unterscharführer Warmbrunn of the 2nd Company described the events of that day: "On 27 June I drove through the enemy lines to assess the situation, which was uncertain. I had volunteered for this mission with the concurrence of my crew. When I drove over a hill I found myself facing a group of thirty Shermans. They showered me with a hail of shells and all systems went out. We owe our lives to the self-control of my driver, who did what we had always practiced, namely placed the Tiger at an acute angle to our armored foe. The crew and I then made our way back through the enemy to our departure point. The mission was worthwhile in spite of the loss of the Tiger." This type of operation was typical, for the Tigers had to take care of almost everything themselves, even their own reconnaissance. Now and then the Schwimmwagen crews of SS-Untersturmführer Henniges' scout platoon guided the Tigers into their positions, having scouted

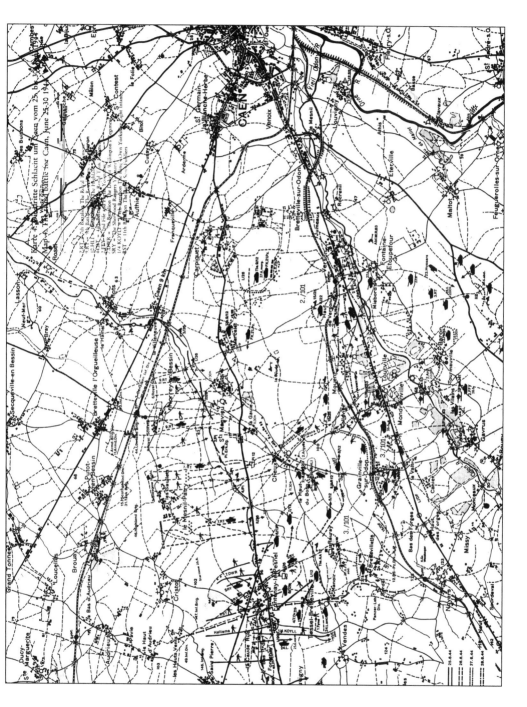

The Third Battle for Caen, 25–30 June, 1944.

them earlier. But the scout platoon could not be everywhere, nor could the armored reconnaissance platoon. SS-Untersturmführer Hahn was wounded in the head by shell fragments and the bone in his left forearm was shattered.

The mission of the 12th SS Panzer Division Hitlerjugend on 28 June 1944 was to prevent the loss of Hill 112 and a further breakthrough by the enemy toward the Orne. The Tigers saw action near Verson, while the tanks of the Hitlerjugend Panzer Regiment fought near Hill 112. Every English attack was answered by an immediate counterattack, often by scraping together the last reserves, as was noted by the English VIIlth Corps. The British 11th Armoured Division was halted on its way to the Orne and on orders from the corps remained in the bridgehead position, since the situation north of the Odon was still uncertain.

The 1st SS Panzer-Grenadier Regiment of the 1st SS Panzer Division Leibstandarte SS Adolf Hitler intervened in the fighting on the Normandy Front for the first time that day. It had taken the division that long to arrive and not until 6 July would the entire division be assembled there. Together with several Tigers, two understrength companies of the 22nd Panzer Regiment, and a company of the 12th SS Panzer Regiment Hitlerjugend, the 1st Regiment attacked toward the west from the area of Verson.

The aims of the attack were to stop the enemy from breaking through to the Orne and simultaneously capture favorable jump-off positions for a counterattack by the IInd SS Panzer Corps. In heavy fighting Mouen was taken from the Monmouthshires holding the town. SS-Obersturmbann-führer Frey and his panzer-grenadiers advanced to Colleville. From there they halted an attack by three armored battalions and a reconnaissance battalion. Later enemy artillery pounded the German units holding out in the town. The number of Tigers lost in this operation is not known. The 2nd and 3rd Companies reported minor losses.

In another part of the front was SS-Untersturmführer Amselgruber of the 3rd Company. The following is taken from a combat report: "28 June 1944. Amselgruber remained in his old location during the night and the entire day, repelled probing English infantry, and was attacked by a superior number of English tanks. Amselgruber was able to knock out two Shermans before his tank was disabled by several hits. Amselgruber's left leg was badly injured as he abandoned the tank; however this failed to prevent him from pulling his gunner, who had been seriously wounded in the belly by shell fragments, from the tank and taking him with him. Under very heavy machine-gun and cannon fire, Amselgruber headed back with the gunner in the direction of our lines, which he came upon after dark. This determined stand by Amselgruber undoubtedly helped give our infantry sufficient time to settle into a new, although only makeshift, position. Amselgruber returned to the battalion, said nothing about his injured leg, and returned to action the following day."

Amselgruber had been attacked from Colleville by tanks of the 9th Camerons; he knocked out two of three tanks and thus stopped the attack. After his tank had been knocked out and Amselgruber was forced to leave his position, the enemy, with strong artillery support, succeeded in taking the town of Grainville-sur-Odon. 28 June 1944 was the last day of Operation "Epsom."

From his bridgehead near Tourmaville the enemy was unable to take Hill 112 against the bitter resistance put up by the Hitlerjugend Panzer Regiment. Persistent attacks by the German battle groups, the need to secure the ground they had won, and the approach of the IInd SS Panzer Corps caused the English to suspend their offensive. The bravery displayed by the 12th SS Panzer Division Hitlerjugend and the 101st SS Panzer Battalion which fought alongside it were decisive factors in the English decision to call off their attack. The steadfastness of the young tank soldiers, who employed everything at their disposal to halt the onrushing enemy and inflict heavy losses on him, was exemplary.

The morning report by Headquarters, Seventh Army on 29 June 1944 stated: "In the afternoon hours of 28 June the powerful armored attacks launched to the northeast, southeast and south from the break-in area were halted by boldly-executed counterattacks by the 12th SS Panzer Division Hitlerjugend bolstered by elements of the 2nd Panzer Division, the Panzer-Lehr Division and the 2nd SS Panzer Division Das Reich. Very heavy losses were inflicted on the enemy and temporarily lost ground was won back. Our own attack on both sides of the Caen-Villers-Bocage road was halted by enemy armored attacks in the line Mouen—bottom land two kilometers east of Tourville."

What were these major battles like for the Tiger crews? Lone Tigers of the battalion were often tied up for days in the sectors held by the Hitlerjugend, completely out of touch with their companies. Every panzergrenadier officer had missions for the Tigers, they were expected to provide support everywhere, and in fact the Tigers were in action nearly everywhere. Rations were irregular and the crews were dependent on the units to which they were attached at that moment. Scattered about in small groups, the Tigers fought everywhere on the threatened front, which exposed them to crushing artillery fire and fighter-bomber attack. They sat waiting that way for hours. Radio silence was ordered, the only contact the crew members had was with each other over the intercom inside the tank.

The Tigers took cover behind hedges, in orchards and in small woods. Camouflage against being seen from the air was the prime necessity. After the artillery fire had abatedand the first enemy tanks appeared, they opened fire from their well-camouflaged ambush positions or charged into the enemy attack. By destroying tanks and Universal Carriers they deprived the infantry of their support and thus prevented incursions into the often thinly-manned German lines.

The Tigers of the 1st Company were constantly forced to operate in terrain unsuited to armored warfare. "I was always fortunate to fight in orchards, and in a tank that was built for long-range tank warfare," SS-Hauptsturmführer Möbius recalled with some bitterness. Massed, fast-moving tank attacks deep into enemy-occupied territory were out of the question in these actions.

The principles of classic armored warfare as taught by Guderian had no place in the overstretched Normandy Front. The type of attack that was practiced before the invasion, in inverted or standard wedge formation, was denied the Tiger companies. The main dilemma of the Tiger Battalion was the lack of unified command under the battalion commander. The tanks were spread all over the front; massed attacks by one or several companies, which had produced the great success at Villers-Bocage, remained little more than wishful thinking on the part of the company commanders.

Adapting to the new situation required an abrupt change in thinking on the part of the tank commanders and their crews, from offensive warfare to flexible defense. Holding fast in fixed defense lines, of which the Tigers were a part, was a fundamental contradiction of the concept of employing tanks as a breakthrough weapon; they spent their strength and their offensive power was diminished by constant losses.

SS-Standartenführer Kurt Meyer, who now commanded the Hitlerjugend Division following the death of SS-Brigadeführer Fritz Witt, summed up the situation: "This tactical patchwork cost the irreplaceable blood of our best soldiers and destroyed valuable material. We were already living on our capital, as yet we had received neither replacements for our killed or wounded comrades nor a new tank or a gun. The crews of the Tigers, who were left largely to their own devices, mastered the situation as best they could. What Panzermeyer described as "tactical patchwork" gave rise in them to the "lick my ass feeling"—a somewhat drastic formulation, but the one which best reflects their frame of mind. This state of mind was aggravated by the inadequate or total lack of contact with the company.

It was with this stoicism and the seemingly fatalistic unconcern that soon followed it that the young men in the Tigers got through those weeks. Only by drawing on their reserves of inner strength were they able to endure the constant series of actions at the front, for every commander of a grenadier unit was glad to have Tigers in his sector. SS-Hauptsturmführer Möbius confirmed the dispersed use of the Tigers: "Massed employment of the battalion in fact never took place, for we were always having to send tanks somewhere. I speak purely from my own perspective—understandable when I say that I only saw the battalion command post twice, as I was always somewhere else with my tank."

This bleeding away of the concentrated power of the 101st SS Panzer Battalion was clearly contrary to the guiding principle of the armored forces: "Strike quickly and don't disperse your forces." However, in view of the strained situation at the front the Tigers could not be pulled out and assembled. The Tigers were truly a rock amid the waves wherever they were committed and were held in high regard by the panzer-grenadiers of the Hitlerjugend. Operation "Epsom" had come to an end. The English had failed to achieve the hoped-for success against the determined German defense.

Some members of the 101st SS Panzer Battalion demonstrated their sense of responsibility toward their crews in the most difficult situations and displayed a previously unsuspected bravery. Typical of those who exhibited this quiet and often nameless heroism which was often seen in the battalion was SS-Sturmmann Erlander, a small, blonde Alsatian who drove SS-Untersturmführer Hantusch's tank in the 2nd Company. When Hantusch's Tiger was hit in the running gear and immobilized, Erlander wanted to leave the tank to repair the damage. Hantusch forbade him to get out under enemy fire. Erlander nevertheless climbed out and tried to restore the Tiger's mobility. The tank was hit again; nothing was found of the courageous driver.

The crew of the platoon commander's tank were able to follow this drama over the radio. It and the company commander's Tiger were equipped with the Fu. 800 radio, which also allowed them to monitor radio traffic from superior units to the battalion and company. The radios also picked up music programs ("Lilli Marleen", German folk concert at 10 P.M.). The remaining tanks were equipped with the Fu. 500 radio set.

How was the morale of the young Tiger crews in those first weeks? Gunner Walter Lau from Wittmann's company remembers distinctly: "No question, during the march into Normandy and even more so in the June days following Villers-Bocage we were certain that we would drive the Tommies from the mainland. Naturally their absolute air superiority and the complete absence of our own air force was depressing.

In Grimbosq Forest we waited for the armored forces to be used en masse and there were in fact attempts to do so. I recall moving into an assembly area with a large number of Panthers and Panzer IVs in June, but there were no massed actions in large tactical battle groups as we were used to in the east. There was some encouragement in late June-early July when we met vehicles of the 2nd Panzer Division and the SS Divisions Frundsberg, Hohenstaufen and Götz von Berlichingen on the far side of the Orne. The mood was confident when we also heard that the Leibstandarte SS Adolf Hitler and Das Reich had arrived. Now, we thought, the tanks would be used en masse. But then the typical fire-brigade employment of the Tigers began all over again.

We were sent here and there with two, four, or at most six tanks—without supporting infantry. This lowered morale but was in no way shattering, for wherever we were committed the Tommies were halted. The word sabotage was much used at that time because there never was full-scale use of the tanks." The battle in Normandy could not be compared to the Eastern Front. Constant alertness was required and the Tiger crews spent the nights in or under their tanks as danger was ever present.

ATTACKS AGAINST THE BRITISH ODON BRIDGEHEAD BY THE IST AND IIND SS PANZER CORPS—29–30 JUNE 1944

A counterattack by the Ist and IInd SS Panzer Corps to smash the British bridgehead on the Odon was planned for 29 June 1944. Taking part from the Ist SS Panzer Corps was a company from the Tiger Battalion, the 12th SS Panzer Regiment, the 12th SS Armored Reconnaissance Battalion, the IIIrd (Armored) Battalion, 26th SS Panzer-Grenadier Regiment, the 12th SS Panzer Artillery Regiment, the 1st SS Panzer-Grenadier Regiment Leibstandarte, the 83rd Rocket Regiment, and two companies of the 21st Panzer Division's 22nd Panzer Regiment. Whether tanks of the 3rd Battalion The Royal Tank Regiment met six Tigers of the 101st SS Panzer Battalion west of Hill 112 on the afternoon of 29 June 1944 cannot be substantiated. In any case the Tigers claimed to have beaten off an attack by English armor. For their part the English occasionally confused Panzer IVs and Tigers in their daily reports.

The attack by the IInd SS Panzer Corps with the Hohenstaufen and Frundsberg Divisions was a success. During the night of 30 June 1944 they took Vieux, Hill 112 was occupied the next morning. The 22nd SS Panzer-Grenadier Regiment Frundsberg took Gavrus. Hohenstaufen became pinned down near Grainville and the attack was called off at noon. The British advance had failed to reach the Orne as planned. Expecting further German counterattacks, they went over to the defensive. The Tigers had once again proved an outstanding success in the fire-brigade role and successfully sealed off numerous penetrations. Much was demanded of the young tank crews, but they proved equal to every task.

Company-strength attacks were no longer possible after the first battles in and near Villers-Bocage. Hitlerjugend Division officers were happy to place Tigers under their command wherever they showed up. The tank commanders were ordered to stand guard behind the main line of resistance or to sally forth beyond the lines to engage the enemy or scout the terrain. Such missions were usually carried out by two to three Tigers. Cooperation with the young panzer-grenadiers of the Hitlerjugend Division was outstanding.

SS-Standartenführer Kurt Meyer, the division commander, wrote: "The conduct of the young soldiers was incomprehensible to us. In a few words they told me of the recent battles and their accomplishments. Their heroic struggle was a matter of course for them. They spoke of the enemy without hate, repeatedly stressing his outstanding fighting spirit. However, deep bitterness showed through in their descriptions when they spoke of the overwhelming material strength of the enemy. Repeatedly I heard: "Damn it all, where would we be now if we had their material? Where is our air force?' We still hadn't seen a German aircraft in the sky."

The enemy air force was the undisputed master of the sky. Out of necessity the Tiger crews improvised defensive measures against the fighter-bomber plague. Usually the enemy aircraft approached the roads from the side, headed straight for the Tigers, and hit them in the flank. If the Lightning, Thunderbolt or Mustang was spotted by the tank crew a long way away, the gunner traversed the turret to the two-thirty position and lowered the cannon to its lowest point. The tank crew opened all the hatches but remained in the fighting compartment. The Tiger thus gave the impression of having been knocked out and abandoned by its crew and was therefore ignored by the fighter-bombers.

The tanks and panzer-grenadiers of the Hitlerjugend Division were constantly harassed by naval gunfire, their own attacks were hindered by the fighter-bombers and assembly areas were pounded by enemy artillery. The continual attacks on supply columns resulted in shortages; many replacement parts for the Tigers became scarce commodities. SS-Hauptsturmführer Möbius remembered the difficult situation facing the companies: "And then came the following notification from the Army High

Command: replacement parts for Tigers are in short supply! We got nothing. We patched up our tracks with wire from fences, because we had no
rings and cotter pins. I then ordered the parts direct from Henschel in
Kassel by express; and there they were, the replacement parts."

The recognized British military historian Chester Wilmot wrote in his
book The Battle for Europe: "The 12th SS Panzer Division, which
defended this sector, fought with a tenacity and a fury the like of which was
not encountered again during the entire campaign." This characterization
of fighting strength also applies to the 101st SS Panzer Battalion, which
saw action in the Hitlerjugend Division's sector and which was intimately
familiar with the abilities of the youthful panzer-grenadiers. So ended the
Third Battle of Caen. By 30 June 1944 the Commander in Chief of Panzergruppe West had already worked out plans for a rationalization of the
front, which led to the evacuation of the bridgehead near Caen-North.
The remainder of the front was to run through Avenay-Villers-Bocage-area
around Caumont.

As well as the Hitlerjugend Division, the Panzer-Lehr Division and the
21st Panzer Division were supposed to begin withdrawing units for a rest,
during which they would form the reserve. On 1 July 1944 the 101st SS
Panzer Battalion's strength was: 1st Company seven Tigers, 2nd Company
eight Tigers, 3rd Company ten Tigers. The men of the battalion were able
to make good use of the brief rest phase; they recovered from stress,
repaired clothing and equipment and faced the coming events with their
usual equanimity. Letters were sent home with the first detailed impressions of the invasion front.

The 4th Light Company also did not see action as a unit. Although the
armored troop carriers of the armored reconnaissance platoon and pioneer platoon carried out their assigned roles in the main line of resistance,
the quadruple flak platoon was not used in the front lines. Nevertheless,
with the constant attacks by fighter-bombers and bombers the gunners of
the three anti-aircraft guns could not complain about a lack of work.

Since the fighter-bombers often attacked crossroads, unserviceable or
knocked-out vehicles were positioned at favorable locations in such a way as
to lure the enemy. When the enemy aircraft dived to attack, a well-camouflaged quadruple flak positioned nearby opened fire and shot the aircraft
down with no danger to itself. As the battle went on, however, the enemy
caught on to this tactic and it became less effective. On I July 1944 the flak
platoon commander, SS-Unterscharführer Kurt Fickert, was awarded the
Iron Cross, Second Class by SS-Obersturmführer Spitz and promoted to the
rank of SS-Oberscharführer. His quadruple flak were often sited to protect

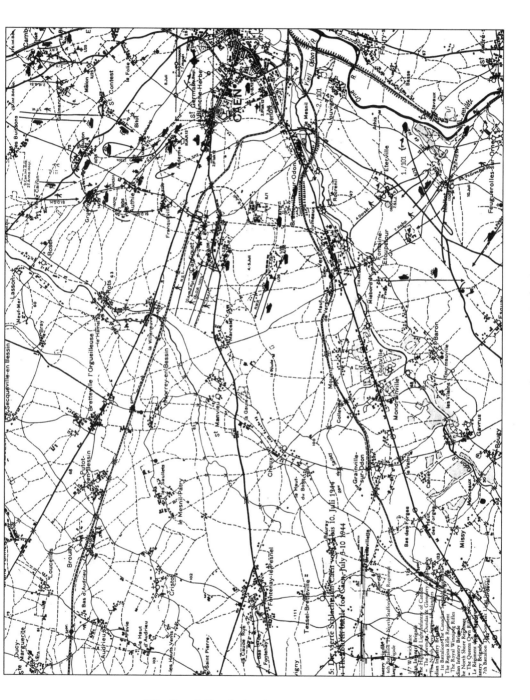

The fourth Battle for Cae, July 3–10, 1944.

installations and bridges. The Luftwaffe flak was often faster when it came to acknowledgement of aircraft shot down. In any case Fickert's quadruple flak participated in the downing of at least five enemy aircraft.

On 3 July 1944 changes were made in the senior command structure. The Commander in Chief of Panzergruppe West, General der Panzertruppen Freiherr Geyr von Schweppenburg, was relieved by General der Panzertruppen Heinrich Eberbach. The Commander in Chief of Army Group B, Generalfeldmarschall von Rundstedt was replaced by Generalfeldmarschall Hans Kluge. The positions of the 12th SS Panzer Division Hitlerjugend followed the line Caen—Luc sur Mer abreast La Bijude, at the south end of Cambes—north of Galmanche—Buron—Gruchy—Authie—west end of Franqueville to Route N 13 from Caen to Bayeux. The first days of July brought no assaults on the lines held by the Hitlerjugend. The enemy's activities were limited to patrols probing the German main line of resistance, while his air force and artillery watched over the front.

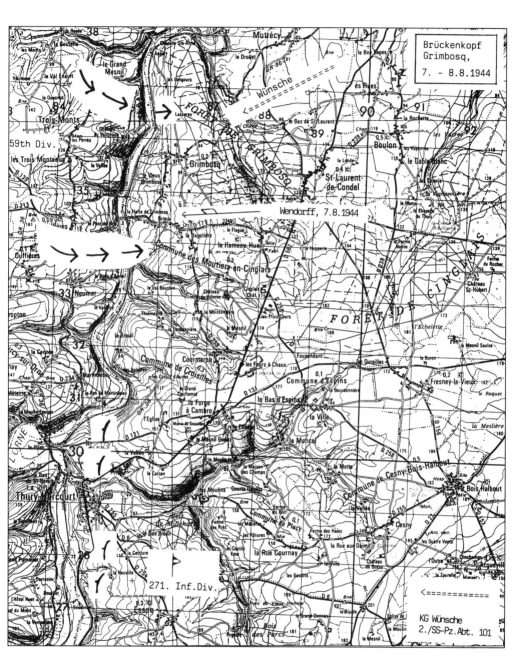

Grisbosq Bridgehead 7–8/8/1944.

The night of 12–13 June 1944 as experienced by the tank crews of Wittmann's 2nd Company east of Villers-Bocage. Heavy artillery and naval gunfire prevented the men from getting any rest after their long march to the front.

The aftermath of Wittmann's devastating attack on 13 June 1944 near Villers-Bocage, where he took on the British 7th Armoured Division alone. Shown here are wrecked tracked vehicles of the 1st Rifle Brigade.

This photograph was taken from the direction of Villers-Bocage. Wittmann conducted his attack in the direction of the viewer and shot up the British column.

The impression left on the roadway by the Tiger's tracks are visible in the foreground of this photo.

View of National Highway 175 looking in the direction of Villers-Bocage. It was here, just beyond Hill 213, that Wittmann drove his Tiger onto the road from the terrain to the left and halted the English advance. Troops inspect a Sherman Firefly tank.

A German armored troop carrier rolls past wrecked vehicles belonging to the 7th Armoured Division.

English soldiers of the 1/7 Queen's Royal Regiment, captured by the 101st SS Panzer Battalion's 2nd Company near Villers-Bocage.

Inspecting a knocked out Stuart light tank.

The Jerboa, a type of desert rat, the symbol of the British 7th Armoured Division from its time in Africa, is visible on the right sleeve of the man nearest the camera in the above photo. In England the division was commonly known as the Desert Rat.

English prisoners.

More English prisoners.

Interrogating an
English prisoner.

The British tanks knocked out by Wittmann in front of Villers-Bocage were
given a thorough inspection.

Men of the 101st
SS Panzer Battalion
examine knocked-out
Cromwell tanks.

Knocked-out Sherman Firefly of the 4th County of London Yeomanry.

Tiger crews in front of a wrecked Cromwell and Sherman Firefly.

Men of the 101st
SS Panzer Battalion
examine articles of
equipment left behind
in the carriers and tanks
by the English.

Visible in these pictures are Cromwell tanks of the regimental headquarters of the 4th County of London Yeomanry knocked out by Wittmann just outside the entrance to Villers-Bocage.

Visible in these pictures are Cromwell tanks of the regimental headquarters of the 4th County of London Yeomanry knocked out by Wittmann just outside the entrance to Villers-Bocage.

Views from Villers-Bocage of the long line of armored vehicles belonging to the British 7th Armoured Division put out of action by Wittmann on 13 June 1944.

Cromwell knocked out by Wittmann on the outskirts of the town.

Photograph taken at the outskirts of Villers-Bocage.

Cromwell knocked out by Wittmann inside the town of Villers-Bocage.

Wittmann's disabled Tiger in the Rue Pasteur in Villers-Bocage in front of Huet Godefroy store. All of the hatch covers are still open. While both photos were taken on 13 June 1944, the photo above was obviously taken later, after British bombing raids further devastated the town. Note the wrecked track on Wittmann's Tiger.

Men of either 101st SS Panzer Battalion's pioneer or reconnaissance platoon in Villers-Bocage.

Tigers 112 of the 1st Company, 101st SS Panzer Battalion (left) and a Panzer IV of the IInd Battalion. Panzer-Lehr Regiment were knocked out deeper in the interior of the town.

The Fourth Battle of Caen, 4–10 July 1944

The enemy attack on Carpiquet, west of Caen, began on 4 July 1944. Carpiquet's most important feature was its airfield. By 1800 hours, after bitter fighting and heavy casualties, the Canadians were in Carpiquet with approximately sixty tanks. The Ist SS Panzer Corps ordered an immediate counterattack. The 1st SS Panzer-Grenadier Regiment of the Leibstandarte was committed during the night but was unable to crack the stubborn Canadian defense. The airfield remained in German hands thanks to the heroic defense mounted by the badly-battered Ist Battalion, 26th Regiment under SS-Sturmbannführer Kruse and several tanks of the Panzer Regiment Hitlerjugend. The operation proved to be a failure for the enemy and further assaults were called off, though admittedly he had improved his position for a major assault on Caen. On the evening of 7 July 1944, 467 bombers attacked the positions of the Hitlerjugend Division. Casualties among the units were light, however the French civilian population suffered badly, with approximately 400 killed.

The major attack on Caen began at 0420 hours on 8 July 1944. The brunt of the assault was borne by the grenadiers of the 25th SS Panzer-Grenadier Regiment. Numerically superior enemy forces broke into Galmanche, Gruchy, Buron and St. Contest. With the agreement of the Ist SS Panzer Corps, during the night the Hitlerjugend began evacuating the Caen bridgehead and withdrew through the shattered city to the south bank of the Orne.

Michael Wittmann returned to the 101st SS Panzer Battalion after receiving the Knight's Cross with Oak Leaves and Swords and his brief leave. His return was met with universal joy. The men thought very highly of him for returning to the front after receiving the high decoration. Wittmann saw this step as a matter of course. The position he had been offered as an instructor at an armored forces school was not at all to his liking and he had therefore turned it down. He ignored Hitler's ban on further tank combat and kept it to himself. That too was typical of Wittmann—he had no intention of hiding behind such an order while his company's tank crews were in combat. Wittmann's return was innocuous; he was simply there again, his inner sense of duty and responsibility had called him back to where he was needed. There was little room for concern about his person.

One of the first to see him again was SS-Rottenführer Lau: "One morning in the Grimbosq Forest I went to the field kitchen to get some coffee. During the short walk there I met Michel Wittmann. I gave my best salute: 'Obersturmführer my congratulations on the Swords!' He smiled and said thank you. I walked alone with him approximately a hundred meters to the field kitchen; as we walked I noticed that there was a second star on his shoulder straps. I apologized for having addressed him by the wrong rank for so long and congratulated him on becoming a Hauptsturmführer.

He smiled again and said something like: 'It was rather a surprise to me too.' That's how he was, our Michel!

I remember asking him his impressions of Adolf Hitler. Michel told me that the Führer had spoken of new weapons that should ease the pressure on us. When we arrived at the field kitchen itself we were joined by other of our comrades, all of whom radiated joy as they congratulated him."

In spite of the award of the Knight's Cross with Oak Leaves and Swords and the fact that Wittmann was now among themost famous soldiers in Germany, in his manner and his essence he remained the same man his men knew and loved. Among those men was nineteen-year-old SS-Sturmmann Hubert Heil, a radio operator in the 2nd Company who had served with Wittmann on the Eastern Front. It was typical of the relationship between the troops, especially the younger soldiers, and the Wittmann myth when he wrote that he ". . . clung to him, like a father. He had won my complete trust through his bravery, his loyal behavior and kindness. Even after he had received the Oak Leaves and Swords he wasn't above taking a sledgehammer into his own hands to spell a crew member and knock out the bolts from a tank track. He never put himself on a higher plane, even though he was the most successful tank commander of the Second World War. Such an exemplary soldier's life and comradely behavior can never be forgotten and they restore to one the feeling of self-worth that they later tried to deprive us of in the post-war period."

As before, Wittmann's outward appearance was unassuming. He still wore his thin, black jacket, which was actually a fitter's jacket worn by the men of the workshop. Now and then he also put on plain, blue work pants. Michael Wittmann may have been the only German soldier who wore the Knight's Cross with Oak Leaves and Swords with a fitter's jacket.

It had been obvious for some time that Obersturmbannführer von Westernhagen's serious head wound was again troubling him, increasingly affecting his fitness for duty. His appetite and ability to sleep were affected and his memory suffered. He wrote: "During the entire time of the invasion battles, as long as I was there, there was neither day nor night for me and so I can't remember specific days or dates but only events (combats) and towns."

Michael Wittmann therefore assumed command of the battalion on 10 July 1944. The king of the Tiger force was now at the head of the battalion, a man whose accomplishments were known to friend and foe alike. Wittmann, who was shrouded in charisma and who his men saw as the bearer of the aura of invincibility, was now forced to turn to other tasks. Instead of leading his company and blasting his way through the largest masses of tanks, he was now responsible for the planning of missions. Wittmann would not have been Wittmann if he hadn't accompanied his men into action anyway, inspiring them with his self-confidence.

Bitter fighting raged near Maltot and Eterville on 10 July 1944. It will first be described from the viewpoint of the hard-pressed panzergrenadiers. The IIIrd Battalion, 1st SS Panzer-Grenadier Regiment of the Leibstandarte SS Adolf Hitler was situated near Maltot. The main burden of this battle was borne by the 11th Company commanded by SS-Obersturmführer Frank Hasse: "On 10 July 1944, the 1st SS Panzer-Grenadier Regiment of the Leibstandarte SS Adolf Hitler was situated in the Louvigny-Eterville sector due southwest of Caen, defending against an enemy pressing from a northerly direction. The IIIrd Battalion, to which SS-Obersturmführer Hasse belonged as commander of the 11th Company, was deployed deep in the defense at the north end of Maltot, south of Eterville. Following an unprecedented, hours-long artillery bombardment, which knocked out a large part of the forces in the position, the enemy succeeded in driving through the village of Eterville into Maltot.

SS-Obersturmführer Hasse, whose company had been pulled out of the line as reserve, was instructed to position his unit on the left wing of the IIIrd Battalion with its front facing west and screen the battalion's open flank. At the same time enemy tanks succeeded in pushing those elements of the IIIrd Battalion still in Maltot further to the west. The enemy's forward elements had by this time already reached IIIrd Battalion's command post located in a château eight-hundred meters southeast of Maltot. This was a very dangerous situation, for the enemy would most likely advance through Maltot to the southeast in order to cross the Orne.

Recognizing this impending threat, Hasse took matters into his own hands; acting contrary to orders he moved against the enemy forces in

Maltot from the east with just one of the platoons at his disposal. Exhibiting extraordinary personal bravery, Hasse led his handful of men against the vastly superior enemy force of infantry and tanks and gained ground in the village toward the west. Hasse was sent an additional platoon and a heavy machine-gun squad from his company. In fierce fighting he and his small force fought off repeated enemy counterattacks supported by tanks, in the course of which four tanks were knocked out at close quarters. Although the Hasse Company was under constant artillery fire, it made repeated attacks, inspired by the tireless SS-Obersturmführer Hasse. By the time help arrived at approximately 0800 hours in the shape of several Tigers and a second company, the 11th Company had already retaken two-thirds of the town. SS-Obersturmführer Hasse remained the heart and soul of the attack until the total capture of Maltot . . ."

Shortly thereafter SS-Untersturmführer Fritz Stamm of the 1st Company of the 101st SS Panzer Battalion, who fought with Hasse in Maltot, wrote: "The day before our departure from Normandy our tanks were still in combat, during the counterattack against Maltot and Eterville. The enemy had one of his worst days ever. His two-and-a-half-hour bombardment in the morning achieved next to nothing, and when his infantry finally advanced through their own smoke they ran unawares into our counterattacking tanks, which only needed to open fire. The enemy was so blinded by his own smoke that his defensive effort against our tanks was completely ineffective."

The departure mentioned by Stamm involved only his badly-decimated company. On 11 July 1944 the 1st Company handed its three remaining Tigers over to the 2nd and 3rd Companies and left the battalion completely. The men of the 1st Company soon reached Paris, where they stayed at the soldiers' hostel on the Champs Élysées run by Gemeinschaftsleiter König. König served with the 13th Company as a gunner during the Kursk offensive. The company subsequently moved through France and the Vosges, where they were fired on from a linesman's cabin by members of the resistance, who soon disappeared however. SS-Hauptsturmführer Möbius did his men a good turn in Strasbourg; he issued passes and told everyone to be in Paderborn-Sennelager on the coming Sunday. Then the company went off on its own.

On 11 July 1944 the Leibstandarte took over the sector held by the Hitlerjugend Division. One of its panzer- grenadier battalions and the panzer artillery regiment remained in the front. The remaining units were pulled out of the line to rest and refit. At the same time several of the battalion's Tigers, coming from St. Martin, west of the Orne, advanced northwest toward Baron. Whether there was any significant combat with the

English 214th Infantry Brigade coming from Miebord cannot be said with certainty. Also in action there were elements of the 12th SS Panzer Regiment. In addition to the Hitlerjugend Division, the Panzer-Lehr Division and the 21st Panzer Division were also finally relieved for a badly needed rest. The constant enemy attacks and the fending off of these attacks, the air superiority and the drum fire of his artillery no longer impressed anyone in the 101st SS Panzer Battalion. Battalion adjutant SS-Untersturmführer Kalinowsky noted laconically on 10 July 1944: "Wittmann is now leading the battalion and has just come back from an attack which drove the Tommy back to his jump-off positions. It was a fierce battle. I myself was only aware of it from the thunder of gunfire in the distance, the explosions, and the trembling of the earth."

When the situation at the front permitted, elements of the combat echelons of the 2nd and 3rd Companies were pulled out of action for a brief rest, allowing them to recover from the stress of endless actions. Tigers of the 2nd Company took the route south over the Orne bridge at Grimbosq and took shelter in the wooded area west of Bretteville-sur-Laize. There they were reunited with friends, were fed and saw to the mechanical needs of their tanks. Heinz von Westernhagen stayed only briefly. As he later wrote, he finally went ". . . on medical leave on 13 July on orders from the commanding general to allow the after-effects of my second head injury to be cured completely. To many his departure came as a surprise, and an unexplained one. There was no farewell, he was simply gone.

When Wittmann took over the battalion on 10 July 1944, the first thing he did was summon his old friend Helmut "Axel" Wendorff from SS-Hauptsturmführer Kling's IInd Battalion of the Leibstandarte's panzer regiment. Wittmann handed over his 2nd Company to Wendorff. SS-Obersturmführer Wendorff, a wearer of the Knight's Cross, was among the most dependable and successful tank commanders of the old 13th Company. With his strong personality he provided the men of Wittmann's old Company with the backing they so badly needed. Wendorff assumed command on 15 July. SS-Rottenführer Lau, a gunner in the 2nd Company who had served with Wendorff in Russia, recalled his return: "His return was a great joy to all of us and I remember vividly, somewhere in Normandy, a solitary man in panzer uniform several hundred meters behind our tanks approaching at quick time. We soon realized that it was our Bubi. I also know that he climbed up onto the tank from behind, and it was clear that Bubi Wendorff was our new company commander."

SS-Untersturmführer Rolf Henniges, who had previously led the scout platoon, also joined the 2nd Company on 15 July 1944. Of course the men of the 2nd Company had watched with distaste as Wittmann moved to the battalion headquarters. In a letter to Frau Wittmann the company's senior NCO, SS-Hauptscharführer Georg Konradt, wrote: "When your husband took over the battalion we were unhappy to see our commander go; he had grown up with us, I would like to say that there was a unique relationship between the commander and his men. We didn't feel his departure very strongly at first, for we received as our new company commander SS-Obersturmführer Wendorff, one of your husband's best friends. The battalion thus reached an all-time high in performance and success." Wittmann attempted to concentrate the actions of the Tigers and prevent their dispersal.

ACTIONS BETWEEN HILL 112 AND BRETTEVILLE-SUR-ODON

SS-Rottenführer Lau described the events of July from the 2nd Company's point of view: "After Hauptsturmführer Wittmann took over command of the 101st SS Panzer Battalion, Obersturmführer Wendorff, who since the end of the winter action in the east in 1944 had been adjutant of the IInd Battalion, 1st SS Panzer Regiment Leibstandarte, came to us as company commander. We were very happy, for Michel Wittmann and Bubi Wendorff—both close friends—were the best-liked and most successful Tiger commanders since the formation of the first Leibstandarte Tiger unit in autumn 1942. We were naturally proud to be his crew: I as gunner, Franz Elmer as driver, Hubert Heil as radio operator and Helmut Hauck as loader. Sometime in the middle of July there were a few days of relative quiet—compared to the constant action of the first weeks of August—for the two or three Tigers of the 2nd Company up front at the foot of Hill 112, a few kilometers south of Bretteville-sur-Odon. In those July days we were under the 12th SS Panzer Division Hitlerjugend as reserve, and by day we sat at readiness in a strip of woods abreast the artillery positions. Almost daily we went to the command post of the Hitlerjugend artillery to receive further orders.

One evening as we drove back from the front at the foot of Hill 112 in the area of Bretteville-sur-Odon we could see a large farm, Le Mesnil. That evening an Untersturmführer of the Hitlerjugend approached the tanks and climbed onto our vehicle. We learned from him that he was defending this farm with barely a dozen grenadiers. Actually he was holding only the left part of the farm as we looked at it, beyond a large gateway, while the Tommies had installed themselves in the right part of the farm. He told us that he was outnumbered by the Tommies and bemoaned the fact that they were running out of rifle ammunition and grenades. He asked us to help out the next day.

The game began late the following afternoon. As agreed, we halted a few hundred meters from the farm. The Untersturmführer then appeared with several grenadiers; he was overjoyed that we were able to give him some hand grenades and several pouches of our machine-gun ammunition. In the course of their conversation, Obersturmführer Wendorff and the Untersturmführer came up with the idea of making things hot for the Tommies dug in on the right side of the farm. Then the Obersturmführer ordered each loader to prepare about twenty high-explosive shells with delayed-action fuses. Both tanks were to fire on his radioed order. Each loader took his wrench and got busy setting the delayed-action fuses, after which both crews waited for the order to come over the radio. The gunners had precise target information, for in no case was the small group from the Hitlerjugend Division to be endangered. We moved a little closer to the farm, to a range of about four-hundred meters and then—after the young Untersturmführer fired a flare signifying that we were cleared to fire—the order rang out over the radio: 'Prepare to fire!' The necessary acknowledgement came back followed by the order: 'Fire!' The two Tigers each fired twenty high-explosive rounds into the part of the farm where Tommy was. Unfortunately we were unable to learn that day what the effect had been and what advantages had resulted for the handful of grenadiers of the Hitlerjugend Division. But several days later we learned from a grenadier of the same regiment that those brave boys had fought to the last round and according to unconfirmed sources not one of the young grenadiers had escaped with his life.

I recall several episodes from those four or five relatively quiet days. It wasn't always quiet in the strip of wood in the area of the artillery positions. We had just received enough rations for a few days. Our food bin—the standard aluminum ammunition box for signal flares—was filled with nourishing things. Radio operator Hubert Heil—as usual the radio operator was responsible for the crew's rations—had placed the food bin on the tank in front of his hatch and was preparing to make sandwiches. Suddenly an artillery barrage. Hatches shut, but the artillery fire was so heavy that we had to move our Tiger several hundred meters to a new position. When quiet returned the food bin was gone. We found what was left of it, run over by our sixty-tonne vehicle. Anyone who knows about the life of a soldier will understand that we rated this as a 'serious loss.' The radio operator was in shit for several days!

Another time we were up front with three tanks, patrolling several hundred meters beyond the front line. Then, suddenly, several fighter-bombers dived on us like hawks. We were defenseless. All that we could do was close the hatches, drive at full speed and stop when they released their bombs. It was the most firsthand and dangerous fighter-bomber attack I experienced in Normandy. The feeling when the bombs came down and our Tiger rocked on its shock absorbers is impossible to describe. But we were lucky, none of the three tanks was damaged. On seeing the craters in the area of our tanks, Bubi Wendorff observed, 'They should turn in their pilot's license, dropping their bombs from so low with us out in the open as if on a serving tray and then missing!'"

Something like that was of course analyzed and somehow we learned that there were two practical possibilities for evading fighter-bomber attacks: 1. If the situation permitted, drive up close to the enemy's main line of resistance. The recipe is said to have come from Panzermeyer. 2. We tried this ourselves in those days when we sortied alone with Wendorff. We saw the fighter-bombers coming in time. Tank halt, all hatches visibly open, turret at 9 o'clock and cannon lowered so that the muzzle almost touched the ground. We were successful; the fighter-bombers pulled up again in the assumption that we were a knocked-out tank."

On 15 July 1944 the battalion adjutant, SS-Untersturmführer Eduard Kalinowsky, wrote to his wife: ". . . Our commander von Westernhagen had to leave us in those days for a hospital stay in the Reich. Michel now leads the battalion until further notice. While the others wreak havoc up front, I'm stuck at the command post, which I am scarcely allowed to leave. There is much work to be done every day and often I get no rest at night either. Michel returned from Führer Headquarters last week and brought lots of news with him, the kind a mere mortal rarely hears. He went back into combat immediately after his return. Last week I received the Tank Battle Badge in Silver; the Iron Cross, First Class was presented to me after my arrival at the battalion.

. . . We simply must stick it out. It is very hard for the soldiers here, for the English and Americans employ an enormous quantity of material, there is almost no end to their air attacks. But these too have abated in recent days and now it's our turn to give them proper hell. Their supplies have now also reached their limit, so that conditions have equalized somewhat. Yesterday at noon a V 1, which we call a Dödel, roared past here. Friends saw it clearly between two wisps of clouds, I only heard it. Vogt was here today. He still has the Headquarters Company, which is giving him no end of trouble. He and comrades Iriohn, who is an operations officer, and Dollinger, who is the signals officer, send you their greetings . . . There is plenty to eat and drink here, for abandoned cattle graze freely everywhere. Over our large portions of meat we often think of the homeland, which could surely use it much more than we . . .

On 14 July 1944, Wittmann instructed his friend Wendorff to take three tanks of the 2nd Company and counter a reported foray by enemy tanks into the Maltot area. Approximately ten tanks were said to have advanced that far. Soon afterward SS-Obersturmführer Wendorff set off toward the designated position with the Tigers of SS-Unterscharführer Sowa, SS-Oberscharführer Lützsch, and SS-Hauptscharführer Höflinger. Wendorff ordered radio silence while on the move so as not to alert the enemy of their presence in advance. The crews were permitted to use the intercom only. The five Tigers soon came to a large farm, which was only one kilometer from the area of the enemy advance. So far the enemy had not shown himself. The Tigers stopped beside the houses and the commanders intently scanned the terrain in front of them, which fell away gently. Visible there was the tall row of hedges surrounding a small village which was supposedly occupied by the enemy. The left side of the village in particular was obscured by dense hedge growth and it therefore offered the enemy excellent cover. All was quiet. SS-Obersturmführer Wendorff formulated his plan quickly. He transmitted an audio signal to his tanks, which meant that use of the intercom inside the tanks was also to cease.

Shortly afterwards the CO's voice came over the air: 'Basalt Leader to everyone, come in!'—'Basalt 1, read you, go ahead.'—'Basalt 2, read you, go ahead.'—'Basalt 3, read you, go ahead.'—'Basalt 4, read you, go ahead.'—'Basalt 1, advance past the village on the right. Basalt 3 and 4 advance left of the village, I'll take the center. Basalt 2 stand guard in front of the village. Panzers forward!' The five Tigers rolled toward the objective at high speed. Wendorff led the way, followed by the tanks of Höflinger and Lötzsch, and behind them Sowa and Brandt. Wendorff was two-hundred meters from the village; several flashes appeared on the left side of the hedge wall—enemy tanks! The first shots just missed us.

Immediate action was called for. Wendorff called out his orders: 'Basalt to Lötzsch and Höflinger, remain abreast of me, objective the hedgerow. Brandt, you stay behind us to the right and keep an eye on the entrance to the village!' All the Tigers kept moving so as not to present a stationary target. Then Wendorff, Lötzsch and Höflinger veered left and fired the first shells into the hedge while on the move. SS-Unterscharführer Sowa, whose Tiger was driving behind them on the left, also fired in the direction of the concealed enemy tanks. The three Tigers reached the hedge, drove through, and spotted two Cromwell tanks. Both were hit, one began to smoke heavily, there was no infantry to be seen. Suddenly the roar of tank cannon firing was heard from the nearby limits of the village.

Shortly afterwards 'Captain' Brandt radioed: 'Enemy tanks at entrance to village, have been hit.' Brandt was lucky, for Sowa's Tiger was in a favorable position and fired several shots in rapid succession at the Cromwell, which was sitting in a niche between several houses at the entrance to the village. 'Got him, enemy tank is burning,' went Sowa's brief radio message. The Tiger of SS-Oberscharführer Brandt had been hit in the lower hull; there were no casualties but the tank's electrical system was knocked out. Moving quickly, Wendorff, with Lötzsch and Hoflinger behind him, reached the center of the village, where they saw the burning Cromwell. Since there were obviously no more enemy tanks there, the three Tigers drove through the village to the other side to investigate the situation there. Suddenly a Cromwell emerged slowly from a side street onto the main street and fired at the trailing Tiger of SS-Oberscharführer Lötzsch, which was hit and stopped immediately.

'Enemy tank behind me, have been hit. Standing in the water,' he radioed, using the code phrase for engine damage. The Tigers of Wendorff and Höflinger stopped. Meanwhile Sowa had also entered the village and put a shot through the Cromwell's turret from about thirty meters. Once again his quick intervention had taken care of a dangerous situation. Further investigation revealed that there were no more enemy tanks or infantry in the village. Höflinger took Lötzsch's Tiger in tow and the five Tigers returned to their starting position unhindered. It was a normal action for them, over which few words were wasted.

Michael Wittmann had got himself an English four-wheeled, open armored car, which he used on personal reconnaissance and scout missions. This practice of familiarizing himself with the attack terrain and identifying the enemy's positions had proved itself in Russia. Wittmann wanted to have as much information as possible before an operation, in order to be able to plan his own attack accordingly.

In those days Party Community Leader König, who was responsible for troop welfare in Paris and who ran the soldiers' hostel on the Champs Élysées, visited the 2nd Company. König had joined the 13th Tiger Company in 1943 as an SS-Sturmmann and was a loader during the Kursk offensive. In Italy he was decorated with the Iron Cross, Second Class, was promoted to the rank of SS-Unterscharführer and left the company. He was not the only party official to have volunteered for front-line service; several served with the Tiger Company for a time.

While talking with the men of the 2nd Company in the Bretteville-sur-Laize forest, König came up with the idea of collecting the black panzer uniforms and taking them to Paris with him. This idea was based on past experience, when the black panzer shirts were frequently burned in action or were otherwise lost. During the Kharkov winter deployment in 1943 the men of the Tiger Company had stowed their panzer uniforms in the luggage bin on the turret of the Tiger, where they were either riddled by fragments or burned up with the bin. The same happened during the Kursk offensive, as König knew from his own experience. In action the tank crews wore tank coveralls and, as of November 1943, leather clothing as well. From then on the smart black uniforms were carefully wrapped in the plastic sheath designed to protect the muzzle brake and were stowed in a compartment for special armor-piercing shells under the floor of the tank. Many uniforms were also lost in the tanks during the winter battles of 1943/44 due to enemy action and the blowing up of disabled vehicles. In an effort to prevent the same thing from happening again, König had the men bring him their black panzer uniforms. They packed a tunic and a pair of pants, a black Italian shirt, a necktie and a new cap and then loaded the clothing onto a truck. The men would thus have their parade uniforms at hand for a victory party in Paris planned by König to mark the victorious conclusion of the fighting in Normandy . . .

Operation "Goodwood": The English Move South, 18–20 July 1944

The Tiger Battalion had also been withdrawn from the front and was now situated in the Grainville-Langannerie area, directly west of National Highway 158 (Caen-Falaise). One company was required to remain at combat and departure readiness at all times. The Tigers took shelter in the forest of Bretteville-sur-Laize, the Fôret de Cinglais, in order to escape detection by enemy reconnaissance aircraft. The men took advantage of the break to recover from the stress of combat; the 2nd Company played football. The maintenance echelons worked on damaged tanks, others were towed to the workshop company by the I8-tonne prime movers. This armored battle group was the Ist SS Panzer Corps' reserve, together with the Ist and IIIrd (Armored) Battalions of the 26th SS Panzer-Grenadier Regiment. The command post was in Fierville-la-Campagne, south of Vimont. On 13 July 1944 the Leibstandarte was pulled out of the front and moved into the Ifs-Bretteville-sur-Laize area. During this period SS-Obersturmführer Hanno Raasch returned to his 3rd Company from the corps hospital in Sees and took command. His hands were still bandaged due to the burns he suffered in the bombing of Evrecy. On 16 July 1944 the Tiger Battalion's flak platoon moved to Le Mesnil, directly southwest of Caen. On 17 July SS-Unterscharführer Warmbrunn, a tank commander in the 2nd Company, destroyed three enemy tanks.

The English offensive code-named "Goodwood" began on 18 July 1944. It was preceded by an air attack carried out by a force of 1,596 bombers; at the same time furious artillery fire pounded the German positions. The enemy broke through the lines of the 16th Luftwaffe Field Division. At midday a counterattack was launched near Bourguébus by the armored troop carrier battalion and the Panther battalion of the Leibstandarte SS Adolf Hitler under SS-Obersturmbannführer Jochen Peiper. The enemy was driven out of the Frémouville-Four area to beyond the Caen-Vimont railway line. The operation was a disaster for the British 11th Armoured Division, which lost 126 tanks; nevertheless it was ordered to continue attacking and capture the Caen-Falaise road west of Bourguébus. The Panthers of the Ist Battalion of the Leibstandarte Panzer Regiment scored an outstanding success that day.

The Hitlerjugend Division was divided into three battle groups: northwest of Lisieux was Kampfgruppe Wünsche, and near Pontigny Kampfgruppe Waldmüller, while the artillery regiment and the flak battalion fought with the 272nd Infantry Division behind the ridge west of Bourguébus. The grenadiers of SS-Sturmbannführer Waldmüller's 1/25 were committed near Cagny and they moved into positions between Emiéville and Frénouville. On the right was the 21st Panzer Division, on the left the 1st SS Panzer Division Leibstandarte SS Adolf Hitler. The Tigers drove north and saw action east of the Caen-Falaise road in the Hubert-Folie-Soliers area.

SS-Unterscharführer Bobby Warmbrunn destroyed a Sherman on that 18 July; he hit it exactly where the turret ring sat on the hull. The turret was blown straight up into the air, turning about itself like the blade of a windmill. Shortly afterwards the company commander, SS-Obersturmführer Wendorff, climbed into the tank and Warmbrunn had to move to the gunner's position. Wendorff knocked out a Sherman west of Hubert-Folie, upstream from La Guinguette. The Tiger was then hit on the gun mantlet as Warmbrunn was taking aim at another tank. The shell failed to penetrate, however, as the armor was very thick there. The enormous force of the impact drove the eyepiece of the telescopic sight right into Warmbrunn's right eye. Wendorff headed back and delivered Warmbrunn to the medical officer. As he was suffering from double vision, Dr. Rabe sent him to Hohenlychen, near Berlin, for special treatment.

The Tigers also saw action farther west, near Thury-Harcourt. Led by company commander SS-Obersturmführer Raasch, several tanks of the 3rd Company carried out an attack against enemy units that had broken into the German lines. In the action Raasch's tank was knocked out by a German Army anti-tankgun and he was killed. SS-Hauptsturmführer Wittmann arrived on the scene in his English armored car shortly afterwards and in his fury bawled out the leader of the anti-tank unit. Raasch lay on the ground at the spot where he had fallen, wrapped in a tent square. He was buried in Bazoches-ou-Houlme. Hanno Raasch had been a popular company commander who enjoyed an outstanding relationship with his men based on mutual trust and comradely behavior. At twenty-three, he had been the youngest company commander in the battalion. The Technical Officer Motor Vehicles I, SS-Hauptsturmführer Heurich, subsequently took over command of the 3rd Company. Several members of the 2nd Company were decorated with the Iron Cross, Second Class: SS-Unterscharführer Adolf Schmidt (medic), Kurt Hühnerbein, Josef Sälzer and Richard Hieb, and SS-Rottenführer Schöppler.

By midday of 19 July Wünsche's tanks and the panzer-grenadiers of SS-Sturmbannführer Krause (Ist and IIIrd [Armored] Battalions, 26th Regiment) had moved next to Kampfgruppe Waldmüller, which was on both sides of the Cagny-Vimont road. SS-Sturmbannführer Olboeter's armored troop carrier battalion (IIIrd [Armored] Battalion, 26th Regiment) moved as far as Emiéville. Lurking in cover behind Waldmüller were the Panzer-jäger IVs of the 1st Company, 12th SS Anti-Tank Battalion Hitlerjugend, which had only recently arrived in Normandy. The Tigers of the 101st SS Panzer Battalion were now deployed in the Leibstandarte's sector and fought on both sides of the Route National from Caen to Falaise.

On 19 July 1944, following a preparatory artillery bombardment, the enemy attacked again. The panzer-grenadiers of the 1st Battalion, 26th Regiment repelled all attacks. Hubert-Folie and Four were evacuated, while La Hogue and Bourguébus were defended and held by the Leibstandarte. Tigers of the 2nd Company also saw action east of Tilly-le-Campagne, near Chicheboville; however, only a few enemy tanks were able to advance that far. In any case the town was again firmly in German hands in the evening.

On 20 July 1944 the Hitlerjugend evacuated Frénouville and the Leibstandarte withdrew from its exposed position near Bourguébus and held onto the line La Hogue-Tilly-la-Campagne. A Tiger of the 2nd Company was knocked out; Günter Boldt, the tank's loader, lost a foot in the incident. His will to live and seemingly superhuman strength enabled him to get out of the burning tank and hobble several meters across a field. SS-Sturmmann Boldt succumbed to his wounds later the same day. At nineteen years of age, the native of Königsberg was one of the old guard of the 2nd Company; with his experience in Russia and on the invasion front he was one of the quiet but essential mainstays of the unit. Boldt had been a member of the Leibstandarte Tiger Company from the time of its formation. He had received the Iron Cross, Second Class on the Eastern Front in March 1944 and the Iron Cross, First Class on 20 June 1944 for his outstanding achievement as Wittmann's loader at Villers-Bocage. Each day brought more dead and wounded; among themselves the tank crews usually spoke very little about the casualties. Everyone knew that he might be the next to be brought back wrapped in a tent square, slung on the side of the tank. The Tigers of the 3rd Company saw action west of the Caen-Falaise road near Ferme Beauvoir. The units of the 272nd Infantry Division were under constant fighter-bomber attack there. Heavy rain hindered the activities of the enemy air force and helped give the German troops a respite.

On the evening of 20 July 1944 the units learned of the attempted coup by the clique surrounding Oberst von Stauffenberg in Berlin and the attempt on the life of Adolf Hitler in the Führer Headquarters. The soldiers regarded this act with disapproval. With the soldiers of the German Armed Forces fighting on every front for the very existence of the Reich and the working people at home making great efforts for the continued existence of the nation, it was not the time to murder the Supreme Commander. It had long been clear to the German people, and the Allies made no secret of their plans, that peace negotiations or even a cease-fire were completely unwanted by them. Their one and only goal was unconditional surrender, which would render Germany totally defenseless and deliver her up to the victors for better or worse. The specter of the Morgenthau Plan, which would reduce Germany to an agrarian state, was only one of many threats made by the Allies. This treacherous act by a clique of conspirators, who were unable to build the least support among the people, had no effect on the fighting morale of the front.

General Montgomery called off Operation "Goodwood" on that 20 July 1944. In spite of his crushing use of air power and his new armored battalions, success was denied him; the only gains made by the offensive were the crossing of the Orne in Caen and a limited territorial gain. The in-depth German defense had proved capable of mastering the situation; behind the panzer-grenadiers the tanks and tank-destroyers waited to be sent quickly to developing points of penetration and engage attacking enemy elements. The Tigers were assembled into fast, mobile groups which formed the backbone of the defense and spearheaded counterattacks. They achieved considerable success in this role, instilling in the troops self-confidence and trust in their weapon. The Tiger Battalion's former operations officer, SS-Untersturmführer Iriohn, was sent to bolster the 3rd Company. Wittmann named SS-Hauptscharführer Höflinger, a tough old soldier from the 2nd Company, to be the new operations officer.

Michael Wittmann made a disheartening impression in those days, he seemed depressed. As an individualist and lone warrior, and one who had achieved success as such, he was not very happy with his new role of battalion commander. He expressed his personal discomfort with an frankness that surprised many.

Food is a vital subject to all soldiers. The worn out, exhausted tank crews were pleased whenever the field kitchen made its way to them, but often they had to provide for themselves. On the subject of food SS-Rottenführer Lau had the following to say: "One had to applaud the cooks of the 2nd Company of the 101st SS Panzer Battalion. They came from Vienna, and Wittmann had got them in exchange for SS-Unterscharführer Mohr's cabbage soup cooks. We made an arrangement with them in July in Normandy. We found a lone pig in a stall and drove our Tigers into a potato field. The pig and two sacks of potatoes were sent by courier vehicle (VW Schwimmwagen) to the train to improve our rations; two days later there was potato salad and sausage from the Viennese cooks."

On 23 July 1944 Generalfeldmarschall von Kluge visited the Hitlerjugend Division, confirming for himself the reports of this unit's high morale. The Tiger crews relaxed, carried out required maintenance and waited for the tanks under repair by the Workshop Company.

On 24 July 1944, following a heavy artillery barrage, the Canadians attacked between Bourguébus and the Orne on a seven-kilometer front. Once again they ran headlong into a brick wall in the Leibstandarte but were able to drive back the 272nd Infantry Division. A counterattack by Hohenstaufen and the 272nd Infantry Division repulsed the enemy and restored the old Tilly-Orne line. SS-Obersturmbannführer Wünsche's battle group was reformed. The Tiger Battalion, which had nineteen Panzer VIs, was placed under the command of Headquarters, 12th SS Panzer Regiment. The battle group also included the 1st Battalion of the 12th SS Panzer Regiment, the 1st Battalion of the 1st SS Panzer Regiment, and the 111rd (Armored) Battalion of the 26th SS Panzer-Grenadier Regiment.

Also that day a group of six Tiger tanks of the 3rd Company under the command of SS-Hauptsturmführer Heurich sat in a wood near Garcelles-Secqueville, south of Tilly-la-Campagne; employing maximum camouflage, they waited for an enemy attack. The area lay under harassing artillery fire and shells fell dangerously close to the tanks. In Tiger 333 SS-Unterscharführer Warnecke ordered his crew to close hatches. The hours of tedious waiting and the constant artillery fire frayed the nerves of all the crews. In spite of the close proximity of the bursting shells, the driver of Tiger 333, SS-Unterscharführer Gerhard Noll, decided to get a better look and opened the driver's hatch, in spite of his commander's warning. At that precise moment a shell struck a nearby tree and exploded; Noll was struck in the back by shrapnel. He died of his injuries later the same day. He was replaced as driver by SS-Rottenführer Paul Rohweder.

On 27 July 1944 the battalion presented decorations to deserving soldiers. In the 3rd Company SS-Untersturmführer Iriohn, SS-Unterscharführer Warnecke, and his gunner SS-Sturmmann Günter Wagner, received the Iron Cross, Second Class. The same decoration was handed to SS-Oberscharführer Peter Kisters, SS-Hauptscharführer Max Görgens and Hermann Barkhausen, SS-Sturmmann Siegfried Ewald, SS-Panzerschütze Reinhold Bytzeck, the commander of the Recovery Platoon Reinhold Wichert, Technical Officer Motor Vehicles II SS-Untersturmführer Georg

Bartel, and SS-Unterscharführer Otto König. By 28 July 1944, the 2nd Company, which had emerged from the earlier 13th Tiger Company, had destroyed 480 tanks and 432 anti-tank guns in the east and west. This represented what was probably a unique run of success by a single panzer company. The Tiger Battalion's strength on 1 August 1944 was: 2nd Company ten Tigers, 3rd Company ten Tigers. The battalion remained corps reserve. During the night of 4 August 1944 the 272nd Infantry Division took over the Hitlerjugend Division's sector; the Leibstandarte was relieved by the 89th Infantry Division.

On 1 August 1944 SS-Unterscharführer Piehler of the Headquarters Company and SS-Sturmmann Wagenfeld of the 2nd Company were decorated with the Iron Cross, Second Class. On 4 August SS-Untersturmführer Hantusch and SS-Rottenführer Falthauser received the Iron Cross, Second Class, as did SS-Sturmmänner Henn, Hauck, Ottmar, Borck and Kreibisch.

Wendorff's gunner Lau described that day, which saw the battalion granted a certain amount of rest: 'In spite of all the rigors and difficulties of those days there was also fun and joy. This was due on the one hand to our youth and on the other to the human and character qualities of our young officers, men like Bubi Wendorff. Only two or three years older than we, up front they were an example to the soldiers entrusted to them, while a few hundred meters behind the lines the welfare of their men took first place. We were conscious of this countless times in the east, south and west, wherever our troops saw action.

We were stationed in reserve in the Thury-Harcourt area, perhaps two kilometers from the main line of resistance. Bubi Wendorff came by a football somehow. Our Tigers, there were about five to seven of them, sat camouflaged in the bocage and we played soccer in a meadow surrounded by hedges. Taking part in the game were the crews of Wendorff, Untersturmführer Hantusch, Oberscharführer Lötzsch, Unterscharführer Sowa and Mölly, and a Sturmscharführer from the Reich Chancellery Motor Pool. Wendorff quickly selected two soccer teams and the game began. Play had to be interrupted now and then when the harassing artillery fire came too close or fighter-bombers were sighted—but soccer and singing were hobbies of Bubi Wendorff. Whenever the situation permitted he made use of both, usually to the benefit of the morale and spirit of the men under his command.

Sometimes, when the situation was quiet and radio silence had not been imposed, he would call to the other tanks: 'Granite to everyone, we're having a musical interlude (Granite was often our radio code name). Then he and his crew began singing his favorite song (over their throat microphones): 'Marianka, you should know that I love you from my heart,

Marianka . . . when will you finally be mine . . .' The other crews joined in enthusiastically.

There probably would have been a tremendous flap if senior signals officers had learned of our singing from radio monitoring, but that wouldn't have bothered a Bubi Wendorff. In regard to this question he merely observed drily, 'Marianka doesn't say anything about the caliber of our guns or about fuel and ammunition usage!' That's the way he was, Obersturmführer and company commander, Knight's Cross wearer Helmut Wendorff."

Michael Wittmann addressed the subject of the situation in Germany in a letter to his family: ". . . for today every SS man knows, . . . that things at home are, if not worse, at least no better than they are for us here at the front. We always have a chance to rest between days of hard fighting; however, the homeland must work every day without once being able to rest for several consecutive days. The company has been under the command of SS-Obersturmführer Wendorff as of fourteen days ago, as I have had to assume command of the battalion since the commanding officer, SS-Obersturmbannführer von Westernhagen, fell III. The company will make itself heard more and more often . . . and promises . . . to continue to do its utmost until victory is ours."

Operation "Totalize," 8–11 August 1944

Despite of the failure of his last attack, Operation "Goodwood," General Montgomery wished to advance further south in the direction of Falaise. Route Nationale 158 was virtually a straight line from Caen to Falaise. The terrain east of the road was well-suited to tank operations in spite of the towns and woods there. There were few natural obstacles which the defenders could incorporate into their defense line.

Given the job of attacking along the road to Falaise was the IInd Canadian Corps, which had available the following units: the 2nd Canadian Infantry Division, the 3rd Canadian Infantry Division, the 4th Canadian Armoured Division, the 2nd Canadian Armoured Brigade, the 51st British Highland Division, the 33rd British Armoured Brigade, and the 1st Polish Armoured Division—a total of two armored divisions, three infantry divisions and two armored brigades.

Facing the Canadian corps on the German side were the 89th and 271st Infantry Divisions. The Hitlerjugend Division and the 101st Tiger Battalion were in reserve of the Ist SS Panzer Corps which was in command there. The 89th Infantry Division's positions extended from La Hogue to the Orne River northwest of St. Martin-de-Fontenay. At the Orne was the 271st Infantry Division, whose positions ran along the river to two kilometers north of Thury-Harcourt; however, some of these positions were no more than a line of strongpoints.

THE GRIMBOSQ BRIDGEHEAD

During the night of 7 August 1944, after a two-hour barrage, the 176th Infantry Brigade of the 59th Division attacked with armor support, crossed the steep bank at Grimbosq and farther south and established two bridgeheads. Two armored divisions crossed the Orne near Le Bas on the morning of 7 August to reinforce the infantry. A counterattack on the Grimbosq bridgehead by the 271st Infantry Division's fusilier battalion failed. The Ist SS Panzer Corps sent Kampfgruppe Wünsche against this penetration. The battle group's composition had changed in the meantime; it now consisted of the 3rd and 8th Companies of the 12th SS Panzer Regiment, the headquarters of the Ist Battalion of the 12th SS Panzer Regiment, and the Ist and IIIrd (Armored) Battalions of the 26th Regiment minus headquarters and one company. Placed under Wünsche's command from the 101st SS Panzer Battalion were the 2nd Company and the Flak Platoon. Only the 3rd Company stayed with the battalion.

The Tiger crews prepared for action immediately and set out toward Grimbosq. The enemy had meanwhile placed pickets in the Fôret de Grimbosq and his bridgehead extended from Lasseray through Grimbosq to south of Brieux. The Tigers were attacked by fifty-four Mitchell bombers while on the move; thirty-six were damaged by flak and some failed to return to England. The armored troop carriers of the IIIrd (Armored) Battalion, 26th Regiment cleared Grimbosq Forest. At 1900 hours the Tigers, Panthers and Panzer IVs assembled in the southern and western parts of the forest in preparation for the attack. The Tigers and panzer-grenadiers made good initial progress and entered Grimbosq and Brieux, while elements of the Ist Battalion, 26th Regiment reached the stream in Le Bas. Twenty-eight enemy tanks were destroyed in heavy fighting, but when the barrage fire became too heavy the panzer-grenadiers dug in. Several Tigers were struck by artillery shells but no serious damage resulted.

The Tigers pulled back and moved into concealed positions, from which they could engage advancing enemy tanks. A number of Panthers of the 12th SS Panzer Regiment's 3rd Company were assigned to guard Grimbosq and a sector at the edge of the town. As well they were to relieve several Tigers still standing guard in the town. The street was so narrow that the Tigers had to be withdrawn first, before the Panthers could reach their stations. In command of the Panthers were SS-Untersturmführer Bogensperger, SS-Unterscharführer Frey and SS-Unterscharführer Freiberg. They waved goodbye to the Tigers and then slowly began to move. On the way they were warned by the grenadiers of the 26th Regiment that the English had infiltrated strong forces into Grimbosq as soon as the Tigers had left and now occupied half the town. In spite of fog and smoke, the Panthers were met by heavy defensive fire which caused casualties among the panzer-grenadiers. In this confused situation the Panthers received orders to pull back to the outskirts of the town with the grenadiers. There the group was joined by a Tiger, but it abandoned its position after taking a seemingly insignificant hit. The three Panthers were showered with a hail of high-explosive, smoke and armor-piercing shells. They succeeded in knocking out a number of the anti-tank guns but were then forced to withdraw. SS-Untersturmführer Bogensperger died with his turret crew, SS-Unterscharführer Frey was wounded.

A renewed attack on 8 August 1944 was supposed to crush the English bridgehead. Following initial rapid progress by the grenadiers and tanks, the attackers came under such heavy artillery barrage fire that they were compelled to halt. The grenadiers were forced to dig in. The artillery of the IIIrd Battalion, 12th SS Panzer Artillery Regiment prepared to lay down a similar wall of barrage fire in front of the anticipated counterattack by the English. The enemy attack, which was strongly supported by tanks, was not long in coming. SS-Oberscharführer Heubeck directed the fire of the artillery from a defile; high-explosive and armor-piercing shells caused some casualties among the English.

All of a sudden Heubeck saw English tanks pressing through the wall of smoke straight towards him. Then he was wounded when a shell fell at his feet; fragments entered his chest and both arms and one pierced a lung. The situation had now become untenable, with most of the grenadiers having been put out of action. Heubeck ordered the radio destroyed and then was taken to a nearby farmhouse. On seeing the first English soldiers outside, he made up his mind not to be taken alive. Then he heard the sound of tanks. As they fell back, his two radio operators had met a Tiger and told the crew of the wounded Oberscharführer. Under cover of smoke the Tiger was able to pick up Heubeck and succeeded in escaping the danger zone unseen by the enemy. The two days of fighting cost Kampfgruppe Wünsche 122 casualties; nine Panthers were lost, none of the Tigers were total losses.

SS-Rottenführer Walter Lau, the gunner in the crew of SS-Obersturmführer Helmut Wendorff, commander of the 2nd Company, recalled the attack on the English bridgehead at Grimbosq. The remaining members of the crew were SS-Rottenführer Franz Elmer (driver), SS-Sturmmann Hubert Heil (radio operator), and SS-Sturmmann Helmut Hauck (loader). "The Tommies had established a small bridgehead at Grimbosq. The village, consisting of roughly ten to fifteen houses, was situated several hundred meters on the near side of the Orne.

We were in a cemetery surrounded by a rather decrepit wall. Five or six Tigers of the 2nd Company took part in the attack; in addition to Wendorff, I remember the tank commanders SS-Untersturmführer Hantusch, SS-Oberscharführer Lötzsch and SS-Unterscharführer Kurt Sowa. An army infantry battalion had been assigned to support us. I recall how Michel Wittmann placed great emphasis on the necessary tactical instructions he gave the battalion commander, a Hauptmann, who had most likely never before taken part in an attack involving Tiger tanks.

Guided by Wittmann, the Tigers had to drive up to the cemetery wall so that both tracks were touching the wall. The five or six Tigers sat along this wall at intervals of twenty to thirty meters. The attack was made by the

Tigers and infantry with no artillery support. Then, on Wittmann's command, the Tigers moved out; they crashed through the wall and drove into the village—two left of the village, two right and one in the middle. When the Tigers reached the village limits, approximately fifty to eighty German prisoners of war emerged from the English positions. They poured past the Tigers to freedom. They were followed by numerous English troops with raised hands. We paid them little notice, left them to the infantry and drove left around the village, because our mission was to crush the bridgehead and destroy the bridge over the Orne. Just beyond the bridge on the right there was a steep grade which made great demands on the engines of the Tigers.

We knew the area very well, for it had been our advance road for some weeks. After breaking through the English infantry positions and destroying several armored vehicles, several of the tanks stood guard. Our tank, which was commanded by SS-Obersturmführer Wendorff, and one other— we drove toward the bridge, not on the road but on the slope—blazed away at the bridge with high-explosive shells from a range of about one to two-hundred meters. I am sure that although we didn't destroy the bridge, no more tanks could cross it.

Meanwhile it had become evening. We still cruised around the area. It was hilly and the Tiger's nose was high as it crested the hills. At the moment the Tiger was still horizontal I spotted an English tank. But at the same moment Franz Elmer pushed the Tiger up the slope and after cresting the small hill the nose dropped. At that moment, without Wendorff's knowledge, I fired at and hit the tank. Shortly afterwards Franz Elmer swung the tank around, having seen an anti-tank gun, and ran over it. Bubi Wendorff was most pleased for his gunner had taken out a tank on his own and the anti-tank gun was eliminated by the driver. Night came slowly and three or four tanks remained on guard. The infantry were in their positions in the houses and we positioned ourselves by the front wall of a stone farmhouse. Artillery fire began. The tank crews standing guard up front suddenly saw English armored vehicles coming toward them. But they weren't combat vehicles, rather a supply unit bound for the English troops in the bridgehead. The handful of vehicles, with two or three officers, several ammunition vehicles and one with rations, were instructed to make their way to Wendorff's position behind the houses. This was a happy occasion for us. I called upon all my schoolboy English, and we enjoyed our best snack on the invasion front.

There was plum pudding, mechanically-peeled potatoes, a wonderful stew and other trimmings. Two of the English officers had been wounded when the tank crews standing guard fired on them with submachine-guns.

We dressed the officers' wounds and then had no idea what we should do with the total of about twenty prisoners. We had an agreement with the headquarters in the rear—I have no idea which headquarters it was to make radio contact every hour, meaning that we set our radios to receive once each hour. At that point Wendorff reported that we had prisoners and that he was going to send them back unescorted in three trucks. In our broken English we then informed the drivers—who were quite incredulous at first—that they should now drive in the direction of the German Reich." SS-Unterscharführer Günther Jacob of the 2nd Company was decorated with the Iron Cross, Second Class on 7 August 1944.

A drawing from the magazine "Signal" depicting Wittmann's attack against the British 7th Armoured Division in front of Villers-Bocage on 13 June 1944. On the right, Wittmann's Tiger rolls past the enemy tanks at extremely close range and then enters Villers-Bocage.

English drawing from the "London Daily News" depicting the battle of Villers-Bocage. The English tank on the left is firing at a Tiger through a half-wrecked house. Behind is another Tiger. An English armed with PIAT, a close-range anti-tank weapon, lurks in the right foreground.

The center of Villers-Bocage, and in the background are the knocked-out Tiger
and Panzer IV.

Close-up photos, taken at the intersection near the marketplace in Villers-
Bocage, of tanks knocked out in the attack by the 101st SS Panzer Battalion's
1st Company on 13 June 1944. Here we see the Panzer IV of the Panzer-Lehr
Division.

The Tiger of the 1st Company 101st SS Panzer Battalion knocked out beside the Panzer IV. The emblems worn by the tanks of the 1st Company are clearly visible, on the left the tactical symbol of a Tiger company, a rhombus enclosing an S, and right the two crossed skeleton keys.

This photo provides a good indication of how narrow the main street of Villers-Bocage was. In the street battle the advantage lay with the defending English.

This Tiger of the 1st Company penetrated even deeper into the core of the town, but was then also put out of action.

Tiger of the 1st Company 101st SS Panzer Battalion, which was knocked out from a garden at the intersection of Jeanne Bacon and Emile Samson streets.

Soldiers of the Tiger Battalion's reconnaissance or pioneer platoons.

13 June 1944, soon after Wittmann's triumph near Villers-Bocage. Wittmann makes his report to Sepp Dietrich. *From left:* SS-Sturmbannführer von Westernhagen, Sepp Dietrich, Wittmann and SS-Hauptsturmführer Herman Weiser, Corps Adjutant of the Ist SS Panzer Corps.

SS-Hauptsturmführer Weiser toasts Wittmann's great success, which eliminated the threat from the left of the Ist Panzer Corps.

The commanding general of the Ist Panzer Corps, SS-Obergruppen-führer and General der Waffen-SS Sepp Dietrich, listens as Wittmann describes the details of his daring act. On the right, Weiser.

On 20 June 1944 some of the men involved in the fighting at Villers-Bocage were decorated. SS-Sturmbannführer von Westernhagen is seen presenting decorations, here to SS-Ustuf. Hahn, 1st Company.

The stress and trials of his action near Villers-Bocage that day are evident in the face of Michael Wittmann. This photograph was taken in Baron-sur-Odon on the afternoon of 13 June 1944.

Members of the 1st Company. 2nd from left Oscha. Bode, von Westernhagen, Kalinowsky and Möbius.

From left from Wittmann's crew: SS-Usch. Walter Müller (driver) and SS-Sturmmänner Günther Jonas (radio operator). Günther Boldt (loader), an SS-Unterscharführer, Wittmann, von Westernhagen, another SS-Unterscharführer and four SS-Sturmmänner. Among the latter were Luscher, Schmidtbauer, Ditl and Schulze, one of the SS-Unterscharführer was Herbert Boden.

SS-Obersturmführer
Philipsen of the 1st
Company, killed near
Cahagnes on
16/6/1944.

SS-Unterscharführer
Werner Wendt
commander of Tiger
132 of the 1st company.

Von Westernhagen decorates
men of the 1st Company. Beside
him are SS-Hauptsturmführer
Möbius and SS-Untersturmführer
Kalinowsky.

SS-Sturmmann Leopold Aumüller and SS-Sturmmann Ernst Kufner; both were in SS-Untersturmführer Amselgrubber's Tiger during the night bombing raid on Evrecy on 15/6/1944. 3rd Company 101st SS Panzer Battalion.

Villers-Bocage after the Allied bombing.

Tigers of Wittmann's 2nd Company west of Caen, June 1944. The Tiger of SS-Untersturmführer Georg Hantusch (in the long coat). The driver (right, with head out) is SS-Sturmmann Erlander.

BATTLES ON THE CAEN-FALAISE ROAD

The Leibstandarte had been relieved on both sides of the road by the 89th Infantry Division, leading the Allies to believe that they would be able to break through to the south more quickly. The tactically senseless bombing of the towns along the advance road began on 7 August 1944: La Hogue, Secqueville-la-Campagne, Garcelles-Secqueville, St. Aignan, Cramesnil, Fontenay-le-Marmion and May-sur-Orne. A half hour later, at 2330 hours, enemy armored and infantry units attacked east of the Caen-Falaise road. Advancing there were elements of the 51st Highland Division and the 33rd British Armoured Division, while the Canadian 2nd Infantry and 2nd Armoured Divisions attacked west of the road. The base of the cloud deck was illuminated with searchlight beams in order to ease orientation, and at 2345 hours 360 guns began laying down a wall of fire 3.7 kilometers wide on both sides of the national highway. In the course of the night Garcelles, St. Aignan and Cramesnil, all in the attack lanes of the 51st Highland Division, were taken. The woods south of St. Aignan were occupied on the morning of 8 August.

The 272nd Infantry Division was able to repulse an attack on La Hogue, but Hill 75 west of Secqueville could not be held and the wood east of Secqueville was also lost. Attacks from St. Aignan to Conteville and Pussy were beaten back with heavy loss to the enemy. On that morning the attackers had reached their planned objectives for the first phase of the attack almost everywhere; only the left flank lagged behind somewhat. Following an attack by 1020 bombers, a barrage from more than 700 guns and a massed assault by more than 600 tanks, a breakthrough of the German lines seemed imminent. Unless the last reserves were committed, the enemy would be able to march down the Caen-Falaise road almost unopposed.

The elements of the 12th SS Panzer Division Hitlerjugend not yet in action, together with the 101st SS Panzer Battalion, were committed at once. SS-Hauptsturmführer Michael Wittmann had only eight Tigers; the 2nd Company under Wendorff was still in action against the British bridgehead at Grimbosq, where approximately five Tigers were involved. Also to see action there were the division and corps escort companies; 39 Panzer IVs of the IInd Battalion, 12th SS Panzer Regiment; 10 tank-destroyers of the 1st Company, 12th SS Anti-tank Battalion; Kampfgruppe Waldmüller; three battalions of artillery, and the 12th SS Rocket Battalion. Elements of the IIIrd Flak Corps and the 83rd Rocket Regiment were still fighting in the Ist SS Panzer Corps' sector. These exhausted and inadequate forces were expected to repulse an attack by an foe who enjoyed powerful tank and air support.

On the morning of 8 August, the commander of the Hitlerjugend Division, SS-Oberführer Kurt Meyer, drove to the threatened sector of the front to see for himself the menacing situation. In view of the completely flat and open terrain, it was clear to him that this massive enemy force could only be stopped behind the Laison River line and on both sides of Potigny. As well, the 85th Infantry Division was on its way but could not possibly reach the area of the break-in that day. It was thus vital to halt the enemy immediately in order to gain time. Panzermeyer personally halted retreating soldiers of the 89th Infantry Division and organized the defense of Cintheaux, situated on the national highway. In Urville Meyer discussed the planned counterattack with General Eberbach, the Commander in Chief of the Fifth Panzer Army. Meyer planned to take the hills south of St. Aignan with Kampfgruppe Waldmüller and the IInd Battalion of the 12th SS Panzer Regiment.

The Corps Escort Company was to attack on the right beside Kampf-gruppe Waldmüller, while the Division Escort Company Hitlerjugend and the 1st Anti-tank Company were to advance through Estrees and take the hill west of St. Sylvain. The tanks of Kampfgruppe Wünsche—which included the Tigers of the 2nd Company—were to break off their attack at Grimbosq during the day, occupy new positions west and northwest of Pontigny, and defend the narrows between Laize and Laison.

"I MUST GO"—8 AUGUST 1944

On 8 August 1944 the 101st Tiger Battalion's 2nd Company was still in the Grimbosq area, while the 3rd Company waited at readiness near Cintheaux to the left of National Highway 158 from Caen to Falaise. That day was plagued by a series of unfortunate incidents that began at day-break. The first was at approximately 0600 hours, when, without orders from Wittmann, SS-Hauptsturmführer Heurich set out towards the north in the direction of Caen with the tanks of his 3rd Company.

The battalion operations officer, SS-Hauptscharführer Höflinger, sub-sequently caught up with Heurich, halted his tanks and passed on instruc-tions to wait for further orders.

Michael Wittmann seemed nervous that morning. At about 0700 hours he and Dr. Rabe drove to headquarters and then to the 3rd Company. Wittmann arrived in Cintheaux at approximately 1100 hours. Present there were the Tigers of SS-Untersturmführer Willi Iriohn, SS-Hauptsturmführer Franz Heurich, SS-Oberscharführer Rolf von Westernhagen, SS-Oberschar-führer Peter Kisters (all of 3rd Company) as well as those of signals officer SS-Untersturmführer Helmut Dollinger, operations officer SS-Hauptschar-führer Hans Höflinger and SS-Unterscharführer Otto Blase of the 3rd

Company. SS-Hauptsturmführer Michael Wittmann had a total of eight Tigers for the coming attack.

SS-Oberführer Meyer described the enemy situation, the German situation and his decision to attack, which was undoubtedly correct: "I met Waldmüller north of Bretteville-le-Rabet and we both drove to Cintheaux in order to inform ourselves as to the current situation. Wittmann's Tigers were standing ready behind a hedge east of Cintheaux, without so far having taken part in the firefight.

Cintheaux was under artillery fire, while the open ground was relatively free of fire. From the north end of the village we saw dense armored columns north of the road to Bretteville-sur-Laize. The tanks were arranged in groups. The same picture offered itself south of Garcelles and at the edge of the forest southeast of the town. The sight of this mass of tanks almost took our breath away.

We couldn't comprehend the behavior of the Canadians. Why didn't this overwhelming armored force carry on with its attack? And why did the Canadian commanders give us the time and opportunity to take countermeasures? First and foremost the feared fighter-bombers were absent. The systematic use of fighter-bombers alone would have caused what was left of our 12th SS Panzer Division to be bled to death on Route Nationale 158 and could have paved the way for a breakthrough by the IInd Canadian Corps. Nothing could have stopped the Canadians from occupying the city of Falaise the same night. Perhaps the gods know why that didn't happen.

It was clear to Waldmüller and me that we couldn't wait for this mass of tanks to attack us. The enemy tanks could not be allowed to advance any further. An enemy armored division stood ready to attack on each side of the road. We could not allow this attack to begin—we had to try to seize the initiative. I decided to defend the town of Cintheaux with the forces already deployed there, and launch a lightning attack east of the road with all the available soldiers and thus throw the enemy plan into confusion. I decided on the wood southeast of Garcelles as the objective. Since a huge quarry south of Cintheaux made an attack by tanks unlikely, I had no fears there. We had to risk the attack in order to win time for the Laison sector. The attack was set for 1230 hours.

During the final conference with Waldmüller and Wittmann, we observed a lone bomber, which overflew the area several times and then released flares. The bomber appeared to us to be a sort of flying command post, and I ordered the attack to begin at once in order to get the troops out of the bombing zone. I shook Michael Wittmann's hand again and made reference to the extremely critical situation. The good Michael laughed his youthful laugh and climbed into his Tiger. One-hundred-and-thirty enemy tanks had fallen prey to him so far. Would he increase this number or himself become a victim?"

What was the nature of the terrain in front of the Tigers? The national highway was bordered left and right by farmland, the terrain was absolutely flat. South of St. Aignan-de-Cramesnil there was a fruit orchard approximately six hectares in size and beginning about 250 meters south of the town a narrow strip of woods which extended to the south, parallel to the national highway. At the same time St. Aignan marked the limit of visibility on the northern horizon.

A few weeks later SS-Hauptscharführer Hans Höflinger, the battalion's operations officer, set down in writing the events of that day: "I was awakened surprisingly early the morning of that terrible day. The reason was that Heurich's company had left its quartering area without orders from the commanding officer and was driving down the road to Caen. Michel wanted to know at once what was going on, and therefore I, as operations officer, had to catch up with the company as fast as possible and enquireas to its mission. This I did straight away, then reported to Michel. After reflecting for a few minutes, which I knew was his custom, he took breakfast somewhat nervously. Then, however, he ordered me to send both staff tanks to the Heurich Company's position. I did so and hurried back at once to Michel in my Schwimmwagen and reported it to him.

Subsequently we drove together—he in the Volkswagen, I in the Schwimmwagen—to Meyer's command post to take part in a situation conference. When this was over we deliberated whether or not to carry out the attack. With us was the battalion signals officer, Untersturmführer Dollinger. Suddenly Michel said to me: 'I must go along, for Heurich can scarcely cope.' Heurich was in fact taking part in his first action that day and that in itself was dangerous. After several hours we drove back to the tanks, which were sitting right on the road abeam Cintheaux. At first I wasn't supposed to go with them, but all of a sudden he changed his order. This made me nervous, for I noticed that Michel was rather uncertain in his decision. Shortly afterwards we climbed in and sent our tanks into cover to avoid being seen from the air."

The crew of Michael Wittmann's Tiger consisted of SS-Unterscharführer Hein Reimers (driver) and Karl Wagner (gunner), both experienced men who had taken part in all of the 13th Company's actions in Russia. His radio operator was SS-Sturmmann Rudi Hirschel, who likewise had Russian experience; the loader was SS-Sturmmann Günther Weber. Wittmann, Dollinger, Iriohn, probably Kisters, and another Tiger advanced to the right of the national highway, while Höflinger and von

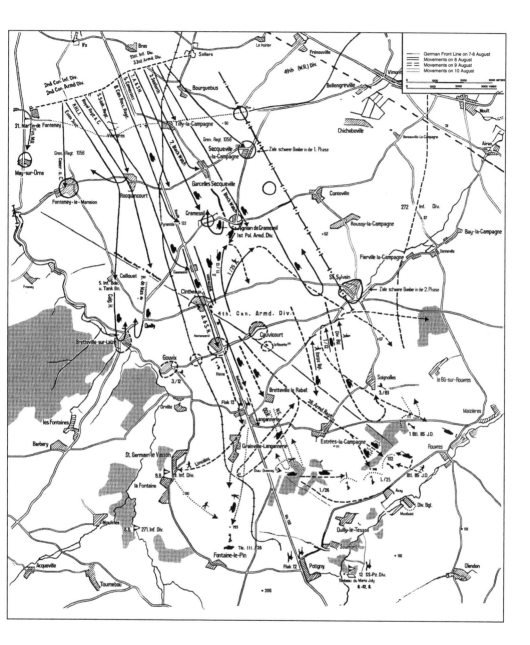

The German Attack on 8/8/1944

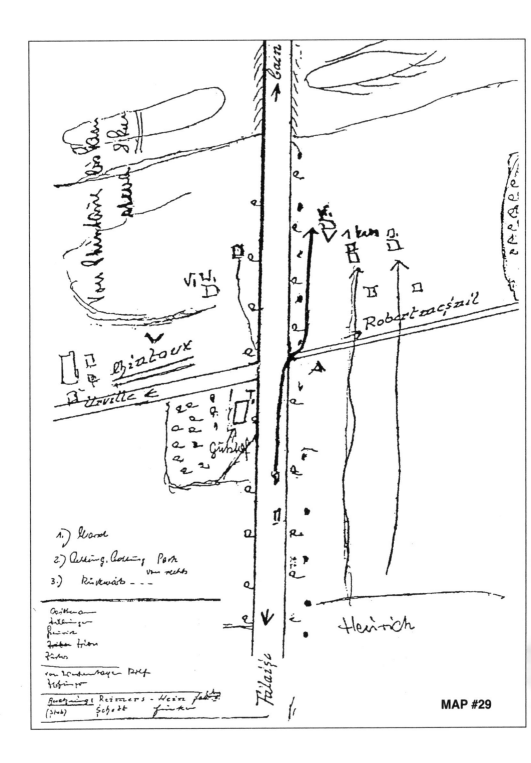

MAP #29

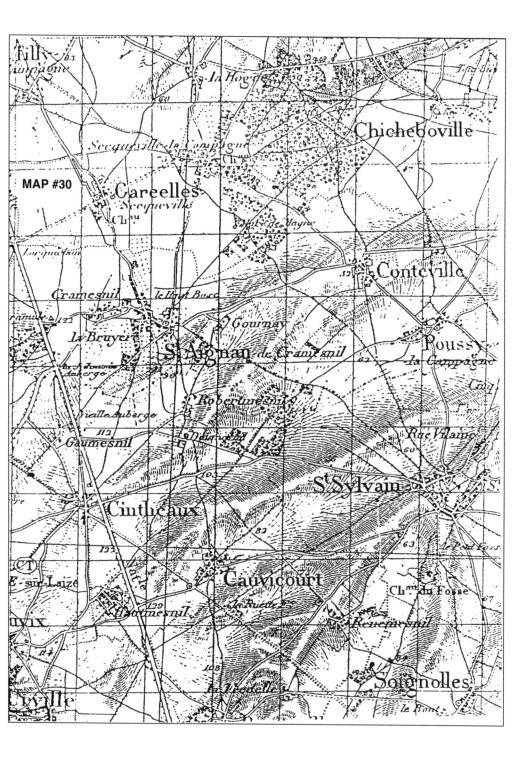

MAP #30

Westernhagen set off to the left of the road. Heurich was also to the right of the road but lagged some distance behind the others. Farther east the grenadiers of Kampfgruppe Waldmüller, 1/25 Hitlerjugend, and the IInd Battalion, 12th SS Panzer Regiment attacked to the north and northeast.

Hans Höflinger now describes the subsequent course of the attack from his experience: 'Then we drove off, Michel right of the road and I left, four others with Michel (other Tigers, the author) and the brother of von Westernhagen with me. Approximately 800 meters to Michel's right there was a small wood which struck us as suspicious and which was to prove fateful to us. Unfortunately, we couldn't keep the wood under observation on account of our mission. We drove about one to one-and-a-half kilometers, and then I received another radio message from Michel which only confirmed my suspicions about the wood.

We began taking heavy fire from anti-tank guns and once again Michel called, but didn't complete the message. When I looked out to the left I saw that Michel's tank wasn't moving. I called him by radio but received no answer. Then my tank received a frightful blow and I had to order my crew to get out as it had already begun to burn fiercely. My crew and I dashed toward the rear and got through. I stopped to look around and to my dismay discovered that five of our tanks had been knocked out. The turret of Michel's tank was displaced to the right and tilted down to the front somewhat. None of his crew had got out. I climbed into von Westernhagen's tank and, together with Heurich, whose Tiger was undamaged, tried to get to Michel's tank. We could not get through. Dr. Rabe also tried it, but in vain . . . I can state the exact time of the incident; it was 1255 hours, near the Falaise-Caen road in the vicinity of Cintheaux."

What had happened? The village of St. Aignan, which lay in front of Wittmann, had been occupied the previous night by 1st Battalion The Black Watch in their Kangaroo armored personnel carriers and the tanks of the Northamptonshire Yeomanry. The English troops subsequently took up position north and east of the village; the regimental headquarters was situated in an orchard north of St. Aignan. A-Squadron of the 1st Northamptonshire Yeomanry established a defensive position, front facing south, in the orchard south of St. Aignan and the adjoining strip of woods, the one Höflinger mentioned in his account.

A-Squadron, which was part of the 33rd Armoured Brigade, was equipped with the Sherman Firefly as well as the standard Sherman. At long range the 75-mm gun of the Sherman was powerless against the armor of the Tiger; however, the Sherman Firefly was armed with a 76.2-mm gun. Using APDS armor-piercing ammunition, it could penetrate 19.2 centimeters of armor plate from a range of 1,000 meters. The APDS was a cage propellant-solid core round. Some of the bombs dropped in the bombing attack mentioned by Panzermeyer also hit the English near St. Aignan but inflicted no casualties.

According to the English war diary, Third Platoon of A-Squadron of the 1st Northamptonshire Yeomanry reported four Tigers approaching Gaumesnil from the south at a range of twelve-hundred yards. Captain Boardman, normally the signals officer of the Yeomanry tanks, ordered the Third Platoon to cease fire immediately since he was en route to them and wanted to direct the fight himself. Tom Boardman recalled that "one of my platoons reported the arrival of these tanks (Wittmann's Tigers, the author) by radio and I drove in my Sherman to that part of the front line.

We ceased fire and I summoned one of our four Firefly tanks, which were armed with a 17-pounder gun. Had I known who was leading those Tigers and the reputation he had, I would have tried to assemble stronger forces than I had. It was bad enough to know that the squadron had only four Fireflies—which were capable of penetrating the armor of a Tiger— and that I had only one of them in my sector."

Wittmann led his Tigers north, parallel to the national highway. Hoflinger's dark premonition caused by the uncertain situation in the area to the right was to be confirmed with fatal clarity. Captain Boardman continues: "I was surprised that the German commander led his tanks through our field of fire and offered us easy targets. The Tigers showed their flanks in front of the orchard where A-squadron was positioned. Our main problem now was that we knew that the guns of our Shermans couldn't penetrate their tanks. I believe Wittmann expected possible resistance from a westerly direction, from the area of Bretteville-sur-Laize."

We know nothing of Wittmann's speculations. It is certain that he was uneasy about the strip of wood and the orchard to his right, which might be harboring anti-tank guns, always feared by him. The Tigers continued to roll north through the fields on both sides of the road toward their objective. Wittmann now pointed out by radio the danger from the right flank. At that time the Tiger commander was unaware that the enemy were already following the progress of his tanks through their telescopic sights. At 1240 hours Captain Boardman gave Sergeant Gordon's tank the order to fire. The Tigers were seven-hundred meters distant. The Firefly's gunner was Trooper Joe Ekins, who hit the rearmost of the three Tigers in his sight with two shots. The Tigers had failed to spot the well-camouflaged Shermans, and it was only after the first shots had been fired and a Tiger knocked out that Wittmann transmitted the message referred to by SS-Hauptscharführer Höflinger: "Move! Attention! Attention! Anti-tank guns to the right!—Back up! . . ."

The second Tiger observed by Ekins spotted the Sherman, veered off to the right and fired several shots in its direction. The Sherman changed its position somewhat to evade the Tiger's fire; one shell struck the turret hatch cover, however, and wounded Sergeant Gordon in the head. He climbed out immediately and Lieutenant James, his platoon commander, took over his tank and went back into position. At 1247 hours his gunner Ekins hit the second Tiger, which exploded in a ball of fire immediately after being hit. The foremost of the three Tigers was fired on by the other Shermans and was likely hit in a drive sprocket, for it began to spin in a circle. Ekins hit it with two shots at 1252 hours and the Tiger began to burn.

Curiously, the English war diary entries mention the destruction of only three Tigers, although two others were knocked out. The fourth advanced farther north and was either knocked out or abandoned due southwest of Cramesnil, on the road from La Jalousie to Cramesnil, near reference Point 117. The fifth Tiger, that of Höflinger, was knocked out on the other side of the national highway. The three knocked-out Tigers, about whose fate there are concrete details on the enemy side, were probably all accounted for by Trooper Ekins.

Captain Boardman's gunner, Eric Rutledge, wrote of the engagement: "I could see them coming through the cornfields. I fired first and they stopped; afterward things became turbulent, for several Shermans got between us and the Tigers and everyone had to watch where he was." Captain Boardman added that ". . . the fire from my tank and the others of the platoon could not penetrate the armor of the Tiger, but apparently damaged the third badly enough that it had to stop."

Matching with accuracy the kills registered by the English with the appropriate Tigers is not without its problems. It is a fact that a total of five Tigers, those of Wittmann, Dollinger, Iriohn, Höflinger and Kisters, were knocked out. Blase, von Westernhagen and Heurich were spared. The turret numbers of two of the knocked-out Tigers are known: 007 and 314. Contrary to all speculation, Tiger 007, a command vehicle, must be allocated to Wittmann, even though his aversion to command tanks—on account of their reduced ammunition capacity—was well known.

Höflinger brought two command tanks to Cintheaux, where the tanks had assembled for the attack. As he and Wittmann later drove to a conference with Meyer, they both later climbed into the tanks that were waiting for them to take part in the attack. Höflinger described how, after it was hit, the turret of Wittmann's Tiger was displaced to the right and tilted forward. That was its condition immediately after the tank was knocked out. Furthermore, it is absolutely certain that the turret was blown off shortly afterward by the Iwce of the exploding ammunition—possibly accelerated by burning fuel in the fighting compartment—and thrown several meters away from the tank. This is confirmed by the only existing photo of 007, taken by a French civilian soon after the engagement. The Tiger therefore began to burn immediately after it was hit, which then caused the ammunition in the turret to explode. Only the tremendous force produced by the exploding armor-piercing and high-explosive shells could have torn the turret, which weighed tonnes, from the hull and then tossed it meters through the air. The crew must have been killed or incapacitated when the tank was hit. The subsequent explosion then extinguished any doubts as to the fate of the five men inside 007.

Several weeks later signals officer SS-Untersturmführer Helmut Dollinger, who took advantage of every opportunity to take part in attacks, described the action: "On 8 August, at about noontime, we attacked the English, who had broken through south of Caen. The enemy secured his point of penetration through the massed employment of artillery, tanks, fighters and bombers. Nevertheless, we succeeded in advancing about three kilometers. Heavy anti-tank guns, which we could not make out at all at first, opened fire on us from excellent positions. The enemy succeeded in knocking out several tanks. As the leading tank, ours was hit and knocked out. The shell struck the turret of the tank. It began to burn at once. I myself was wounded in the forehead. I lost consciousness for a few minutes, but before I did so I was able to give the order to bail out.

When I came to again and got out myself, we came under heavy artillery fire. Beneath the tank I found my driver, the artillery observer and the second radio operator (SS-Sturmmann Alfred Bahlo, the author), who advised me that Oberscharführer Schott was lying on the rear deck aft of the turret. We got him down immediately and were just able to drag him beneath the tank, since the artillery opened fire again and the anti-tank guns also began firing at the tank. Oberscharführer Schott was still fully conscious. He told me that he was in no pain and just asked me to dress his wounds. His right arm had been torn off and several fragments had entered his right side.

After much effort, we managed to carry him out of the firing zone. Everyone in the crew had been wounded. I was able to summon a doctor and a Volkswagen. Oberscharführer Schott had by now lost consciousness. His face was peaceful and clear. He showed no sign of pain. These were difficult moments, for we knew that he was beyond human help. The doctor then loaded us both into his Volkswagen. Oberscharführer Schott died near Falaise without regaining consciousness. At that time I myself was also unconscious again."

A member of the crew of Untersturmführer Dollinger's Tiger, SS-Sturmmann Alfred Bahlo provided the following account: "I was medium-wave radio operator (communications with the division) and machine-gunner in Dollinger's tank. My commander Dollinger was an Untersturmführer and signals officer of the panzer battalion. Oberscharführer Schott was the ultra-short-wave radio operator (communications with the other tanks) and loader. This division of roles took place only in the so-called headquarters tanks. The driver and gunner were both Unterscharführer, I've forgotten their names.

The hit which our panzer took penetrated the right side wall. The shells in the fighting compartment exploded and Oberscharführer Schott was badly wounded. I myself received a minor injury in my neck. Where the defensive fire came from I do not know; there was talk later of a Canadian anti-tank front.

Untersturmführer Dollinger, the driver and I got out of the tank, followed later Oberscharführer Schott, who was seriously hampered by his serious injuries and whom I helped climb out. I attempted to get one of the retreating tanks to take Oberscharführer Schott with them. This failed because Untersturmführer Iriohn (the third tank) did not open his turret hatch, and the fourth tank was knocked out right in front of my eyes immediately afterwards. Untersturmführer Dollinger and I then carried Oberscharführer Schott on a makeshift stretcher to the Caen-Falaise road, where we loaded him into a Kübelwagen which then drove away. On the way we passed the knocked-out panzer of Hauptsturmführer Wittmann; the turret was blown off. I then made my way on foot to the aid station."

After evaluating all available documents on the German and English sides and interviewing the handful of survivors of this action (neither Hauptsturmführer Heurich nor his driver Unterscharführer Hofmann have been able to provide verifiable statements), one can assume that the tank which, according to British sources, was hit at 1247 hours, was 007. SS-Hauptsturmführer Dr. Rabe's account and the English war diary both mention that this was the only Tiger that blew up after being hit.

The eight minute time discrepancy compared to that given in Höflinger's account is of little significance as the source of the error appears to be completely genuine and time discrepancies can never be ruled out. As well, Höflinger's account was written several weeks after the events in question; it is also thoroughly possible that the error in time might lie in the English war diary.

In a letter to Wittmann's wife written eight weeks later, SS-Hauptsturmführer Dr. Rabe, one of the few eye-witnesses to the events in question, described what happened: "Now, dear Frau Wittmann, I may describe the events of 8/8/1944. Since 7/8/1944 we had been at the Grimbosq bridge-head, where Obersturmführer Wendorff was in command of the 2nd Company which was deployed there. The 3rd Company, which was at rest, received the order to attack at 6 A.M. on 8/8. It was to advance north along the Caen-Falaise road, near the village of Cintheaux, at 11:30 A.M. At about 7 A.M. Michel and I drove to headquarters then to the 3rd Company and arrived at Cintheaux at about 11 A.M. The last time I saw Michel was when he climbed into his tank at 11:30. The attack was delayed somewhat because the British made a carpet bombing attack. We suffered no losses however. At that point in time I was in a defile approximately 500 meters behind the tanks.

When the attack was rolling, I drove forward several hundred meters and covered the last stretch on foot. There was quite heavy anti-tank and artillery fire. I wanted to get to Michel's tank. When I had got to within about 250 to 300 meters I saw flames suddenly shoot from the tank and the turret fly off and fall to the ground. The tank then burned out completely. I still tried to reach it, but I couldn't cross the open field as the Tommy fired at solitary me with their anti-tank guns. It is unlikely that Michel got out before the hit, as I would have to have seen him. None of the remaining crew members came back either.

It must therefore be assumed that Michel was killed in action. I tell you this, dear Frau Wittmann, because I believe that it would be a disserv-ice to offer you false hope. It is difficult for us to believe that our Michel is no more, but we dare not hope that it might be different. I don't need to tell you that Michel will always be our model, he is after all famous in all of Germany!

My most heartfelt greetings, your Dr. Rabe."

SS-Rottenführer Herbert Debusmann likewise made mention of the fifth knocked-out Tiger. Later, while a prisoner of war, he worked in the same area clearing mines and was able to examine the Tiger more closely. As he remembers it, the Tiger, which belonged to the 2nd Company, was situated approximately 2,000 meters north of Tiger 007, but somewhat far-ther away from the national highway. There was no sign of an obvious fatal hit and the Tiger was still fully armed. After the attack the battalion still held out hope that Wittmann perhaps might have got out. Dr. Rabe attempted to work his way to Wittmann's tank as he believed that someone might have been able to free themselves through the escape hatch in the floor. Rabe came under heavy fire the instant he left the ditch at the side of the road and was thus unable to get any closer to the Tiger.

When evening came and Wittmann had still not returned, SS-Ober-sturmbannführer Wünsche initiated a search for him. SS-Untersturmführer Horst Borgsmüller of the panzer regiment headquarters staff was given the assignment: "I was ordered to search for Wittmann and his crew to the right and left of N 158. My driver, Sturmmann Klein, and I first drove in the direction of Hautmesnil. Dusk fell and I couldn't make out anything clearly. After a while we began taking machine-gun fire from right of the road. The search in the field and at the aid stations was fruitless. From some grenadiers I heard that Tigers had been knocked out by enemy anti-tank guns to the right of the road. Obersturmführer Wendorff of the Tiger Battalion could also tell me nothing. On orders from Hauptsturmführer Isecke I drove into the night once again, in the direction of Grainville. Obersturmbannführer Mohnke's command post was located there. The latter warned me to drive on as the enemy was already close by. We carried on a little farther. Flares went up and we came under fire, once again from the right."

The uncertainty about the fate of Wittmann and his crew gnawed at the nerves of the men, as the senior NCO of Wittmann's 2nd Company, SS-Hauptscharführer Konradt, wrote: "It was the most difficult battle. We had to pull back somewhat, but the tank of our dear Hauptsturmführer could not; hit badly, it remained on the battlefield. Recovery was impossible, the enemy was too strong and had already reached the tank. We had to withdraw, not knowing what had become of the crew. We couldn't comprehend that our Michael Wittmann was no longer with us."

The fate of Germany's—and indeed the war's—most successful tank commander was fulfilled on that 8 August 1944. Michael Wittmann was described as appearing somewhat nervous before the attack; he was forced to act quickly in order to steal a march on the imminent enemy attack. Wittmann didn't have to go along on the 3rd Company's attack, he knew that. But he went with the Tigers anyway, not wanting to let SS-Hauptsturmführer Heurich, who lacked experience in commanding a tank company, go it alone. In the end he alsochanged his orders and allowed Höflinger, a fellow Bavarian with whom he had fought in Russia and who he only recently appointed operations officer, to go along on the attack. Heurich, the former Technical Officer Motor Vehicles, now in command of the 3rd Company, naturally lacked experience in tank combat on the battlefield. It is however impossible to determine and therefore in the end pointless to speculate whether Wittmann would have gone along on the 3rd Company's attack if a more experienced commander than Heurich had been present to command the company's attack.

"I must go with them, for Heurich can scarcely cope." This sentence, spoken by Wittmann before the attack, was typical of him. He wanted to lend his support to the others. Wittmann knew the seriousness of the situation, as well he had received the latest intelligence from Panzermeyer that morning. He simply couldn't sit by idly at his battalion's headquarters and do nothing. Acting on an impulse, he climbed into his Tiger and set off with the others. "I must go with them . . ." he said.

To many the news that Wittmann had been killed in action was simply incomprehensible. The Senior NCO of Wittmann's 2nd Company, SS-Hauptscharführer Konradt, tried to put into words the pain felt by the entire battalion: "How hard the company was hit by the loss of our dear Hauptsturmführer is indescribable, I cannot describe it aptly. Still the hopes of the entire company are that he is still alive and has been taken prisoner, wounded, by the English." These vague hopes also helped feed unsubstantiated rumors; Konradt continued: "An Oberscharführer just back from hospital claims to have heard that the Calais Soldiers' Transmitter (English transmitter) that our Hauptsturmführer had been captured wounded by the English. But I consider this information to be unconfirmed and therefore have no wish to make a statement based upon it." Nevertheless, Wittmann's soldiers and comrades clung to the straw called hope. It was also suspected that SS-Unterscharführer Hein Reimers, who is known to have been Wittmann's driver on 8 August, was in British hands as a prisoner of war. In a telex dated 16 August 1944, Wittmann was emphatically reported as missing and the same entry appears in his personnel file.

"I was amazed that Frau Wittmann considered her husband missing in action, especially since I myself visited her and informed her that her husband had died a hero's death in his exploding tank on 8 August 1944." So wrote Heinz von Westernhagen in regard to this, ending all speculation. The battalion commander, who was spending time at home, was informed of Wittmann's death soon afterward, and a few days later he sought out Frau Wittmann in Erbstorf and gave her the sad news. Numerous legends surround Wittmann's death, all the possible and impossible versions course through the relevant literature. Various versions are offered: he was killed when his tank was knocked out by Canadian tanks, or by the Shermans of the 1st Polish Armored Division, another states that he fell victim to rockets fired by a Typhoon fighter-bomber. In any case Wittmann and his crew remained missing.

It was not until the spring of 1983, when his skeletal remains and those of his crew were found, that all the speculations were put to rest. One thing that remains uncertain, however, is whether the English put a price on Wittmann's head. Proof that the English did in fact engage in this degenerate practice is contained in a July 1944 situation report by the 49th Infantry Division: "A reward is offered for SS-Obergruppenführer Sepp Dietrich, the notorious commander of the Ist SS Panzer Corps, dead or alive."

The news of Wittmann's death raced through the Ist SS Panzer Corps like wildfire. The men of the battalion and the divisions of the panzer corps were dumbstruck. All were shocked, and deep, genuine sadness gripped soldiers of all ranks. Depressed, the members of the battalion headquarters staff sat in their small Norman house. They could not comprehend that Wittmann had been killed, after all he had been with them only a few hours earlier. Paralyzing dismay spread. It was as if the war would stop for a moment. 8 August 1944 was the blackest day in the history of the Leibstandarte's Tiger battalion. Wittmann's death created a gap that could never be filled.

But the myth of Michael Wittmann was not extinguished by his death. Wittmann is not forgotten in the conversations and memories of the survivors of the great conflict, he remains alive among these men as an undiminished example. To these men their Michel remains what he always was: their rousing and beloved leader, ever a concerned superior who judged with heart and feeling in every situation and who was always accessible to his men. He was a trusted officer, one you could talk to—even if you were only an SS-Sturmmann.

Wittmann embodied the modern officer of the Waffen-SS, who lived with his men in a comradely community and thus firmly blotted out the clearly-defined stations—officer, noncommissioned officer and enlisted man—of earlier days. He was a man who was essentially unchanged by the highest awards for bravery the Reich could offer and the popularity that went with them, remaining the honorable, considerate and responsible officer he had always been. Wittmann was incorruptible in the face of all enticements; that is why he turned down the offer of a secure position at an armored command school and instead returned to his company in Normandy.

Wittmann wanted no privileges for himself. He also had no time for the flattery of his person and was unreceptive to ingratiation. He was in many respects an extraordinary man and soldier, one who fit no existing cliche. In spite of his rather common origins and tough early years, Michel Wittmann was an educated and multifaceted man. There was no standing still for him, he worked constantly to better himself and thus acquired new knowledge and skills, read books and occupied himself with things useful to him. Of medium height, 1.76 meters tall, he was of slim build with pale eyes and medium blonde, almost brunette hair. His voice was pleasant and his Bavarian origins were not immediately evident in its melodic pattern; he spoke High German.

To strangers he appeared rather reserved, but in no way timid. Wittmann was undoubtedly an idealist and had clearly defined moral codes which he passed on to the men under him. He was in this respect—as in all others—extremely precise, which helped make him a good superior, for in addition to their military training he considered the bringing-up of his young soldiers to be part and parcel of his role. His men considered him an optimist and he was never seen to lose his head, not even during the heaviest fighting on the Eastern Front in 1943 and 44. He had faith in his skill and his weapon and used this to lead his men through the toughest battles against a numerically-superiorfoe in unfavorable weather conditions with weak forces. He always operated deliberately and never from an ad hoc approach. He commanded with spirit and intelligence and in combat he was the best. Resorting to blind action was foreign to him and he never charged into the enemy without a plan. When forced to make a quick decision he tried to reach the best solution, reflected for a moment and in those few seconds developed his plan.

Results showed that Wittmann, the individualist, achieved his greatest and most spectacular successes when he fought alone. Tactically, he employed his Tiger brilliantly; he never spared himself, instead he always led from the front, even in uncertain situations. His successes were not the result of his rank, and they cannot be ascribed solely to his talent and his undoubtedly outstanding ability—his conscientiousness was equally important as one of the blocks that formed the foundation of his success.

The mastery of the tank as a weapon and care of the tank were important to him and he placed great emphasis on them. He could become "disagreeable" in the face of slackness, perhaps a hangover from his time in the Reichswehr and later as an NCO instructor. Unforgiving he was not, however. He addressed mistakes and that ended the matter as far as he was concerned. Fairness was of great importance to him. He never abandoned himself to frivolities after the daily actions, in which he never spared himself and often spent himself to the point of total exhaustion. Instead he busied himself with coming missions.

He could be characterized as spiritual, leaning toward introverted, without however appearing reserved or aloof. Wittmann the Bavarian was uncomfortable in a boisterous circle where there was excessive drinking and he either avoided such parties altogether or spent only a very brief time at them. He showed no tendency to indulge in the jokes and obscenity of the soldiers, they weren't a part of his world, though he was not seen as a prude.

He could be merry without alcohol, for he was usually in a positive mood, in good spirits and demonstrated a sense for the beautiful. He was as intensively concerned about the welfare of his men as he was about their training. He questioned tank crews just back from an action and worried when a Tiger crew became overdue. He was receptive to his men and received them not as subordinates in the earlier sense of the word. Once, while scouting terrain in Russia in 1943, he told the men with him that he could imagine running a farm in that area with its fertile soil. Wittmann talked with his men about private matters too and also had the ability to just listen. His authority was based not just on his success in combat, but also on his ever correct behavior, his honesty and his performance—all of these things enabled him to become an acknowledged leader and model.

On one occasion, after he had won the Knight's Cross, Wittmann was helping his crew pound the bolts into the tracks of their tank in the endless mud. Army soldiers passing by were astonished that an officer and Knight's Cross wearer was standing in the mud with his men, pounding in bolts with a hammer. For Wittmann that was nothing unusual, he also helped clean the tube of the Tiger's eighty-eight. Even after he had received the Knight's Cross with Oak Leaves and Swords his men still saw him working on track bolts with a hammer. His discipline and sense of duty and his sense of responsibility combined in his good relationship with the men under his command, which made for a close-knit fighting team. To the soldiers he was more than their superior officer, he was a clever tactician in combat, a brave fighter, and their best friend. He lived for that. His very human manner and his personal example, which he offered daily, allowed him to win the hearts of his men. When they were with him they always had the feeling that he was one of them. Wittmann lived by the axiom "Be more than you appear" and he remained true to that concept until the end. Thus was created the Wittmann saga.

Within five months Wittmann had been awarded the Knight's Cross, Oak Leaves, and Swords, promoted from SS-Untersturmführer to SS-Hauptsturmführer and become one of the best-known soldiers in Germany. The successes that resulted in the decorations were his quite personal successes. He was decorated for what he had done while acting on his own, not for the command of a unit. This was so even in 1941, when he commanded an assault gun. Wittmann was undoubtedly an ideal company commander, but commanding the battalion from July 1944 was less to his taste. He talked about this too, even to nonmembers of the battalion. Michael Wittmann, who everyone just called Michel, was an idealist who knew exactly what he was fighting for. All these attributes—and much more—made him Germany's outstanding tank soldier and deservingly ranked him with the long list of the nation's greatest soldiers.

The 8th of August 1944 was not yet over, however. A combat report said of SS-Hauptsturmführer Dr. Rabe: "On 8 August 1944, during an attack by the Tigers attached to the 21th SS Panzer Regiment, the leader of the battalion, SS-Hauptsturmführer Wittmann, was knocked out of action. Dr. Rabe, who as was his custom had accompanied the attack in his vehicle, assumed command of the battalion on his own initiative and deployed the remaining three Tigers against an enemy counterattack from the area west of St. Aignan with an infantry battalion, ten tanks and numerous anti-tank guns. Under Rabe's direction, the Tigers destroyed seven enemy tanks and halted the attack. The time thus gained enabled a new defensive line to be established during the night."

The three Tigers mentioned in the report match exactly the number of serviceable Tigers given in the preceding accounts. The 2nd Company was still en route after being withdrawn from the English bridgehead position near Grimbosq. SS-Hauptsturmführer Dr. Rabe wrote of the events that day: "Toward evening I drove to Brigadeführer Kraemer (Chief of Staff, Ist SS Panzer Corps, the author) and reported the day's events to him. As I was the battalion's senior serving officer he instructed me to lead back the remnants of the battalion and placed me under Wtinsche's command."

SS-Rottenführer Walter Lau, gunner in the Tiger of the company commander, SS-Obersturmführer Wendorff, wrote of the 2nd Company and its action near Grimbosq on 8 August 1944: "We withdrew at dawn on 8 August 1944 while it was still quite dark. Infantry came to relieve us. A heavy artillery barrage began as we reached the fuel trucks waiting one and a half kilometers to the rear. We simply rolled the 200-liter drums into the ditch and hastily took cover, for we feared they would be hit and explode. However, once again all ended well and we were ableto refuel our tanks, though with great difficulty. We resumed our drive toward Grimbosq while it was still morning and moved into a good firing position in a defile just outside a town. As we were familiar with the terrain on both sides of the Orne, we knew roughly where the enemy had dug in on the opposite bank. We fired a few shots to get the Tommy to reveal his position then blanketed him with high-explosive and armor-piercing shells. Suddenly we were struck a tremendous blow, a hit, accompanied by a terrible explosion. It felt as if the Tiger had rolled backward some meters under the force of the impact of the enemy shell. The engine noise died—dead silence—the smell of burning?—should we get out? What was the right thing to do in this situation? We very quickly determined that bailing out was not necessary, but we could not restore the Tiger's mobility. Obersturmführer Wendorff instructed the crew of another Tiger to take us under tow. The loader and gunner of the other Tiger, which was now behind us, coupled the two tanks with stout cables and heavy bolts. Then it happened. A shell burst next to loader Paul Sümnich, a good friend of mine from Pomerania, and blew off both his legs. We recovered our seriously-wounded comrade and tended to his wounds as best we could pending medical attention at the clearing station. We were first towed up the slope at high speed and soon afterward reached the road where we had refuelled under artillery fire at dawn. The Tigers of the 2nd Company then assembled on this road. Obersturmführer Wendorff took over another, intact Tiger. I can still remember his words as he asked me and Fran Elmer, our driver: 'Well tall one (I was called that because I fully met the Leibstandarte height requirement), are you coming with me?' Of course we were glad to and the three of us climbed into a serviceable Tiger. I believe it must have been a tank of the IIIrd Platoon, either 232 or 233. Sturmmann Hubert Heil, the radio operator, had been wounded and did not come. This interlude and the move to another tank has stayed in my memory because it was at that time that the news came through; voice trembling and tears in his eyes, Bubi Wendorff said: 'Michel Wittmann has been killed.' At that time the version as it was told to Wendorff was that during an attack by several Tigers Wittmann had been caught in a hail of bombs and that there was nothing left of his tank and its crew.

That day was an extraordinarily depressing one. Bubi Wendorff did not say a word. An operations officer delivered orders for those Tigers still serviceable—I believe there were two—to be deployed at another location approximately one hour's drive away." Hans Frahm of the 2nd Company was posted missing in action on 8 August 1944, while Willi Freitag was killed in a motor vehicle accident near Tassailly.

Preparations for the further defense against the threat of an enemy breakthrough were made on the hills north of the Laison by the Hitlerjugend Division. The 12th SS Panzer Regiment Hitlerjugend, together with the Tigers of the 101st SS Panzer Battalion and thirteen Tigers of the 102nd SS Panzer Battalion, took up positions in Quesnay Forest, two kilometers northwest of Quilly-le-Tesson.

SS-Sturmmann Ernst Kufner of the 3rd Company described his experiences in those grave days: "7 August once again found me in a tank as replacement radio operator. During the drive into an assembly area near Cintheaux, during the night of 7–8 August, a Tiger drove into our tank in a defile. Both tanks were removed from the advance road and parked in a barn beside the road. The next day, 8 August 1944, the gun was boresighted, this having become necessary after the collision. Toward evening of 8 August both Tigers drove to our unit at the front.

On the way we met some comrades from our company. They said that Hauptsturmführer Wittmann's tank had been knocked out and that the crew had been killed. We drove to the command post and there into an assigned position beside the road. I can remember well how the English used hundreds of searchlights to light up our sector of the front when darkness fell. We heard tank engines, a sign that they were going to attack again the next day. Toward midnight our tanks were refuelled and the battle group, consisting of two Tigers and eight Panzer IVs, moved into the area near Quesnay.

At about 02.00 hours we rolled into position in an orchard. We camouflaged our tanks and waited for the English to attack. Ground mist developed at dawn. We could hear tank engines but couldn't see the tanks themselves. When the mist cleared we saw the enemy tanks and supply vehicles and knocked out several from a range of 1,500 meters. Other enemy tanks bypassed our sector of the front. That morning we destroyed seven tanks and numerous supply vehicles and fired on the infantry with high-explosive shells. By about midday the English had outflanked us and were already approaching from the rear and from the side. We drove back into the village and hid ourselves beneath the tin roof of an open barn. Fighter-bombers had already spotted us.

The two tank commanders deliberated. In command of the second Tiger was our senior NCO, Hauptscharführer Hack. He had joined the tank's crew as replacement commander. After much consideration we decided to drive through a forest. The main gun was placed in the 6 o'clock position and we cleared a path through the forest with our tank. At the end of the forest was a field, across which the English were already moving. We had no time for further deliberations, the commander of our tank instructed the driver by way of the intercom to increase speed.

Our two Tigers drove past the English, only a few meters away. They raised their hands and we trembled in the tank. Not a shot was fired. After several-hundred meters we disappeared behind a hedge. The English were frightened for they suspected more German tanks in the forest. We arrived at the regimental command post towards noon. Our arrival was met with great joy for we were already considered missing. Our tank had suffered transmission damage after driving through the forest, but we were able to make temporary repairs. From the command post we were towed by an 18-tonne prime mover."

In spite of their superior numbers and unlimited air superiority the Canadian armored and infantry divisions failed to achieve the desired breakthrough into the German rear. The handful of Tigers played a significant part in the German defensive success; together with Waldmüller's panzer-grenadiers and Wünsche's battered panzer regiment they stopped the enemy in a hard-fought battle.

Morale in the 101st SS Panzer Battalion was poor in the days after 8 August 1944. SS-Obersturmführer Wendorff's gunner, Walter Lau, remembered those difficult days on the Caen-Falaise road: "The moral breaking point came with the 20th of July, which confirmed many true and false rumors. I recall that in the days after the 20th of July until the beginning of August there were many grim-faced discussions between Obersturm-führer Wendorff and Hauptsturmführer Dr. Rabe under the tank or in a quiet corner. These surely concerned the events of the 20th of July.

The absolute morale low point was then the death of Michel, which coincided with the more or less evident realization that the brave remnants of the proud Hitlerjugend Division and we would not be able to withstand the onslaught."

As the table below indicates, at least two officers, eight NCOs and nine enlisted men were killed in the period 7–12 August 1944, while one officer, one NCO and two enlisted men were wounded. Only known losses are given for the 7th and 8th; the true number was probably higher, especially on the 8th. At least two officers, eight NCOs and eleven enlisted men were listed as missing in action, for a total of twenty-one.

| | | Killed | | | Wounded | | |
Date	Company	Officers	NCOs	Men	Officers	NCOs	Men
7/8	2nd	-	1	-	-	-	-
8/8	2nd	-	3	7	-	-	2
8/8	HQ	1	-	-	1	-	-
8/8	3rd	1	-	-	-	-	-
9/8	Workshop	-	-	-	-	-	-
11/8	2nd	-	-	1	-	1	-
11/8	3rd	-	-	1	-	-	-
11/8	HQ	-	2	-	-	-	-
12/8	3rd	-	1	-	-	-	-

Following the conclusion of the battle of Villers-Bocage several of the 1st Company's Schwimmwagen drove into the town to recover those killed on 13 June 1944. On their left is Panzer IV 634. Next to the vehicle number on the rear of the turret is the Schönburg family's coat of arms; Prince Schönburg, commander of the IInd Battalion, Panzer-Lehr Regiment, was killed a short time before.

Photographs of the town of Evrecy, which was totally destroyed by English bombers during the night of 15–16 June 1944. The 101st SS Panzer Battalion suffered heavy casualties in the bombing; as well 130 French civilians lost their lives.

The Tiger of Knight's Cross wearer SS-Untersturmführer Alfred Günther, destroyed by a direct hit by a bomb. Günther lost his life in the explosion.

Another view of SS-Untersturmführer Günther's Tiger.

SS-Sturmmann Günther Boldt,
the nineteen-year-old loader.
Here he is seen in the loader's
hatch of Wittmann's Tiger 231
in July 1944.

SS-Unterscharführer Waldemar
Warnecke, commander of Tiger
333 of the 101st SS Panzer
Battalion's 3rd Company,
knocked out six British tanks on
the Caen-Villers-Bocage road in
one day in June 1944.

SS-Rottenführer Paul Rohweder,
Warnecke's driver.

SS-Panzerschütz August-Wilhelm "Büding" Belbe, Warnecke's gunner.

A Tiger of the 2nd Company leaves its camouflaged hide in the forest, where it was invisible to enemy aircraft, and rolls to the attack. Standing on the right and wearing the leather jacket is SS-Untersturmführer Heinz Belbe.

The young panzer-grenadiers fought side by side with the Tigers of the 101st SS Panzer Battalion; their close front-line comradeship was based on mutual respect, both groups knowing that they could depend on each other.

A panzer-grenadier.

Panzer-grenadiers of the 12th SS Panzer Division "Hitlerjugend" shortly before an attack. In the foreground is SS-Sturmmann Otto Funk of the 15th (Reconnaissance) Company, 25th Panzer-Grenadier Regiment "Hitlerjugend".

Grenadiers of the Hitlerjugend Division in a Norman village.

A grenadier during a
short break between
battles.

2nd Company, SS-Sturmmänner Hubert Heil (radio operator) and Erich Tille (gunner), SS-Unterscharführer Franz Elmer (driver) and Helmut Hauck (loader).

A tank of 2nd Company.

2nd Company.
Left to right: a driver,
SS-Untersturmführer
Hantusch and Belbe,
SS-Hauptscharführer
Höflinger and SS-
Unterscharführer
Warmbrunn.

These were the young
soldiers of the Leibstandarte
Tiger Battalion—filled with
the joy of life and full of
youthful idealism in spite of
the difficult fighting.

June 1944 Michael Wittmann on a farm which housed the command post of his 2nd Company. Pensiveness is reflected in his face.

On 29 July 1944, the Battalion Technical Officer in Charge of Motor Vehicles I, SS-Hauptsturmführer Franz Heurich, assumed command of the 101st SS Panzer Battalion's 3rd Company after the death of SS-Obersturmführer Hanno Raasch earlier in the day. On 15 July 1944 SS-Obersturmführer Helmut Wendorff returned to the Tiger Battalion and took over Wittmann's 2nd Company, as Wittmann was by now commanding the battalion.

Helmut Wendorff

Hanno Raasch

SS-Sturmmann Günter
Boldt, Wittman's loader,
was killed on 20 July 1944.

Franz Heurich

SS-Oberscharführer
Georg Lötzsch.

SS-Oberscharführer Jürgen Brandt and Lötzsch, 2nd Company.

Gemeinschaftsleiter Ewald König visits the 2nd Company in the Bretteville-sur-Laize forest in July 1944. As a representative of the Strength Through Joy organization, König was responsible for the soldiers's hostels in France. He had earlier served in the Tiger Company as a loader. *From left:* Mölly, König and Brandt.

Brandt and SS-Unterscharführer Mölly, both Tiger commanders since 1942.

Tiger in Rouen, August 1944.

Battles Northeast of Falaise, 9–16 August 1944

In position near Hill 140, northwest of Assy, on 9 August 1944 was an armored battle group of the 28th Armoured Regiment of the 4th Canadian Armoured Division and infantry of the Algonquin Regiment. It had been instructed to occupy Hill 195 northwest of Potigny and from there break through to Falaise. The Hitlerjugend Division's 1st Operations Officer, SS-Obersturmführer Meitzel, discovered this threat on the early morning of 9 August and informed SS-Obersturmbannführer Wünsche, who immediately committed his Tigers and Panthers to retake the hill. The panzers were able to clear the hill, destroying a number of enemy tanks in the process, and thus relieved the acute threat to the new defense front then being formed.

Also on 10 August 1944, the Canadians tried to at last get their stalled attack going again; the first step was to take the Quesnay Forest, where there were still some German tanks. The attack began in the evening but was repulsed by the tanks and panzer-grenadiers of Kampfgruppe Krause (1126); Canadian losses were heavy. Northwest of Rouvres, SS-Obersturmführer Hurdelbrink of the 1st Company, 12th SS Anti-Tank Battalion Hitlerjugend was able to destroy eleven tanks of the 1st Polish Armoured Division which had advanced that far. Seven more Polish tanks were knocked out by SS-Oberscharführer Roy and two by the armorer-artificer, SS-Unterscharführer Ortlepp. This raised the company's score of enemy tanks destroyed since 20 July 1944 to 86. The Tigers of the 101st SS Panzer Battalion once again engaged the enemy near Hill 140. The opposing tanks moved off into a valley basin on the heels of a bombing attack. While the Tigers waited in well-camouflaged ambush positions, the Panthers of the 3rd Company, 12th SS Panzer Regiment rolled down the valley road to envelop the enemy armored force. This move resulted in the destruction of more than 50 enemy tanks by the German panzers and an 88 mm flak. The 28th Armoured Regiment lost 47 tanks at Hill 140 on the 9th and 10th of August 1944. SS-Rottenführer Ryll of the 2nd Company and SS-

197

Unterscharführer Tilly of the 4th were decorated with the Iron Cross, Second Class that same day.

A surviving report by the 101st SS Panzer Battalion states: "The Tigers of the battalion had to take up screening positions behind the main line of resistance during the night of 9–10 August and on the 10th. Rabe drove from tank to tank under the heaviest fire, not allowing himself an hour's rest; he maintained contact with the tanks and passed instructions to the crews. The battalion destroyed thirty-eight enemy tanks during this period." The Tigers of the 2nd Company made contact with the enemy north of the Laison, near Bû-sur-Rouvres, on 11 August, as did elements of the 3rd Company on the following day. SS-Hauptscharführer Barkhausen of the 3rd Company was killed in action, SS-Oberscharführer Lötzsch was wounded.

The foremost elements of the 2nd Canadian Corps were on Hill 195, three kilometers northwest of Potigny. In spite of the lavish use of tanks and air power they had managed to advance a total of only fifteen kilometers to the south, opening a corridor which extended from Bretteville-sur-Laize to St. Sylvain. The enemy called off Operation "Totalize."

During the night of 12 August 1944 the 85th Infantry Division took over the Hitlerjugend Division's entire sector. The Hitlerjugend became corps reserve and moved into the area northeast of Falaise. Under its command were the 101st and 102nd SS Panzer Battalions, which together had only eleven serviceable Tigers. SS-Rottenführer Lau described the actions in that area from the point of view of the tank crews: "We were on a road. We drove up to a wood on the left side. From the forest emerged Panzermeyer and his operations officer. By coincidence I knew the latter, Untersturmführer Puls; he had been a Jungbannführer in the Hitler Youth in Rostock. How Obersturmführer Wendorff received his orders I do not know, but in any case we drove with Wendorff on the right side of the wood, looking in the direction of the front, and on the left side drove Untersturmführer Henniges' tank. He was, by the way, seeing his first action in those days, having joined our company shortly before as a young Untersturmführer.

Panzermeyer knew, and he had also told us, that there were quite a few Canadian tanks beyond the wood; they were our target. All of a sudden we saw eight Canadian tanks race left to right across an open field, approximately 600 to 800 meters in front of us, toward another wood. Load armor-piercing, open fire, and the first shot was fired. I felt Obersturmführer Wendorff nudge me with his foot, for the first shot missed. The enemy tanks were moving fast and I now knew the required amount of lead to use, on the second aiming spike next to the main spike. The next seven shots left seven Canadian tanks immobilized on the field. Suddenly an armored vehicle, marked with a large red cross and flying red cross flags, drove up to the tanks, some of which were on fire. Wendorff said, 'Tall one, cease firing!' We had never experienced such a thing in Russia. At about the same time Panzermeyer and his operations officer came out of the wood, from where he had watched us, and said drily: 'You handled that well.' Then he passed up a pack of twenty-five R 6s. Wendorff and I were heavy smokers.

The Poles broke through in the evening hours, possibly at the Laison Valley. We were sitting on a slope and beneath our tank lay Panzermeyer with his operations officer. When he fetched Wendorff from the turret we knew that something was being cooked up. Then, toward evening, between 19.00 and 20.00 hours, Wendorff peered in and said in his typical fashion, 'Listen to me people. We have a little job to do.' He explained to us that Panzermeyer was putting several anti-aircraft tanks on the rise and these were supposed to pin down the Tommies. Farther down the slope there was a so-called 'belly battalion,' an alert unit made up of rear-area personnel. They gave us several bags of hand grenades; we were to drive through the English lines, with the anti-aircraft tanks pinning down the infantry, and make things hot for the enemy in his positions. This was surely done in order to bring some quiet to the area and thus gain a few hours to prepare our defense.

We crept along a hedge, and when we had driven through the forward German lines and overrun the first enemy infantry positions it was time to use the 'pineapple' hand grenades. The grenades were lobbed quickly from all the hatches, at least by the commander and the loader, and I had a downright uncomfortable feeling as they did so. What if a grenade slipped from their hands and fell into the fighting compartment? But nothing happened. When we were through the English lines we saw a gathering of tanks and other vehicles, which, it appeared, were being refuelled.

The commander barked out, 'Twelve o'clock, armor-piercing, open fire!' After several shots the whole area was in flames, for fuel trucks had obviously driven alongside the tanks. According to the driver, who kept track of the proceedings, we were able to destroy eight tanks there. When those of the morning were added, our total for the day was at least fifteen kills. We later calculated that that should be enough to earn Franz Elmer and me the Iron Cross, First Class. There were also the kills we had to our credit from Russia and from the first days on the invasion front in the area of Villers-Bocage.

The situation now became ticklish, however; the glare from the fires shone into our fighting compartment through the gaps. We withdrew and drove back to our departure point. Panzermeyer was among those there.

He was full of praise. Several days before this SS-Unterscharführer Adolf Schmidt (our SDG), who was always up front with us, had told us that a thigh wound was the worst that could happen. Tragically he was himself severely wounded in the thigh. As our engine had begun to sputter and we ourselves could barely stand, we were sent back to the workshop. First we drove to the battalion command post. Hauptscharführer Höflinger, the operations officer, greeted Wendorff, who immediately stretched out on a mattress in a garage and fell into a deep sleep. I myself always had something left over for good food and asked SS-Hauptscharführer Höflinger for something to eat. He obtained some wonderful goulash from our Viennese cook and some boiled potatoes. Our hunger was so great that we emptied two full mess tins.

Then it was off to the workshop, where we spent two full days while the tank, especially the engine and the running gear, underwent a general overhaul. The cannon was supposed to be bore-sighted anew. As senior gunner, it was customary for me to see to that. I therefore stuck a small pennant in the ground at a distance of approximately 400 meters, removed the breech mechanism and, using the cross hairs, bore-sighted the cannon myself.

Those two days were the first that Obersturmführer Wendorff had spent with the company's rear-echelon for a long time and he and Senior NCO Konradt processed death reports as well as decorations and promotions. Several winks from Wendorff made it clear to me and to Elmer that the Iron Cross, First Class was a sure thing. Franz Elmer became an Unterscharführer that day. Afterward we drank plenty of Calvados. I know that Schorsch Lötzsch, whose tank was in the workshop, and Kurt Sowa were also there at that time. We were old chums from past days and we made a happy bunch in the workshop."

To his men Bubi Wendorff—also called Axel—was a valued and liked company commander. Wittmann had put the company in the right hands when he decided on his best friend and comrade. With his crew he joined an extremely close front-line comradeship based on trust in the reliability of everyone. This intelligent, richly gifted young officer planned to give up his military career after the war and run his father's farm in the Uckermarck together with his young bride Hannelore—he carried a wedding photograph with him at all times.

General Montgomery's objective was the encirclement and destruction of the German forces and the capture of Falaise. The German troops between the Seine and the Loire were to be destroyed. The British 2nd Army was given the task of taking Falaise as the Canadians had so far failed

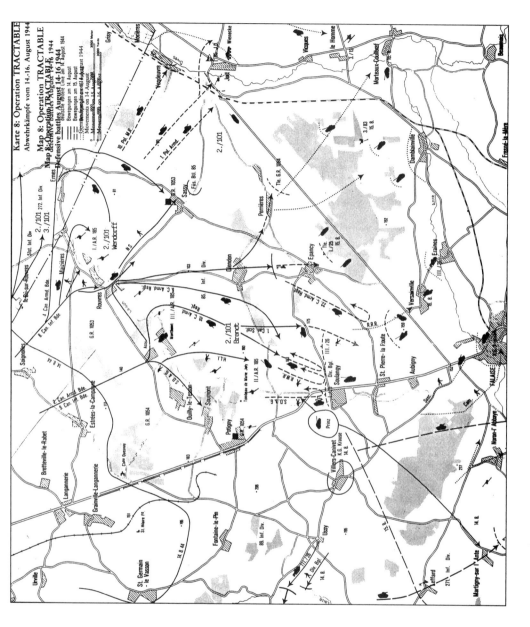

Operation Tractable

to do so. The extreme right boundary of the Ist SS Panzer Corps extended from a point in the vicinity of Ernes, east of Maizières, through the southern tip of the forest north of Le Bû to the east end of St. Sylvain. In the front line was the 85th Infantry Division. The Laison Valley formed a natural anti-tank obstacle in the Hitlerjugend Division's sector, and the division's tanks could only be employed in the open areas.

The 4th Canadian Armoured Division, with the attached 8th Infantry Brigade, was supposed to smash the German positions on the hills north of the Laison Valley between Maizières and Mountboint. Its objective was Versainville, 2.5 kilometers northeast of Falaise. The Canadian attack began on 14 August on the road from St. Sylvain to Bretteville-le-Rabet. At 11.37 hours the artillery fired marker rounds for the bombers, then laid down smoke to cover the movements of the Canadians. Fifty-three bombers subsequently attacked German positions in Montboint, Rouvres and Maizières. The Canadian tanks moved off at 11.42 hours. The infantry positions north of the Laison were unable to hold for long against the onrushing tanks; the wooded Laison Valley finally slowed the Canadian advance. At the same time, elements of the 51st British Highland Division took Le Bû and from there drove on toward the southeast. The tanks of the 4th Canadian Armoured Brigade crossed the Laison in and north of Ernes and swung in an arc toward the southwest, taking the German artillery southeast of Maizières in the rear. The few remaining Tigers of the 2nd and 3rd Companies of the 101st Tiger Battalion—the 1st Company had been in Germany for a month—were embroiled in heavy fighting against a far-superior enemy in the Assy-Maizières sector. SS-Obersturmführer Helmut Wendorff and another Tiger of his 2nd Company engaged the troops of the 3rd Canadian Infantry Division. The enemy broke through near Assy. Just beyond the village his armored vehicles ran into units of the 85th Infantry Division, whose accurate defensive fire halted the Canadians near Château Montboint. The combined fire of two Tigers inflicted considerable losses on the attackers, whose own tanks had not yet caught up with the infantry.

The following account by Walter Lau, gunner in company commander SS-Obersturmführer Wendorff's tank, begins the previous day: "Then came the 13th of August 1944. The tanks—there were six as I recall—drove forward in the evening, as I learned later in the direction of Maizières. Present there were the tanks of Wendorff, Hantusch, Lötzsch, Brandt, Sowa and Mölly. To avoid being seen from the air, we drove into the shelter of an orchard, an advantageous situation in that the apples hung down into our hatches. One man stood watch in the turret, while the rest ate the apples, which were not quite ripe.

An army operations officer appeared at dawn and briefed Wendorff on the situation using the map. Sitting right next to Wendorff in the gunner's seat, I was able to hear everything, and I recall that a breakthrough was feared eight to ten kilometers in the direction of Maizières against the 85th Infantry Division. The enemy had massed strong tank forces and the sector had no anti-tank defense. We were to drive there as quickly as possible.

Our six tanks moved out of the orchard, with Wendorff's the last. We then drove past the others and I saw Kurt Kämmer, a veteran driver, and Rudi Lechner, a gunner with whom I had spent a lot of time, waving once again. We then took the lead, and I know that Hantusch and Lötzsch were also there. We drove off, and as we were behind the front I took off my pistol belt, laid it on the recoil guard, leaned sideways in the gunner's seat and put my feet up. We had slept little all night—on account of the apples— and since, according to the operations officer, we still had eight to ten kilometers to drive to the front, I was able to close my eyes for a brief spell, for things would be hot up front and sleep would be out of the question. The radio operator had no need for further preparations and he could close his eyes too. The loader had joined us only the previous day, his name has escaped my memory. He was Wendorff's batman and was eager to come along on a mission. (It was SS-Sturmmann Peter Mayer, the author.)

And so, thinking we were still behind the front, we clattered into our new sector. We may have gone several kilometers in the direction of Maizières, when suddenly Wendorff roared, 'Man, two Shermans, Tall One, fire!' I whipped off my headset, quickly put on my throat microphone and put my feet down onto the pedals. The loader quickly released the gun, which was locked in position while we were on the move. Left hand on the traversing mechanism, right hand on the elevating mechanism. I heard the round slide in and the breech snap shut. All the while Wendorff shouted, 'Tall one, shoot, shoot, shoot.' But I saw nothing, so I traversed the turret to one o'clock and through the monocular sight I could almost see the grooves in the gun of the enemy tank. The Sherman was sitting on a bend in the road at point-blank range; looking through the sight I estimated thirty to fifty meters. I targeted it quickly and the eighty-eight barked. The first shot was on target and the explosion blinded me. The Sherman was surely nothing more than a black spot on the road.

Then Wendorff called out again: 'Beside it, the second Sherman!' I traversed the turret by hand and found the second Sherman at two o'clock. At the same instant there was a tremendous bang which I will never forget as long as I live. After a while I came to. All was deathly still. There was an awful stench in the tank and I could hardly see. As I discovered months later, the telescopic sight (which fortunately for me was monocular) must have struck me in the eye, for I was completely blind in my right eye, the eyeball was crushed. As well I felt pain in my hands, feet and face—burns as it turned out. I also heard a roaring sound, leading me to believe that there might be something wrong with my ears. My first thought, after how long I do not know, was the usual one, to reach up and grasp the two grips for the gunner just in front of the commander's cupola, through which I entered the tank. But I could not reach them, for Wendorff was sitting there. I felt his lifeless knee and leg. I shouted 'Obersturmführer' several times and then tried to move him, but there was no reaction and I concluded that he was either severely wounded or dead.

I found it terribly difficult to breathe during these movements; I was getting no air and lost consciousness repeatedly. I vaguely remember the radio operator, Fred Zimmermann, calling to me and other members of the crew. With the turret at two o'clock he was right under me.

We were able to communicate with one another. His feet were caught in the steering gear and he couldn't open the hatch as the cannon was sitting over it. Judging by the wounds that I had and by the fact that the loader and Wendorff were dead on the spot, the shot must have struck the hull from the right. Perhaps Wendorff's, the loader's and my wounds had been caused by articles flying about in the fighting compartment. If the shot had penetrated it would very likely have ended my life too.

The last thing I heard was Zimmermann saying that the engine was burning. I couldn't see it, but I could smell it. Fred Zimmermann said, 'I'm going to end it.' In those seconds, minutes, maybe a half hour, I reached for the cannon because I had laid my pistol belt on the recoil guard. As was normal when a tank was knocked out, the hydraulics had failed and the recoil guard had tipped up and in. My pistol belt was jammed between the recoil guard and the roof of turret. I asked Fred Zimmermann to give me his pistol. When I was finished it would fall down to him. But Fred refused. I made one last effort to reach my belt but failed. I desperately tried to reach Wendorff's pistol, but apparently he was sitting on it and I could not. Meanwhile I called to him several times and it was my impression that he was dead; I felt no blood however. In the course of this effort of moving my arms I lost consciousness. I had only just come too again when I heard a crack. Fred Zimmermann no longer answered my calls and I assumed that he had ended his life. Unconsciousness returned painlessly. My head fell against the foam rubber padding of the telescopic sight—twenty years later I still had black flecks from it on my forehead. I remained unconscious for some time. All this happened between 05.00 and 07.00 hours."

The battalion had lost Michael Wittmann and another wearer of the Knight's Cross within one week. Helmut Wendorff belonged to the select group of outstanding officers and individuals of the former 13th Company and the 101st SS Panzer Battalion. He had destroyed at least eighty-four enemy tanks. SS-Rottenführer Walter Lau, who had served close to Wendorff in Russia as loader and later gunner, recalled: 'I am convinced that Michel Wittmann and Bubi Wendorff characterized the Tiger arm of the Leibstandarte in the eyes of all the comrades of the 13th Company, SS Panzer Regiment Leibstandarte and the later 2nd Company, 101st SS Panzer Battalion. In many actions at Kharkov, Belgorod, in the tank battle at Kursk, and the deployment from November 1943 to March 1944, I served at various times as loader and then gunner with then SS-Untersturmführer Wittmann, and for a longer time with SS-Untersturmführer Wendorff. The crews changed quite often, so that one could only say that he belonged to their crews temporarily.

And now a word about our beloved Bubi Wendorff. In my lifetime there are three personalities I can never forget. In first place, surely, Michel Wittmann, then Helmut Wendorff and Hannes Philipsen. Philipsen perhaps somewhat less, because he always had the bad luck to be wounded quickly; altogether he spent only a few weeks with the 13th Company and later the 1st Company. But to me Wittmann and Wendorff will always be synonymous with the Tigers of the Leibstandarte. Bubi Wendorff was much loved by us, for he was a fine man. Raised in the Napola, he knew that he had to exemplify bravery, and he concealed all emotions. I have seen times when, though he was surely hungry himself, he would tell us that he had already eaten at headquarters so that we would receive a little more. Another example that was characteristic of him: we were driving point in Russia. It was standard practice there for an Untersturmführer, usually also a platoon commander, to drive his Tiger up a slope to where it was in plain view of the enemy, in order to discover the location of his anti-tank front. One day we drove forward that way and attracted the attention of the anti-tank guns. We came under tremendous fire. Later, while refuelling, we counted a total of twenty-eight hits on the Tiger. Some were of course minor, but others were big enough to put one's fist into. All were in the frontal armor. At the moment when shells were raining down on the Tiger, however, Bubi Wendorff said in his Berlin dialect, 'Man, it's like being in the middle of a war here.'

Bubi Wendorff was surely not the type of officer one could characterize as razor blade sharp. Michel Wittmann was of course highly respected, honored and also loved, but I would also like to add of Michel Wittmann that, from my own point of view, he was not a pleasant customer to deal with in many situations.

In comparison Wendorff was a quiet type. When, during training near Kharkov, he saw that all was going well, he would give the command: 'Face the horizon, move, move. Lie down. You may smoke.' That was typical of Bubi Wendorff. His intelligence was also remarkable. No one fell asleep while he was lecturing on a certain tactical problem at the sand table or on ideological themes. He knew how to offer something. Personally, in the tank he was a comrade second to none. He explained our missions to us, shared our hardships and tried to make life as bearable as possible. Of course he too could get angry now and then. During the first march to Belgorod we found a gramophone and one record somewhere. On one side of the record there was an operetta melody and on the other a schmaltzy tango. The record was played from morning until night, all day long. One fine day we had the gramophone sitting on the turret and once again the music blared for hours. Bubi then took the set, along with the record, and smashed it against a rock."

SS-Obersturmführer Wendorff's Tiger was knocked out three kilometers west of Maizières. Only driver Franz Elmer managed to escape the tank. There was uncertainty in the battalion as to the fate of the crew. Wendorff, Lau, Zimmermann and Mayer were entered in the loss report as "probably fatally wounded." Wendorff was subsequently reported missing in action, while several weeks later SS-Untersturmführer Hantusch, now in command of the 2nd Company, informed Walter Lau's parents that their son had been killed on 14 August 1944. Wendorff's recommendation for the award of the Iron Cross, First Class to Lau, who had participated in the destruction of twenty-six enemy tanks, almost exclusively in Normandy, was approved on 23 August 1944.

Walter Lau's mother had been wearing mourning clothes for some time when, in September 1944, she received a letter from her son from England. He had been pulled out of the tank badly wounded and delivered to an English field hospital on the evening of 14 August 1944. He was subsequently taken to England in an unconscious state. After Wittmann's death, the loss of Wendorff was another heavy blow to the 2nd Company. The Senior NCO, SS-Hauptscharführer Konradt, wrote soon afterward: "We had lost the last of the old Tiger officers and now had an orphaned company."

At 14.00 hours on that 14 August 1944 461 bombers bombed the towns on both sides of the national highway. Once again, as on 8 August, Canadian units were also hit.

The battalion recorded of the 2nd Company: "On 14 August 1944 near Assy, following the loss of the company commander, SS-Obersturmführer Wendorff, SS-Oberschatführer Jürgen Brandt assumed command of the company's remaining three Tigers and sent them to the attack against large numbers of enemy tanks. Brandt himself destroyed five Shermans. On 15 August 1944 SS-Oberscharführer Brandt and a company of infantry secured Hill 160, east of the Caen-Falaise road. The hill was surrounded by the enemy and the infantry were overrun and taken prisoner. Brandt broke through the encirclement by running over an anti-tank gun. One-hundred-and-sixty enemy tanks attacked at about noon the same day. After destroying twelve tanks, the two Tigers deployed there were forced to withdraw in the face of far superior numbers. On account of mechanical trouble the second Tiger had to be taken under tow by SS-Oberscharführer Brandt under heavy artillery fire."

Brandt's opponent had been the 1st Canadian Armoured Regiment. The Tigers of the 2nd Company had to repulse heavy armored attacks at Hill 160, east of Potigny, and further to the east as well. In the course of the battle the Tigers destroyed several enemy tanks three kilometers southeast of Sassy. The 2nd Company's casualties were one dead and five wounded, including Unterscharführer Sowa. The situation grew increasingly critical on the right and left flanks of the Ist SS Panzer Corps on that 15 August 1944. The enemy armor was also gaining ground toward the south, west of the Route Nationale. By evening elements of the Canadian 4th Infantry Brigade were two kilometers from Falaise. In the course of 16 August the British and American spearheads closed to within only eighteen kilometers of one another. The encirclement of the Seventeenth Army, the bulk of the Fifth Panzer Army and Panzer Group Eberbach was imminent. Acting on orders, during the night of 17 August 1944 the elements of the Hitlerjugend Division holding east of Falaise withdrew behind the Ante River line and barred the usable crossings near Bloqueville, Damblainville and Eraines. Located there were the remaining Tigers, the tanks and tank-destroyers, and the armored troop carrier battalion of the Hitlerjugend Division.

On 15 August 1944 SS-Obersturmführer Hannes Philipsen of the 1st Company, who had fallen two months earlier, was named in the Honor Roll of the German Army and awarded the Honor Roll Clasp. He was the sole member of the Leibstandarte Tiger units to be honored with this rare and highly-regarded decoration. Despite the fact that the Tiger crews were constantly in action, not a single Iron Cross, First Class and only twenty-six Iron Crosses, Second Class were awarded in the entire period from 16 July to 14 August 1944. This inexplicable contradiction becomes even more crass when one considers that in the same period members of the 101st SS Artillery Battalion were awarded a total of thirty-six Iron Crosses, Second Class and four Iron Crosses, First Class. Had those in higher places placed less value on the accomplishments of the 101st SS Panzer Battalion, which fought in every sector of the front, than those of the corps artillery?

THE 101ST SS PANZER BATTALION MOVES EAST, 17 AUGUST 1944

The quadruple flak platoon of the 4th Company shot down a fighter-bomber near Falaise and subsequently moved into the Orbec area. The platoon commander, SS-Oberscharführer Fickert, noted in his diary on the 17th of August 1944: "Destruction of the flak platoon on the stretch Vimoutiers-Orbec. Under machine-gun fire from enemy fighter-bombers from 14.00 to 22.00 hours. Shot down a Spitfire. SS-Unterscharführer Hölscher fatally wounded. Wounded myself for the third time; forehead and lower jaw."

Only SS-Unterscharführer Werner Müller was able to save his quadruple flak by taking cover in a wood adjacent the road. On 16 August the 4th Company had two dead and one wounded—SS-Oberscharführer Gerhard Klatt, leader of the company headquarters squad—in Cernay, near Orbec. Three members of the company were wounded northeast of Vimoutiers on 17 August. The Workshop Company was also on the march toward the east; on 19 and 20 August in Orbec it had four wounded and two missing, one of which, a Sturmmann, made his way back to the company. The 101st SS Panzer Battalion was not caught in the Falaise Pocket; it is not certain whether the two Tigers which were in action with Kampfgruppe Olboeter on 19 August near Roc and south of Bierre belonged to the battalion. The pocket was closed at the latest on 19 August 1944. There were, however, some fairly large gaps in its eastward front, and it was there that a breakout offered the greatest chance of success. At 22.30 hours the same day the 3rd Parachute Division launched a breakout; both of the Tigers mentioned above were assigned by the Hitlerjugend Division to support the paratroopers. Tigers and Panthers blasted open a gap near Trun, through which the encircled elements were able to break out to the east. The main body of the Leibstandarte broke out near Chambois. In many cases units had disintegrated; groups of soldiers, in some cases leaderless, streamed toward the east. The few tanks and assault guns exerted a magical attraction on the grenadiers. The commanding officer of the Leibstandarte, SS-Brigadeführer and Generalmajor der Waffen-SS Teddy Wisch, was seriously wounded by mortar fire but was brought out of the pocket in an armored troop carrier.

In the days that followed, the few Tigers attempted to cross the Seine and make their way to predesignated assembly points. Contact between the tanks was lost. SS-Unterscharführer Waldemar Warnecke of the 3rd Company brought his Tiger 333 to the bank of the Seine. Sadly, however, it had to be blown up there on account of engine damage and a defective main gun. At the bank of the Seine was SS-Oberstgruppertführer Sepp Dietrich. Warnecke and his crew continued their journey in a Schwimmwagen.

The units of the Tiger battalion fought their way toward the Seine in small groups, often mingled with other units, in the remaining vehicles. Elements of the 3rd Company marched through Bernay on 22 August and ultimately reached the Seine near Elbeuf. Men of the Headquarters Company crossed the broad river near Poses. Other members of the battalion (2nd, 4th and Workshop Companies) reached the far bank in Rouen and Oissel. There, too, there were losses to the frequent fighter-bomber attacks. The fighter-bombers loitered overhead constantly, on the lookout for prey, especially at the Seine crossings.

SS-Hauptsturmführer Heurich led several of 3rd Company's Tigers to the Seine; he was able to get them across with the help of a ferry and reached the assembly point in Songeons, the unit's former quartering area before the invasion. He was decorated with the Iron Cross, First Class for his efforts. Because of the totally uncertain situation, shortly afterwards Heurich took a vehicle and drove west again; in doing so ran into a long column of American tanks. He had his driver race past at full speed then jumped for cover. Resistance was pointless in view of the enemy's superior numbers and Heurich was taken prisoner. He was taken to Caen, then England and finally to the USA. The Technical Officer Ordnance, SS-Untersturmführer Berger, also became a prisoner of war.

SS-Sturmmann Ernst Kufner of the 3rd Company described his experiences during the retreat from Falaise. His Tiger broke down with transmission trouble south of Cintheaux on 9 August and was taken in tow by a prime mover. "In the late hours of the evening our tank was taken in tow by a prime mover equipped with a flatbed trailer, and we continued in the direction of Falaise. By the time we reached Falaise the workshop company had moved. The city was already under English artillery fire. The tank and the prime mover took shelter in a forest on the periphery of Falaise. That was 10 August 1944.

We had to watch all day as the main line of resistance was pounded by tons of heavy bombs dropped by four-engined bombers. Individual aircraft even came down and strafed with their machine-guns. We resumed our journey in the direction of Rouen during the night of 11 August. With the arrival of dawn the tractor and tank had to be camouflaged at the side of the road. Combat vehicles which thought they could continue driving down the road became easy prey for the fighter-bombers. The enemy aircraft were in the air from dawn until late in the evening and kept the road under constant surveillance. They never failed to find badly-camouflaged vehicles beside the road. Once we had to look on as even ambulances were attacked and destroyed.

In mid-August we reached the city of Orbec during the night. Two fighter-bombers dropped 'Christmas trees' as we were crossing the empty city square. The square was brightly illuminated. The driver quickly moved the tractor into a side street; however the trailer with the tank and its crew were left on the brightly-lit square. The fighter-bombers attacked our tank with bombs and guns. The attacks followed a certain rhythm as the fighter-bombers had to circle for each new attack. We were able to get out of the tank safely, however, and took cover in a side street. The prime mover, its cargo and we all survived the attacks undamaged.

We continued on in the direction of Rouen. The journey ended on the line of hills before the Seine; however, we failed to find the workshop company. Our tank commander enquired as to whether there was a possibility of getting the tank across the river by ferry. This was not possible as there was no 60-tonne ferry.

We spent about two days with our tank. The driver of the prime mover and flatbed trailer had left us. The Rouen sector commander gave us authorization to blow up the tank. First we removed the machine-guns and wrecked the radio with track bolts. Cleaning wads soaked in gasoline together with hand grenades in the turret soon showed an effect. After an hour we were ready to leave; however we were stopped by an infantry unit which was supposed to establish a blocking front before the Seine. Our pay books were taken from us. After lengthy negotiations we were let go. We crossed the Seine on a ferry in the late afternoon of 17 August 1944. We skirted the city of Rouen, which we let pass to our right, and reached the Rouen-Songeons road (N 31). I don't know if Songeons really was planned as the 3rd Company's assembly point. Instinct led us there. We hitched rides whenever possible on vehicles of other branches of the service. We frequently had to take shelter in foxholes at the side of the road due to fighter-bomber attack and afterward climb aboard other vehicles. We reached Songeons unharmed and happy."

A missing report was also filed on 14 August. Fatal casualties in the period 13–19 August thus totalled one officer, five NCOs and twenty-two enlisted men. SS-Untersturmführer Helmut Dollinger, SS-Oberscharführer Georg Lötzsch, SS-Unterscharführer Adolf Schmidt and SS-Rottenführer Walter Lau, all of the 2nd Company, were decorated with the Iron Cross,

First Class. Awarded the Iron Cross, Second Class were SS-Unterscharführer Rolf Henniges, SS-Rottenführer Gustav Grüner and Wilhelm Brock, SS-Sturmmänner Hubert Heil, Otto Koch, Günther Braubach and Otto Gollan, and SS-Panzerschütze Wilhelm Dahlmann. In the 3rd Company Rolf von Westernhagen was decorated with the Iron Cross, First Class. The Iron Cross, Second Class was handed out to SS-Unterscharführer Otto Blase, Paul Rohweder, Werner Albers and Jurgen Merker, SS-Sturmmänner Willi Hagen, Paul Pilz and Georg Christian, and SS-Panzerschütze Heinz Becker.

Date	Company	Killed			Wounded		
		Officers	NCOs	Men	Officers	NCOs	Men
13/8/1944	HQ	-	-	2	-	-	-
14/8/1944	2nd	1	-	4	-	1	-
15/8/1944	2nd	-	-	1	-	-	-
15/8/1944	4th	-	-	-	-	-	2
16/8/1944	4th	-	1	2	-	1	-
17/8/1944	4th	-	-	-	-	1	3
19/8/1944	Workshop	-	-	-	-	-	3

The End of the Normandy Campaign

BATTLES AT THE SEINE, VERNON BRIDGEHEAD, 23–30 AUGUST 1944

The fighting in Normandy was not yet over for all members of the Tiger Battalion. Several hastily-formed armored groups saw combat against the Americans at the Seine. Veteran Tiger commander SS-Oberscharführer Jürgen "Captain" Brandt of the 2nd Company served in one such group, together with one other Tiger. Tigers of the 2nd Company fought against the advancing Americans west of Vernon beginning on 23 August 1944. The company suffered two casualties in the fighting of 27 August; SS-Rottenführer Fritz Falthauser was killed and Fritz Jäger was wounded. The battalion noted of these battles: "On 28 August 1944 SS-Oberscharführer Brandt's two Tigers destroyed two 57 mm anti-tank guns, four munitions vehicles, an armored car armed with a 37 mm gun and several heavy machine-guns, light machine-guns and mortars in an attack on the enemy bridgehead near Vernon.

On 29 August 1944 the enemy outflanked our pickets and positioned strong forces approximately two kilometers behind the tanks. In order to allow the infantry to withdraw under the protection of one of our tanks, Brandt attacked the enemy in the flank and almost completely destroyed a battalion of infantry which was in the act of deploying. On 30 August 1944 approximately thirty English tanks attacked. The enemy attack was halted after Brandt had destroyed two and damaged one. On the evening of the same day the enemy made frontal and flanking attacks with his eighty to one hundred tanks. The two Tigers each knocked out three tanks, leading the enemy to abandon further attacks and instead attempt to encircle the battle group. The Tigers then had to be blown up on account of a lack of fuel and ammunition. SS-Oberscharführer Brandt has so far destroyed forty-seven enemy tanks." (From the recommendation for the award of the German Cross in Gold to Brandt.) These last kills by Brandt near Brunehamel, 7.5 kilometers northeast of Rozoy, stopped the Americans briefly. Though mentioned in the account, English tanks were not employed there.

TIGER II, "KING TIGER"

The prototype of the Tiger II was demonstrated to Adolf Hitler on 20 October 1943, while the Tiger I was still in production. The new version of the Tiger adopted a similar exterior shape to that of the Panther, with a sloped frontal plate which was more effective in deflecting armor-piercing shot. There were more than external changes, however, especially in the area of the turret; the Tiger II differed fundamentally from its predecessor. The new tank was armed with an outstanding gun which was clearly superior to those of all enemy tanks. The 88-mm KwK 43 L/71 could destroy any enemy tank in the field from more than two kilometers and at 2,500 meters it could effortlessly penetrate fourteen centimeters of strong steel armor. With its frontal armor of 18.5 centimeters, and 15 centimeters on the sides, the Tiger II was almost invulnerable from those ranges. The ammunition used by the Tiger I was improved by adopting a more powerful propellant charge, and the new round was of greater diameter. Consequently the ammunition used by the two variants was not interchangeable.

Compared to the Tiger I the new Tiger was thirteen tonnes heavier, and with a total weight of 69.7 tonnes was the heaviest battle tank of its day. The increased weight did result in a further drop in the power-to-weight ratio, however. The Tiger II's significantly higher fuel consumption and smaller fighting compartment led to a reduction in ammunition capacity from the ninety-two rounds of the Tiger I to seventy-two to eighty-four rounds. Fuel capacity was 860 liters, which gave the tank a range of 130–140 kilometers on roads and approximately 90 kilometers over medium terrain. Approximately 1,000 liters of fuel were consumed in covering 100 kilometers exclusively off-roads. The Maybach engine gave the tank a cruising speed of fifteen to twenty kph on roads and approximately fifteen kph off roads. Maximum achievable speed was thirty-eight kilometers per hour.

Production of the Tiger II also took place at the Henschel Firm in Kassel. The first fifty Tiger IIs were equipped with the Porsche turret, which was designed in 1942 for the unsuccessful Porsche Tiger. All subsequent Tiger IIs received the turret built by Krupp, which was designated as the production version. It differed from the Porsche turret in having a reduced frontal area and was more heavily armored. The Krupp turret had no external gun mantlet and could accommodate six more rounds of ammunition. It also lacked the Porsche turret's bulge for the commander's cupola on the left side of the turret.

The 501st SS Panzer Battalion was equipped exclusively with Tiger IIs, all of which had the production turret. The most commonly used designation, "King Tiger" (Königstiger), which was also used then, came about as the result of pure chance. When an officer, Hauptmann Fromme, saw the Tiger II at Henschel, he was at first so perplexed by its size that in his surprise he said, "That's not a Tiger any more, that's, yes that's . . . a King Tiger." A total of 484 Tiger II tanks were manufactured.

THE 1ST COMPANY OF THE 101ST SS PANZER BATTALION RETURNS TO FRANCE WITH THE TIGER II

On 11 July 1944 in Normandy, the 1st Company handed over its last three Tigers to the battalion and drove via Paris to Strasbourg. There SS-Hauptsturmführer Möbius issued the men passes stipulating that they had to be in Paderborn-Sennelager by 15 July 1944. The men had to make their own way and celebrated their arrival in Germany at a number of inns in the Paderborn and Bielefeld area. The presence of the Leibstandarte Tiger crews, fresh from the Normandy front, was naturally something special for the population. By 15 July all were in Paderborn. The 1st Company was to be retrained on the latest version of the Tiger, the Tiger II. In charge of instruction was a Feldwebel of the 500th Tiger Training and Replacement Battalion, which was stationed at Sennelager.

On 19 July 1944 SS-Untersturmführer Fritz Stamm of the 1st Company described the situation on the Western Front and in Germany in a letter to his father, who was likewise in military service: "Not until the night before last Sunday did the enemy attack again and was able to enter several villages. But on Sunday and Monday he was forced back again, as his losses during the attack were so high that he could not hold the line he had won. I am convinced that when you receive this letter he will again have attacked and been driven back a few more times. Perhaps he will have gained two or three kilometers, but he will not get through. After all they're English over there and not Russians. They will come to realize that there's nothing to be won on the invasion front. But at that same moment we will have the tiller of the war firmly back in our hands. To ensure that this moment comes, we must do nothing other than what we have done, defend with all force.

Almost a year ago I came home from Bitsch. That was just after the betrayal in Italy happened. If I compare the mood that reigned in the homeland then with that of today, I can happily state that calm has returned to the people, without which we could not withstand this struggle in the long run. When I also see how they are working here at home, and with what composure development of wonderful new weapons is being pursued, then my confidence is strengthened, which is no less than what I expected of my visit in the homeland. With its accomplishments such a nation in fact has no need to be ashamed before the front. Who would conquer such a people may not depend on his guns and tanks alone, but the enemy does nothing else."

Gunnery practice was conducted at Sennelager using several training Tigers. At the same time the tank commanders and drivers were sent to the Henschel works in Kassel, where they worked shift work on the Tiger production line beside the workers and were also paid like them. This was intended to increase technical understanding of and build confidence in the new Tiger II. The wait in Sennelager for the Tiger II grew longer. On 20 July SS-Hauptsturmführer Möbius telephoned Führer Headquarters and enquired as to the whereabouts of the tanks. Following the 20th of July Möbius brought the seventeen-year-old son of Berlin Chief of Police Graf von Helldorf to the company. He joined SS-Oberscharführer Franzl's crew as loader.

On 5 August 1944, SS-Untersturmführer Stamm wrote: "One can only admire the behavior of our people at home, what with the enemy in the west also able to achieve a success and the bombing terror again claiming many victims in our cities. I had the opportunity to spend a few days working in a large armaments plant, where the workers spend twelve hours a day on the line. We visited another facility that had been almost completely bombed out some time ago. The new factory sheds were nearing completion and production went on oblivious to all difficulties. Work resumed two days after the bombing attack under more difficult conditions and in a very few weeks had surpassed the old level. It is exactly the same there as at the front, where a division performs just the same in the tenth and twelfth week as in the first, though its strength has long ceased to be what it once was. It is with this spirit that we will also master the new crises on all fronts.

Furthermore the attempt on the Führer's life has started a stone rolling which has already shaken many. It is finally serious total war. We now intend to commit everything in order to have the last shot with this stone. Kurt will probably have written that he paid me a visit. Mother and Waltraud were also here for a few days and travelled from here to Menden. I will steam off again in three or four days too and hopefully will be able to get back into my tank again in two weeks. In closing I hope that this letter reaches you very soon, dear father, and I send you my most heartfelt greetings. I wish you all the best for the future and hail and victory! Your Fritz."

From 28 July to 1 August 1944 the 1st Company took possession of fourteen Tiger IIs at the ordnance depot in nearby Sennelager. On 5 August 1944 the Tigers and wheeled vehicles were loaded aboard a transport train and departed for France. In addition to SS-Untersturmführer Fritz Stamm, the company's platoon commanders were SS-Oberscharführer Franz Zahner and Knight's Cross wearer SS-Standartenjunker Franz Staudegger.

BATTLES NORTHWEST OF PARIS AND THE RETREAT TO BELGIUM 25 AUGUST–6 SEPTEMBER 1944

After several days of rail transport the 1st Company's Tiger IIs detrained north of Paris; the customary fighter-bomber attacks began at once. The 1st Company made its first contact with the Americans near Troyes and Gisors on 25 August 1944, suffering one killed and three wounded. The 1st Company was the only element of the battalion present in that area. Tigers of the 1st Company also fought near St. Souplettes. On 26 August the 1st Company's target was the American bridgehead near Mantes, northwest of Paris. While driving in an easterly direction south of Fontenay-St. Père, just short of a forest, SS-Untersturmführer Fritz Stamm's Tiger was hit by a shell fired by an anti-tank gun. The hit wrecked the tank's right track and rendered it immobile. Heavy anti-tank fire from the village subsequently blanketed the Tiger. SS-Rottenführer Kurt Koch, Stamm's driver, got out of the tank, his clothing on fire. He rolled in the ditch to extinguish the flames then ran back and jumped into a bomb crater where he lay exhausted. From his vantage point he saw the burning Tiger blow up moments later; no other members of the crew were able to escape. Koch was taken prisoner but soon managed to escape.

SS-Untersturmführer Fritz Stamm died in his tank. A young and enthusiastic officer had fallen. At twenty-one, he was the youngest officer in the battalion. His fate remained unclear and he was officially listed missing on 10 October 1944. "Tank hit and set on fire, nothing known of the crew," was how the entry in the loss lists read. With him died his gunner, radio operator and loader; the latter SS-Panzeroberschütze Alfred Weyl, had only recently been decorated with the Iron Cross, Second Class in Normandy. With their potent high-velocity 88 mm cannon, the Tiger IIs proved superior to all American and English tanks. While quite capable of destroying enemy tanks, they could themselves be vulnerable in unfavorable situations. On 27 August 1944 the 1st Company fought near Esternay; SS-Oberscharführer Karl Müller and six men, including SS-Rottodnführer Foege and Luley, were subsequently posted missing.

On 28 August, west of Magny-en-Vexin, Tigers of the 1st Company attacked the enemy bridgehead near Vernon on the Seine. The company suffered considerable losses in tanks to tank and anti-tank fire from the flank. King Tigers also saw combat near Sailly, in the course of which SS-

Hauptscharführer Fritz Hibbeler (an SS-Obersturmführer in the Führer Escort Detachment) was killed. The 1st Company also saw action on the 29th and 30th of August and the 2nd and 6th of September. The retreat took several elements of the Tiger battalion through Amiens-Mons and Liege to Belgium, while farther south others retired east by way of Dinant and the Meuse. During the withdrawal into the Reich several members of the 3rd Company encountered elements of the 1st Company. SS-Sun-Imam; Lünser, once Staudegger's gunner and now a member of 3rd Company, met Staudegger, who asked about the situation at the front. Both subsequently went their separate ways.

The 1st Company now joined the retreat east into the territory of the Reich. On 31 August there were still elements of the company in Lamecourt and on 2 September near Le Quesnoy. The company was down to four serviceable Tigers. The company's route subsequently led it through Bavai, where tank commander SS-Junker Erwin Asbach was posted missing, on 3 September, and to La Chapelle on 5 September. SS-Hauptsturmführer Möbius was standing at the Meuse near Huy with one Tiger on 6 September, while near Mons SS-Unterscharführer Arno Salomon was able to free a trapped army unit. In the midst of the general retreat, battle damage and mechanical breakdowns inevitably led to the loss of Tigers and the 1st Company was soon decimated. A number of members of the 1st Company were listed as missing in action.

THE 101ST SS PANZER BATTALION'S RETREAT THROUGH FRANCE AND BELGIUM INTO REICH TERRITORY, 28 AUGUST–9 SEPTEMBER 1944

After crossing the Seine, some members of the Tiger Battalion set out for the quarters they had occupied prior to the invasion. One such was SS-Sturmmann Ernst Kufner of the 3rd Company, who had reached Songeons: "Elements of the 3rd Company were ready to depart in supply vehicles. I took my now customary place in the armorer-artificer's three-and-a-half tonne tracked vehicle. The retreat took us through Amiens to Mons and from there via Namur and Liege to Aachen. Untersturmführer Amselgruber held a company briefing near Mons, Belgium. The drivers had trouble with the tires in Belgium. At night partisans scattered nails over the road; these were designed in such a way that there was always a sharp side facing up. This led to the tire damage.

In Germany we stopped at the tri-national border between Holland, Belgium and Germany. We spent several days there and then drove through Jülich into a village in the vicinity of Düren. At the beginning of September we were already being harassed by the fighter-bombers there. One fighter-bomber was shot down over the village. The pilot took to his parachute and came down in the top of a tree next to our quarters. The farmers, who had been attacked in their fields by the fighter-bombers, wanted to lynch the pilot; however, we protected him from the angry mob and about two hours later handed him over to Luftwaffe officers. In mid-September we were transferred to the village of Verl, near Gütersloh. The company was refurbished, and new soldiers arrived to make good the heavy losses in Normandy. The company took on a new face. The retreat from Normandy to Germany had to be made in the train's remaining supply vehicles; the tanks had all been lost in Normandy. Crossing the Seine was impossible for the tanks; nevertheless, there was a rumor making the rounds to the effect that one or two of the company's Tigers had been in action in the Mons area."

On 28 August 1944, a group from the 3rd Company was surprised by the enemy near Gournay-en-Bray; one man was captured and SS-Unterscharführer Richard Müller and four men were listed missing. A further Unterscharführer went missing near Arras. Several veterans of the 1st Company also managed to reach their old quarters. Two NCOs were reported missing on 30 August, SS-Unterscharführer Behrendt (tank driver) and SS-Oberscharführer Johann Seifert (motor transport sergeant); both were seen on 28 August in Gournay-en-Bray. On 31 August SS-Unterscharführer Sepp Engshuber of the 3rd Company went missing in Lamcourt. SS-Sturmmann Alfred Lünser of the 3rd Company was one of the few still on his way east in his Tiger. After he and his crew crossed the Seine near Elbeuf they continued on alone. Luftwaffe and army soldiers took the opportunity to hitch a ride on the tank, which repeatedly had to take cover from the fighter-bombers. For days they drove east as part of the German western army's general retreat. They solved the fuel problem in a simple fashion: they parked the Tiger across the road so that no vehicles could get by. When an army Major asked them why the Tiger was sitting there, Lunser replied that they needed fuel. When the Major reluctantly brought two 20-liter containers from his vehicle the quick-witted Lünser informed him that they couldn't even start the Tiger with that amount of fuel. The crew subsequently received ample fuel with which to continue their journey. The men lived off what they had in their boxes, as well as plenty of Dextro-Energen (glucose) tablets. The Tiger eventually arrived at a crossroads where an officer in a motorcycle coat was giving directions to the oncoming vehicles. All the vehicles and soldiers heading east on foot he directed to the right, and only the Tiger to the left, toward the northwest.

After travelling some distance the Tiger crew suddenly found itself facing a wave of American Sherman tanks which abruptly opened fire. Lünser jumped from the stricken Tiger into the ditch. The tank's Danish loader was wounded badly and taken prisoner. Lünser was able to escape detection by the enemy in a rhubarb field and after darkness fell he made his escape. He came upon a group of German soldiers and joined up with them. The sole officer was night-blind and had to be led.

Several days later, on 11 September, Lünser was cornered by a group of Belgian partisans near Dinant on the Meuse; they opened fire and he was hit several times in the thigh. It was Sunday and church bells could be heard ringing from a nearby village. Soon afterward the Americans arrived on the scene and took him away in an ambulance. After three-and-a-half years as a POW in England and America, in February 1948 Lünser was reunited with his family, which had been driven from Silesia, in Oldenburg. His fate was similar to that of many of the 101st SS Panzer Battalion as they fled east in those weeks.

The weak forces of the Ist SS Panzer Corps Leibstandarte established a strongpoint-style front on the line Fourmies-Chimay. As the Americans had already crossed the Oise and were threatening Avesnes, Fourmies and Chenay, the corps prepared to make a stand near Trelon-Chimay. The defense line consisted of little more than weak strongpoints and was incapable of withstanding heavy attacks. The 101st SS Panzer Battalion suffered its first losses on Belgian soil in Mons and Brussels on 28 August 1944. As a result of the vigorous pursuit by the Americans, especially on the corps' right wing, the Ist SS Panzer Corps had to be withdrawn in stages to the line Beaumont-Renlies-Froidchapelle-Bois de Chimay.

A powerful American armored advance from Avesnes through Maubeuge to Mons also resulted in losses to the 101st SS Panzer Battalion. In Jemappes, near Mons, Tiger 113 of the 1st Company had to be abandoned on the Avenue Foch. SS-Untersturmführer Peter Harsche and SS-Oberscharführer Robert Bardo of the Headquarters and Supply Company also went missing in Jemappes that day, 2 September 1944; one enlisted man was captured and six others listed missing. The Headquarters Company lost two more men in Mons. Mons had been designated a reporting point but was now abandoned as such.

The units strove to reach the Reich by the most direct route. After losing most of its guns in the hours-long fighter-bomber attack near Vimoutiers on 17 August, the 4th Company's quadruple flak platoon was left with one Vierlingsflak (gun commander SS- Unterscharführer Werner Müller). The platoon was led by SS-Oberscharführer Fickert to Elbeuf, Oissel on 21 August and on 24 August across the Seine at Rouen. Two days later the platoon arrived in Gournay-en-Bray and from there set out for its former quarters in Cremeville. Its subsequent route took the platoon through Amiens (27 August), St. Albert (28 August) and Arras (29 August) to Mons, where it arrived on 30 August. There were other elements of the 4th Company there, but time was short and the march was continued through Liege (1 September). On 2 September the flak platoon reached German soil near Aachen.

On 3 September, the 101st SS Panzer Battalion received the official order from Army Group B to transfer into the Reich for a complete overhaul. First, however, details of a special mission given to Bobby Warmbrunn of the 2nd Company. SS-Unterscharführer Warmbrunn returned to the battalion on 17 August from the SS hospital at Hohenlychen, where he had received treatment for the eye injury he suffered on 18 July. He still wore an eye patch and was unfit for front-line service; therefore was given a special mission. Prior to leaving for the invasion front several boxes of documents had been deposited in Paris; they contained, among other things, detailed drawings illustrating the Tiger's vulnerable spots, which might provide the enemy with important clues to combatting the tank. These boxes had to be prevented from falling into enemy hands.

On 21 August 1944 he drove to Paris in a Schwinnmvagen for the first time and returned with some documents. Warmbrunn himself describes his second foray to Paris, in which he helped a female German agent escape the threatened city: "23 August. Once again into partisan-dominated Paris to retrieve documents on the Tiger tank and how to combat it. Had one truck and two men with me, in order to also bring back the rest of the company's paraphernalia. The struggle through Paris lasted six hours, for we were hindered by a goods train blockade. As I had been able to guess what would be awaiting me in Paris, I took smoke canisters, signal flares and flare pistols with me. We had an easy time of it as the partisans assumed the smoke was poison gas. We reached Reims on 26 August. The word in the Hotel Strasburg was sleep only. We arrived in Metz on 28 August 1944 and sent the truck home from there. I took the Tiger documents to the office in Berlin in a two-handled case while the remaining papers were carried by an escort; we both travelled to Berlin by train.

Due to the strain and my own lack of concern my wounded eye burned like fire. After completing my assignment I immediately went to Hohenlychen for treatment. They sent me on leave on 9 October 1944 with instructions for the eye doctor in Munich. After the final examination I returned at my own request to the front-line forces as an experienced instructor of Tiger crews."

The battalion's total losses during the fighting north of Falaise and the retreat east, with the initial losses at the Seine recorded on 22 August, which ended in the Mons-Brussels area in the first week of September, were thus one officer, four non-commissioned officers and twelve enlisted men killed, two NCOs and eighteen enlisted men wounded, and three officers, nine non- commissioned officers and forty-one enlisted men missing.

The 1st Company's losses included two officer candidates among the NCOs, while SS-Hauptsturmführer Heurich and SS-Untersturmführer Berger, both of whom were captured by the Americans, do not appear in the loss lists of the corresponding period.

Also not mentioned are two members of the Headquarters Company, Untersturmführer Harsche and Oberscharführer Bardo, both of whom were absent from their unit as of 2 September 1944. These names have not been included in the final tallies.

It is to be assumed that most of those listed missing in action were taken prisoner during the retreat, while some fell prey to partisan ambushes. Seventeen Italian auxiliaries and four Italian volunteers were reported missing during the entire period of the fighting in Normandy.

SUMMARY OF THE BATTALION'S LOSSES

Date	Company	Killed			Wounded			Missing		
		Officers	NCOs	Men	Officers	NCOs	Men	Officers	NCOs	Men
20/8	4th	-	-	-	-	-	-	-	-	1
20/8	Workshop	-	-	-	-	-	-	-	-	2
22/8	3rd	-	-	-	-	1	-	1		
22/8	Workshop	-	1	-	-	-	-	-	-	-
23/8	2nd	-	-	-	-	1	-	-	-	-
23/8	HQ	-	-	-	-	-	1	-	-	-
24/8	Workshop	-	-	-	-	-	1	-	-	-
25.8	1st	-	1	1	-	-	3	-	-	-
25/8	2nd	-	-	1	-	-	-	-	-	-
25/8	4th	-	-	-	-	-	-	-	-	1
25/8	Workshop	-	-	3	-	-	3	-	1	3
26/8	1st	1	-	2	-	-	2	-	-	2
27/8	1st	-	-	-	-	-	-	-	1	6
27/8	2nd	-	-	2	-	-	2	-	-	-
27/8	HQ	-	-	1	-	-	-	-	-	-
28/8	1st	-	1	-	-	-	-	-	-	-
28/8	3rd	-	-	-	-	-	-	-	2	5
28/8	4th	-	-	1	-	1	2	-	-	-
28/8	Workshop	-	-	-	-	-	2	-	-	2
30/8	1st	-	1	-	-	-	-	-	2	1
30/8	HQ	-	-	-	-	-	-	-	2	

Date	Company	Killed			Wounded			Missing		
		Officers	NCOs	Men	Officers	NCOs	Men	Officers	NCOs	Men
31/8	1st	-	-	-	-	-	-	-	-	1
31/8	3rd	-	-	-	-	-	-	-	1	-
01/9	1st	-	-	-	-	-	-	-	-	1
01/9	3rd	-	-	-	-	-	1	-	1	2
02/9	1st	-	-	-	-	-	-	-	-	1
02/9	HQ	-	-	1	-	-	-	-	-	8
03/9	1st	-	-	-	-	-	-	-	1	1
05/9	1st	-	-	-	-	-	-	-	-	1

TOTAL NUMBER OF LOSSES IN THE WEST

Killed			Wounded			Missing		
Officers	NCOs	Men	Officers	NCOs	Men	Officers	NCOs	Men
7	24	63	7	25	80	3	10	49

That makes 156 killed, 112 wounded and 62 missing, 330 casualties alto-gether. As well seventeen auxiliaries were listed as missing. These figures do not reflect the battalion's total losses, however, as there are no loss records available for the period 17–21 June 1944. Total casualties suffered in that period may be estimated at approximately sixty.

SUMMARY OF THE BATTLE IN NORMANDY

The style of warfare seen in Normandy differed fundamentally from previ-ously known practice. The German Armed Forces faced an enemy whose unlimited air superiority completely altered the operational conditions of the German panzer divisions and forced them to submit to completely new tactics and rules of conduct.

Not just the command of, but also the supplying of the frontline forces had to confront the remaining possibilities. The aircraft, not the enemy tank, as was the case on the Eastern Front, became the bitterest enemy of the German divisions. The 101st SS Panzer Battalion did not carry out a sin-gle concentrated attack with its forty-five tanks in Normandy. The danger was too great in many places on the threatened front and the Tigers had to fill the gaps there. Determined, massed attacks by tanks into the area occu-pied by the enemy, which in the first days of the invasion would have brought about a change in the overall situation, were impossible for the 101st SS Panzer Battalion, as they were for all the German panzer divisions.

The panzer divisions were held back at first and then committed too late without a unified command, and this was decisive in the failure to smash the Allied beachheads during their weakest phase. The hedgerow terrain typical of the Normandy battle zone often forced individual tanks to wait for a coming enemy attack in camouflaged positions for days on end. This style of armored warfare as such contradicted the fundamental mission of the Panzertruppe. The Tigers sat alone for days in the main line of resistance waiting for the next attack, constantly exposing themselves to the fire of the enemy artillery, which was also more of a threat to tanks than is generally accepted. The time spent waiting for an attack was hard on the crews. They were not allowed to leave their tank on account of the artillery fire; therefore food and ammunition could only be brought forward at night. When the enemy did attack, on the heels of an artillery barrage or an air attack, the lone Tigers, sometimes in close proximity to the panzer-grenadiers, could attack from their well-camouflaged ambush positions and halt the attack by destroying the enemy tanks as they appeared. This battle tactic more closely resembled that of the anti-tank units.

The enemy attempted to split up the close fighting team of tanks and panzer-grenadiers with his heavy artillery fire. When they succeeded in this the Tigers were exposed to increased danger from lone tank-killers. Swift counterattacks by small groups of Tigers, often only one or two tanks, frequently smashed the enemy attack and drove the attackers back to their own lines. In spite of the imposing tally of enemy tanks destroyed by the Tigers, in the end they represented no more than local successes against an enemy with a seemingly infinite superiority in men and materiel. The panzer units wore themselves down in maintaining a defense in Normandy and were completely decimated.

In spite of all setbacks the 101st SS Panzer Battalion fought with admirable courage and acquitted itself well with all the units it served with. The signs were all there, for the Allies had not left Germany unaware of their intentions in the event of their victory; everyone knew what awaited Germany if the will of the enemy powers, namely unconditional—meaning powerless and abject—surrender was fulfilled. Though the enthusiasm was long gone, at the latest after the fighting in Normandy, the inner sense of duty rooted in every soldier, the love of people and country, held the troops together firmly and gave them the strength to endure the greatest burdens. The pronounced comradeship that was particularly evident in the ranks of the Waffen-SS proved itself over and over again in the 101st SS Panzer Battalion during the Normandy fighting. A typical example is provided by SS-Untersturmführer Amselgruber. After knocking out several enemy tanks, his Tiger was hit and he was then wounded while bailing out.

In spite of furious artillery fire and the shells falling all around him, Amsel-gruber rescued his gunner, who had been seriously wounded in the belly by shrapnel, and at great risk to himself dragged him through the shellfire back to the German lines.

This act was a matter of course to Amselgruber; no great words were wasted over assistance given to a comrade. This applied to all tank crews. This strong bond of unreserved comradeship, the implicit feeling of being able to depend on one other, was also an important element, causing a feeling of belonging to grow and strengthen. The unit became like a home. Not as important, but nevertheless also of a certain significance, was obviously the justifiable pride in one's arm of the service, in the legendary—to both friend and foe alike—Tiger and the respected armored command. The cuff title that the men of the 101st SS Panzer Battalion wore made nothing easier for them. To them it represented both a quiet, inner obligation and an incentive. The wearers proved themselves worthy, especially in front-line service.

And thus the 101st SS Panzer Battalion lived and suffered through the hell of the materialschlacht, the war of materiel. The Allied plan to destroy a large part of the German Army in the Falaise Pocket was frustrated, and after crossing the Seine the German units successfully withdrew to the east. There, in spite of the heavy losses, they soon settled down again and established a continuous defense front on the western frontier of the Reich. In concluding this description of the war in Normandy a word from General der Panzertruppen Heinrich Eberbach, who commanded the Fifth Panzer Army to which the Ist SS Panzer Corps belonged: "As commander, it was my responsibility to carry out my orders and at the same time do the best for the men entrusted to me. I suffered their deaths as if they were my own children."

On 15 August 1944, SS-Obersturmführer Hannes Philipsen, platoon commander in the 1st Company, 101st SS Panzer Battalion, was named in the Honor Roll of the Army and posthumously decorated with the Honor Roll Clasp. He is seen here with his fiancee Gudrun Fromm in January 1944.

On 25 June 1944 at the Berghof, Adolf Hitler presented Michael Wittmann with the Knight's Cross with Oak Leaves and Swords. He was at the peak of his career and, as Germany's most successful tank commander, was widely known.

Hilde Wittmann, bottom left, with her family.

Michael Wittmann with his father-in-law during his last home leave in July 1944 after he received the Swords.

Michael and Hilde Wittmann in July 1944.

Tiger of the 101st SS Panzer Battalion in Normandy. Turret is in the five o'clock position.

Tiger of the 2nd Company, 101st SS Panzer Battalion; on the right is SS-Untersturmführer Hantusch.

Tiger 211 in Normandy.

Knocked-out Tiger 223, in front, an English soldier.

Panther commander of the Hitlerjugend Panzer Regiment.

Panzer IV of the 5th Company, 12th SS Panzer Regiment Hitlerjugend, which fought alongside the Tigers near Maltot on 10 July 1944.

A Tiger, well camouflaged to prevent being spotted from the air.

SS-Hauptsturmführer Wittmann, commander of the 101st Panzer Battalion, discusses the final details before an attack on 18 July 1944.

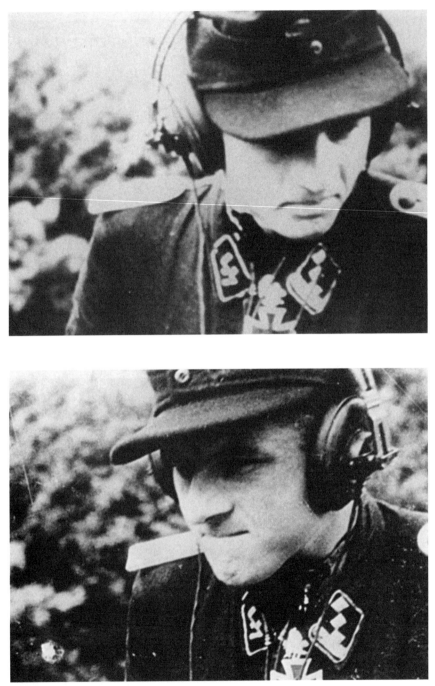

Michael Wittmann in the turret of his Tiger shortly before an attack. His face betrays intense concentration and tension. These are the last photos taken of Wittmann before his death.

SS-Unterscharführer Karl
Wagner, Wittmann's gunner
on 8 August 1944.

SS-Sturmmann Rudi Hirschel,
the radio operator.

SS-Unterscharführer
Hein Reimers, the driver.

SS-Sturmmann Heinrich Peyers of the 4th Company of the 25th SS Panzer-Grenadier Regiment Hitlerjugend in the car with which he drove Wittmann to the final briefing on August 1944.

One of the only known photographs of Tigers knocked out near Gaumesnil on 8 August 1944. Shown here is Tiger 314 of the 3rd Company.

The remains of Wittmann's Tiger 007. The turret lies approximately five meters from the hull of the tank. Next to the exhausts may be seen what is left of the umbrella antenna, a feature of command tanks only. Another knocked-out Tiger is visible in the photo about 500 meters to the north.

Reorganization of the 101st SS Panzer Battalion, 28 September–1 December 1944

The first elements of the 101st SS Panzer Battalion began arriving in the Düren-Jülich area on 10 September 1944. Stragglers also found their way there. All in all the battalion gave the appearance of a battered but unbroken band of soldiers. Some men drove straight to Paderborn, like SS-Unterscharführer Mollenhauer, with the orderly office and two other vehicles of the 1st Company. The 1st Company had managed to bring another Tiger II back from France. SS-Unterscharführer Salamon reached the Siegburg-Troisdorf area with it in the last days of September, and from there the tank was brought to Schloss Holte by rail. From there it was transported to Sennelager-Augustdorf for training purposes; later the Tiger returned to Schloss Holte, where it was once again to serve the battalion.

On 13 September 1944 the battalion transferred to Meschede in the Sauerland, where it took up quarters in a local school until 22 September. Elements of the 4th Company reached Schöneberg via Aachen and Düsseldorf on 12 September and Eschwede the following day. Meanwhile new quarters had been arranged and the transfer began soon afterward. The 1st Company came to Oerlinghausen. The officers lived in the city's hotel, some of the non-commissioned officers were billeted in private quarters, and as well men stayed in the youth hostel, two classrooms of a school and the Ravensburg guest house. The 2nd Company took up quarters in a branch office of the Bodelschwingh Institute in Eckardtsheim. The 3rd Company was housed in a school in Verl, the 4th Company in Wilhelmsdorf as of 16 September, and the Workshop Company in Stuckenrock. Battalion Headquarters and the Headquarters and Supply Company were located in Schloss Holte, where the officers received private quarters, as did several of the non-commissioned officers. The rest were put up in the Schloßkrug Castle guest house and the school.

SS-Hauptsturmführer Möbius assumed command of the battalion on 1 September 1944; on 12 September command of his Ist Company passed to SS-Obersturmführer Wessel. The 2nd Company had been led by SS-Untersturmführer Hantusch since the latter part of August, after a brief stint as commander by SS-Obersturmführer Brandt following Wendorff's death. SS-Untersturmführer Hahn took command of the 3rd Company in Verl. SS-Hauptsturmführer Dr. Rabe, who had led the battalion since Wittmann's death, returned to his own field as battalion medical officer. SS-Obersturmführer Spitz's 4th Light Company had also been able to bring little of its vehicle complement back with it from Normandy. As before, the Supply and Workshop Companies were led by SS-Obersturmführer Vogt and Klein.

The following orders were issued by way of a telex from the SS Operational Headquarters on 21 September 1944: ". . . (3) the SS units transferred east of the Rhine for rest and refitting—1st, 2nd, 9th and 12th SS Panzer Divisions as well as the 501st SS Heavy Panzer Battalion, and corps units of the 1st SS Panzer Corps—are removed from their command relationship with the General der Panzertruppen West and with respect to their rest and refitting are under the command of Headquarters, Sixth Panzer Army now being formed (6) Commander in Chief SS-Oberstgruppenführer and Generaloberst der Waffen-SS Sepp Dietrich . . . 6. As per Subparagraph 3, pending the activation of Headquarters, Sixth Panzer Army, SS panzer units in refit are to submit their personnel and material needs relating to the refit directly and immediately to SS Operational Headquarters. Message centers for arriving stragglers, men on leave and those in official travel status: 1st SS Panzer Division: Siegburg, . . . , 12th SS Panzer Division: Arnsberg, . . . , 501st Heavy Panzer Battalion: Sennelager troop training grounds near Paderborn.—Corps units 1st SS Panzer Corps: Siegburg."

AFTER THE RETREAT FROM NORMANDY

Some members of the battalion were able to fight their way through from France to Germany by adventurous routes. Split up into small groups, elements of the unit moved east; many were overtaken by the Americans and were repeatedly forced to dodge out of the way to avoid contact. One group from the 3rd Company, for example, drove in its own supply vehicles through Amiens-Liege and from there to Aachen, then arrived at the battalion's assembly point. Some men were captured by the Americans in September, others fell into the hands of French partisans. The companies had suffered heavy losses in personnel and lost all their tanks. The retreat into the Reich and their experiences in the course of it were the main topics of conversation among the men in those days.

Convalescents from the hospitals soon began arriving at the various companies, as well new soldiers were transferred to the battalion. It was there that the men first learned the true extent of the losses suffered in Normandy and on the way back to the Reich. Many, too many, good comrades had fallen, leaving behind gaps in their ranks. With the loss of Michael Wittmann the battalion had lost its leading figure. Wendorff, Philipsen and Günther had fallen with Wittmann in Normandy—four old friends who had fought side by side since 1940. But there were comrades absent from the other companies too. The men recovered from the strains of the past weeks, glad to have escaped with their lives; however, in their subconscious they harbored the disquieting question of who was supposed to stop the Allies, who were advancing toward the German frontier everywhere. The news from the Eastern Front was also anything but encouraging. The enemy was on the advance everywhere.

The panzer soldiers had other needs now, they were alive and they enjoyed it. They wanted to forget the past grim weeks and months in Normandy, with the barrages and the drum fire of the artillery, the carpet bombing and constant fighter-bomber attacks, constantly harried and pursued. Returning comrades who had been wounded in the fighting were given a rousing welcome. They felt safe and well with their "bunch" and therefore wanted very much to return to their own battalion to avoid being transferred to an unfamiliar unit. Many men had lost members of their families in the night bombing of Germany—parents, brothers, sisters, wives and good friends. The Tiger battalion had become their home now. They lived and fought as part of it, now even more doggedly than before. They had seen clear evidence of the enemy's will to destroy and ravage. Germany would be granted no peace, the Allied powers' sole demand was her unconditional surrender.

All that life held and made it worth living, all the property of everyone, family, home and possessions, in short the entire nation with all its worth was in the most extreme peril. The armaments industry was running in high gear in order to provide the fighting fronts with every available weapon immediately and in the greatest possible quantities. The English bomber fleets flew at night and the American bombers came by day, their objective to break, not just the German military economy, but the morale and the will to resist of the German people as well.

The men of the 101st SS Panzer Battalion were not spared these burdens. Bielefeld was struck by one of the enemy raids at about 14.00 hours on 30 September 1944. By 14.45 the city lay under one great pall of smoke and dust. At 17.00 men of the 1st Company were taken to Bielefeld to help in the clean-up. There they all saw firsthand what sort of war the Allies were waging. It was a war of bombs and phosphorous against women, children and the elderly. Depressed by the misery they had seen, the men of the 1st Company subsequently returned to Oerlinghausen. A power blackout was imposed after 22.30 hours as the power station had been hit.

On 30 September 1944 SS-Untersturmführer Rolf Henniges and SS-Unterscharführer Kurt Sowa were decorated with the Iron Cross, First Class. SS-Unterscharführer Karl Wagner, who had died with Wittmann but was still officially listed as missing in action, was awarded the Iron Cross, Second Class. In the Headquarters Company, SS-Sturmmann Gerhard Kaschlan was decorated with the Iron Cross, First Class, SS-Rottenführer Horst Uhlig and SS-Sturmmann Alfred Bahlo received the Iron Cross, Second Class. Members of the 1st Company awarded the same decoration were SS-Unterscharführer Günther Kunze, Alfons Ahrens, SS-Rottenführer Horst Daniel and SS-Sturmmänner Oskar Batsch and Ernst Wedehin.

In the 2nd Company the Iron Cross, Second Class was received by SS-Unterscharführer Bernhard Ahlte, SS-Rottenführer Johannes Kern, Fritz Jager and Kurt Lange, and SS-Sturmmänner Willibald Schenk, Aribert Wideburg and Willy Martschausky. SS-Hauptscharführer Willy Hack, the 3rd Company's senior NCO, was decorated with the Iron Cross, Second Class, as were SS-Unterscharführer Kurt Diefenbach and Richard Müller, SS-Rottenführer Paul Rohweder, SS-Sturmmänner Ewald Graf and August-Wilhelm Belbe, and SS-Panzerschützen Heinrich Eiselt and Rudolf Stallmann. In the 4th (Light) Company, leader of the scout squad SS-Unterscharführer Konrad Mankiewitz, Manfred Krebs, anti-aircraft gun commanders Gottlob Braun, Heinrich Hölscher and SS-Rottenführer Werner Müller, SS-Sturmmänner Herbert Turck, Manfred Blumberg, Gustav Look, Karl Schwab, Erich Will and Paul Müller of the Workshop Company all received the Iron Cross, Second Class.

SS-Obersturmbannführer Heinz von Westernhagen paid the battalion a surprise visit at Schloss Holte at the beginning of October 1944. He wrote: "Since I had no news of my battalion, recently I drove down to see my gang, especially since I was on official business in that area anyway. . . ." In Schloss Holte he learned that the notifications sent to the families of the battalion's fallen, missing and captured men had not reached the recipients. He wrote: ". . . that mail service between the front and home was completely interrupted during the last eight weeks. The units at the front received no mail at all, it was lost or was only now received by the addressee." Von Westernhagen instructed several officers to write letters to the families immediately. He himself regretted this deplorable situation and wrote of ". . . the wretched fighting retreat that shattered all our lines of communication. As a rule it is not our way to be so silent."

Wittmann's former gunner, Knight's Cross wearer Bobby Woll, had been in Eckardtsheim for some time already. Problems arising from his old head wound had sent him from Normandy to a hospital and then to Germany. He did not return to France after his recovery. His former unit, the 3rd SS Panzer Division Totenkopf, belatedly awarded him the Demyansk Shield for his actions in the Demyansk Pocket in 1942.

On 1 October 1944 Woll was promoted to SS-Oberscharführer. He had to drive home on 26 October as his parent's home in Wemmetsweiler had been badly damaged by bombs. SS-Untersturmführer Helmut Dollinger, the former battalion signals officer, led the 2nd Company in the interim. In addition to tank training, the men received instruction in the use of the Panzerfaust anti-tank weapon. In the second week of October the battalion's designation was changed; it was now called the 501st SS Heavy Panzer Battalion. The designations of all corps units of the Waffen-SS now began with the number 5. The battalion received its first six new King Tigers on 17 and 18 October.

On 21 October 1944, the 1st Company held a social evening in the town hotel in Oerlinghausen. The maintenance echelon provided a storage battery to ensure adequate electrical power. It was a sumptuous party and its carefree gaiety allowed the men to forget their cares. To mark the occasion the 1st Company had a humorous rag magazine printed, in which the officers and men of the unit were lampooned. The "overly refined" Knight's Cross wearer Franz Staudegger was of course drastically caricatured, as the following extract from the sarcastic remarks made about him reveals:

". . . But he is at war, he has no thoughts of women and also never misbehaves. His goal now is to smash the enemy, indeed, we really can't complain about that. Where you lead us, there we will follow and if things become difficult, we will stand by you. If others flee and you stand fast, you are not alone, the future will see. In the struggle against fraud and falsehood, we will always stand behind you, your Second Platoon." In October 1944 SS-Standartenoberjunker Heinz Buchner ran across the battalion by chance and decided to stay; he subsequently received an official transfer. Buchner had served as a gunner in the 13th Tiger Company in 1942.

On 27 July 1943, at which time he held the rank of SS-Panzerschütze, he received both Iron Crosses for his efforts in Operation Zitadelle. Buchner was Staudegger's gunner the day his actions won him the Knight's Cross. On 30 January 1944, Buchner became an SS-Unterscharführer and in May 1944 arrived at the SS-Junkerschule Klagenfurt, where he was promoted to SS-Standartenjunker on 1 June 1944. This was followed by the tank course in Fallingbostel and on 1 July he was promoted to SS-Standartenoberjunker. He then came to the 501st SS Panzer Battalion by fortunate circumstances via the SS Panzer Training and Replacement Regiment Riga and Paderborn. On 20 October 1944, he was promoted to SS-Untersturmführer as a member of the battalion.

The platoon commanders in Wessel's 1st Company were SS-Untersturmführer Henniges, SS-Standartenjunker Staudegger and SS-Hauptscharführer Lötzsch. The "Panzer General" had been decorated with the Iron Cross, First Class in Normandy and transferred from the 2nd Company. The men of the company gave the appearance of a cheerful pack of rascals who maintained good relations with the population. The same applied to the other companies. One appropriately self-ironic advertisement in a humorous rag magazine read: "Seeking large tent, as we plan to appear publicly with our circus soon. Offers to 1./s.SS-Pz.Abt. 501."

On 9 November 1944 decorations were awarded for outstanding feats in Normandy and promotions were announced. Because of the distance between quarters the presentations were made by company commanders and there was no parade involving the entire battalion. SS-Untersturmführer Dollinger of the 2nd Company was promoted to SS-Obersturmführer. The commander of the 4th Company, SS-Obersturmführer Spitz, was promoted to the rank of SS-Hauptsturmführer. In the Workshop Company, SS-Untersturmführer Glaeser, the commander of the Workshop Platoon, was promoted to SS-Obersturmführer, as was the commander of the Recovery Platoon, Reinhold Wichert. Wichert had distinguished himself on several occasions in Normandy as a tank recovery specialist and had been decorated with the Iron Cross, Second Class and the War Merit Cross First Class with Swords.

On 14 November 1944 SS-Hauptscharführer Dr. Wolf Rabe was awarded the German Cross in Gold for his performance as battalion medical officer and acting battalion commander in Normandy. He had been put up for the decoration by SS-Oberstgruppenführer Sepp Dietrich on 17 August 1944. In addition to his main function of caring for the wounded, Rabe on many occasions accompanied the fighting troops in his Kfz. 81, so as to be close at hand in the event of casualties. In doing so he frequently took part in combat operations himself, briefing tank crews and deploying them against the enemy. For this the almost two-meter-tall doctor from Vienna became the first member of the Tiger battalion to receive this prestigious award.

On 20 November SS-Hauptscharführer Hans Höllinger and SS-Unterscharführer Sepp Franzl were decorated with the Iron Cross, First Class. Among the personnel of the Workshop Company, the Iron Cross, Second Class was received by SS-Rottenführer Ludwig Schulz, Karl-Heinz Fetz,

Rudolf Walter and Josef Hammerl, and SS-Sturmmänner Erich Klein-schmidt, Heinrich Hoidn, Walter Raddatz, Hans Eggensberger, Rudolf Alt-mann, Ulrich Beilfuß and Oskar Ganz.

On the following day SS-Obersturmbannführer Heinz von Western-hagen returned to the battalion again and was received by the men with great joy. Even after his four months of convalescent leave his state of health had not improved as much as he imagined. The effects of the head wound hampered him severely, even though his soldiers saw little evidence of it. "For this reason I am also forgetful like an old man, but I will try . . ." The commander lived in a villa in front of the castle, which was also the site of the battalion orderly office. SS-Untersturmführer Eduard Kali-nowsky continued to serve as adjutant. On 14 November 1944 SS-Unter-sturmführer Heinz Belbe returned to the battalion after his convalescence and joined the battalion staff as special duties officer. SS-Oberscharführer Sernetz, who had been assigned to battalion headquarters, was employed as operations officer. SS-Rottenführer Herbert Debusmann, former special duties officer, had become the command post clerk. Under his tutelage the battalion war diary, which had previously been written out longhand, was now typed up entirely by machine. His predecessor, SS-Unterschar-führer Hartwig, had been removed for disciplinary reasons, because he could not be found during the stop in Meschede when a night alert was called. SS-Oberscharführer Kolle remained the battalion clerk and was also responsible for death notifications.

As of November 1944 the battalion staff was provided with a senior NCO, who was to take under his wing the approximately thirty enlisted men—consisting of the messenger echelon as well as drivers, radio opera-tors and clerks. The battalion commander listened at length to the men who had fought in Normandy as they filled him in on his battalion's fate following his departure on 13 July 1944. The descriptions of the battles that had decimated the battalion visibly made a deep impression on him.

On 22 November von Westernhagen submitted a recommendation for the award of the German Cross in Gold to SS-Untersturmführer Thomas Amselgruber of the 3rd Company. He had known Amselgruber since 1942 when he had served with the assault gun battalion of the Leibstandarte SS Adolf Hitler; in all the battles in which he took part he proved to be a very brave tank commander. Sepp Dietrich confirmed von Westernhagen's view in his comments: "I heartily endorse this recommendation. Amselgruber has proved to be a highly capable fighter in all situations."

Relations with the residents of the villages were excellent. Walter Bingert, Willi Otterbein, Meixner, Hermann and Georg Przybilla all got married. They were followed on 10 November by SS-Obersturmführer

Wessel, their company commander, who married a female officer of the Reich Labor Service. The wedding took place beneath the mighty oaks in the castle grounds. There was subsequently a party in the town hotel in Oerlinghausen. In November 1944 the companies of the Tiger Battalion received a visit from SS-Obersturmbannführer Jochen Peiper, commanding officer of the Leibstandarte Panzer Regiment. On 19 November the 2nd Company threw its company party.

Several SS-Standartenoberjunker had joined the battalion in recent weeks but assumed no corresponding command positions. Among their number were Oberjunker Lenz and Kirschbaum. The latter had served with the 4th Company as a Rottenführer and was now placed in charge of the company headquarters squad. SS-Standartenoberjunker Hubert Hartmann, who had previously headed the workshop company's weapons workshop, became the new Technical Officer Ordnance (TFW).

Hartmann was born in Breslau on 17 December 1921 and belonged, as did some other members of the battalion, to the cadre of the Leibstandarte's assault gun battery. It was there that his career in ordnance engineering and mechanics began and he was employed accordingly. In 1942 Hartmann was decorated with the General Assault Badge, War Merit Cross Second Class with Swords, the Iron Cross, Second Class and the Eastern Front Medal, and on the 1st of September that year was promoted to the rank of SS-Unterscharführer. After further service with the assault gun battalion, at the end of 1943 he was transferred to the Ordnance Engineering and Mechanics Training Institute. After the course was over, on 20 May 1944 he was promoted to the rank of SS-Standartenoberjunker and subsequently transferred to the 101st SS Panzer Battalion.

Following the return of battalion commander von Westernhagen there were a number of personnel changes in the course of reorganization. SS-Hauptsturmführer Möbius did not take over the 1st Company, but was instead transferred to the 2nd Company as company commander. He took several highly-qualified men with him, among them SS-Hauptscharführer Lötzsch, who had previously belonged to the 1st Company for a short time. Also transferred to the 2nd Company was SS-Untersturmführer Walter Hahn. Möbius selected as his platoon commanders Dollinger—the former signals officer—, Hantusch and Hahn.

SS-Obersturmführer Jürgen Wessel had been transferred from the 2nd Company to command the 1st Company on 12 September 1944. The Ist Platoon was commanded by SS-Untersturmführer Rolf Henniges, who had joined 2nd Company during the fighting in Normandy, while SS-Untersturmführer Heinz Buchner led the IInd Platoon. Another transferee from the 2nd Company, SS-Oberscharführer "Captain" Brandt, commander of the IIIrd Platoon. Interestingly, the twenty-year-old SS-Untersturmführer Buchner had as section leader in his platoon SS-Standartenjunker Staudegger. Buchner had been a member of Staudegger's crew during Operation Zitadelle in 1943 while a Panzerschütze and now he was an Untersturmführer and Staudegger's platoon commander. Twenty more Tigers were delivered between 26th November and 3rd December, raising the battalion's complement to thirty-four Tiger IIs (eight Tigers arrived on 11th November).

The battalion's first Tank Battle Badges with action numbers were issued on 1 December. SS-Oberscharführer Brandt, SS-Unterscharführer Warmbrunn, SS-Rottenführer Paul Bender and SS-Untersturmführer Hahn are all known to have received the Tank Battle Badge, Level Two for twenty-five days in action. The same day von Westernhagen recommended veteran panzer soldier "Captain" Brandt for the German Cross in Gold; Brandt was credited with forty-six enemy tanks destroyed. Training continued unabated and restored the battalion to full strength. One disadvantage was that there was not a single opportunity to conduct live firing exercises. In November 1944 an order was issued for the 4th Company to form another flak platoon. Together with the platoon commander, SS-Oberscharführer Fickert, that month the men of the new platoon were sent from Wilhelmsdorf to Schwabhausen in Thuringia to take part in an armored flak course.

In September 1944 SS-Hauptscharführer Appelt took over the Armored Reconnaissance Platoon in place of SS-Hauptscharführer Poetschlak, who had fallen sick. Martin Appelt was born in Lugau, Schwiebus District in the Mark Brandenburg, on 4 September 1911. In the years before the war he served with the Leibstandarte and later the Führer Escort Detachment. Appelt went on to become a tank commander and served in the 6th Company of the SS Panzer Regiment Leibstandarte. He was decorated with the Iron Cross, Second Class on 20 March 1943 after the capture of Karkov, and after Operation Zitadelle, on 16 September 1943, with the Iron Cross, First Class. Wounded and hospitalized, Appelt received the Wound Badge in Silver and was subsequently sent back to the Tiger battalion.

SS-Untersturmführer Walter Brauer continued to lead the Pioneer Platoon. The Scout Platoon was disbanded; some of the men were retrained as gunners and transferred to the panzer companies, like SS-Unterscharführer Mankewitz and Heidemann. SS-Unterscharführer Warnecke of the 3rd Company was sent to the Armored Forces School in Königsbrück for officer training, taking part in the SS Panzerjunker Special Course.

The last days of November passed in feverish haste, the order to march had arrived. The battalion was going back into action again! The headquarters and the headquarters company entrained at Schloss Holte at 06.00 hours. The 1st Company entrained in Asemissen and the 3rd Company in Brackwede.

The companies spent the 1st-3rd December travelling by rail into the Weilerswist area, southwest of Cologne. The 2nd Company entrained in Sennelager on 30 November and reached Cologne during the night of 1 December 1944. It rolled through Duisburg on 2 December and reached its destination area on the 3rd. Some members of the battalion remained behind in Schloss Holte, among them SS-Hauptscharführer Höflinger, SS-Oberscharführer Woll and SS-Unterscharführer Warmbrunn.

Support Base Schloss Holte, as it was officially designated, stayed in existence until the end of the war. Support base commander was SS-Obersturmführer Schönborn. The tank soldiers left there trained recruits, gunners, commanders, loaders and drivers. SS-Oberscharführer Bobby Woll was still unable to take part in active service on account of his still incompletely-healed head wound.

ORDER OF BATTLE:
Headquarters, 501st SS Panzer Battalion, 16/12/1944

007
Commander
Ostubaf. Heinz von Westernhagen

008
Adjutant
Ustuf. Eduard Kalinowsky

009
Signals Officer

Headquarters & Supply Company, 501st SS Panzer Battalion, 16/12/1944

Company Commander: Ostuf. Paul Vogt

Fuel Transport Column

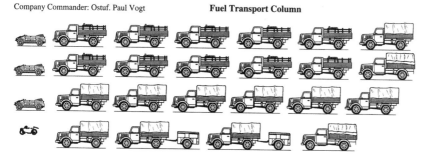

Ammunition Transport Column

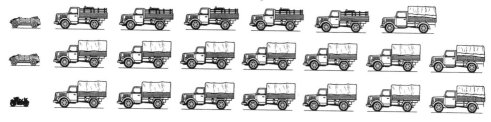

Signals Platoon

Medical Echelon: Hstuf. Dr. Wolfgang Rabe

Rttf. Arthur Bergmann
Strm. Jochen Borchet
Pz.Schtz. Heinz van Rossum
Pz.Schtz. Gottfried Salzmann
Pz.Schtz. H. Rudolf Schneider
Pz.Schtz. Konrad Sollfrank
Uscha. Wolfgang Unruh
Pz.Schtz. Albert Habenicht

Strm. Karl-Heinz Heim
Pz.Schtz. Herbert Kriese
Pz.Schtz. Franz Krippel
Strm. Kurt Krötzsch
Uscha. Lothar Kühn
Pz.Schtz. Johann Müller
Rttf. Edmund Laule
Rttf. Haupt

Uscha.Willi Röpstorff (Fahrer Kdr.-Pz.)
Rttf. Herbert Debusmann
Rttf. Otto Hahn
Rttf. Künast
Rttf. Posattel
Uscha. Arthur Görtz
Senior NCO: Hscha. Willi Hamm
Maintenance Technical Sergeant:
Oscha. Alfred Lasar

1st Company, 501st SS Panzer Battalion, 16/12/1944

105
Company Commander
Ostuf. Jürgen Wessel

104
Company HQ Squad Leader
Oscha. Sepp Franzl

Ist Platoon

111
Ustuf. Rolf Henniges

IInd Platoon

121
Ustuf. Heinz Buchner

IIIrd Platoon

131
Oscha. Jürgen Brandt

112
Oscha. Hein Bode

122
Oscha. Paul Steinwender

132
Uscha. Willi Otterbein

113
Oscha. Fritz Zahner

123
St.Jk. Franz Staudegger

133
Oscha. Werner Wendt

114
Oscha. Helmut Fritsche

124
Oscha. Arno Salamon

134
Uscha. Helmut Dannleitner

GUNNERS:
Uscha. Poerner
Uscha. Hartwig
Uscha. Alfons Ahrens
Uscha. Hermann
Uscha. Georg Przybilla (105)
Uscha. Hess
Strm. Fischer
LOADERS:
Strm. Heinz Noß (133)
Pz.Schtz. Graf v. Helldorf (104)
Strm. Oskar Batsch (105)

RADIO OPERATORS:
Pz.Schtz. Hans Keck (133)
Uscha. Fritz Belbe (105)
Strm. Mader
Strm. Helmut Schrader
Rttf. Lorenz Mähner
Rttf. Paul Berder

DRIVERS:
Rttf. Kurt Koch
Strm. Theo Janekzek (133)
Uscha. Gerd Beutel
Uscha. Walter Bingert (105)
Rttf. Lemaire
Rttf. Anesi
Strm. Helmut Lange
Rttf. Heinz Boltz

Senior NCO: Hscha. Günter Lueth
Technical Sergeant (radio): Oscha. Quenzer
Account & Pay NCO: Uscha. Peter Schnitzler
Field Kitchen: Uscha. Cosyns
Clothing Stores: Uscha Walter Streubel

Maintenance Echelon: Uscha. Heinrich Wölfel
Armorer-Artificer: Uscha. Wolfgang Schneider
Ordnance & Equipment: Uscha. Bernhard Bauer
Clerk: Uscha. Karl Mollenhauer

2nd Company, 501st SS Panzer Battalion, 16/12/1944

205
Company Commander
Hstuf. Rolf Möbius

204
Company HQ Squad Leader
Uscha. Eduard Stadler

Ist Platoon

IInd Platoon

IIIrd Platoon

211
Ostuf. Helmut Dollinger

221
Ustuf. Georg Hantusch

231
Ustuf. Walter Hahn

212
Ischa. Paul Klose

222
Oscha. Kurt Sowa

232
Uscha. Ewald Mölly

213
Uscha. Franz Faustmann

223
Uscha. Walter Müller

233
Hscha. Georg Lötzsch

214
Uscha. Ludwig Eser

224
Uscha. Grätzer

234

GUNNERS:
Uscha. Sepp Rößner
Rttf. Willibald Schenk
Uscha. Mankewitz
Uscha. Rudi Lechner

RADIO OPERATORS:
Strm. Hubert Heil
Uscha. Heinz Stuß

DRIVERS:
Uscha. Franz Ellmer
Rttf. Fritz Jäger (204)

Senior NCO:
Hscha. Georg Conrad

Maintenance Echelon:
Uscha. Adolf Frank

LOADERS:
Strm. Stark
Pz.Schtz. Hermann

3rd Company, 501st SS Panzer Battalion, 16/12/1944

305
Company Commander
Hstuf. Heinz Birnschein

304
Company HQ Squad Leader

Ist Platoon

311
Ustuf. Thomas Amselgruber

312
Oscha. Heinrich Ritter

313
Hscha. Peters Kisters

314

IInd Platoon

321
Ustuf. Winfried Lukasius

322
Uscha. Herbst

323
Oscha. Fritz Renfordt

324

IIIrd Platoon

331
Hscha. Rolf von Westernhagen

332
Uscha. Otto Blase

333
Oscha. Heimo Traue

334

GUNNERS:
Rttf. Otto Garreis
Rttf. Heinz Bannert

LOADERS:
Strm. August-Wilhelm Belbe

RADIO OPERATORS:
Strm. Werner Dörr
Strm. Duwecke
Strm. Richard Garber
Strm. Willi Hagen

DRIVERS:
Uscha. Ludwig Hofmann
Rttf. Herbert Bölkow
Rttf. Konrad Peuckert
Strm. Ulrich Kreis
Rttf. Paul Rohweder (331)
Uscha. Bernhard Ahlte

Senior NCO:
Hscha. Wilhelm Hack

Motor Transport Sergeant:
Oscha. Herbert Tramm

Maintenance Echelon:
Uscha. Georg Sittek

4th Company, 501st SS Panzer Battalion, 16/12/1944

Company Commander: Hstuf. Wilhelm Spitz
Company HQ Squad Leader: St.O.Jk. Kirschbaum

Armored Reconnaissance Platoon: Hscha. Martin Appelt

Pioneer Platoon: Ustuf. Walter Brauer

St.Jk. Heinz Fiedler   Oscha. Richard Ackermann   Uscha. Thomsen

"Wirbelwind" Anti-Aircraft Platoon: Oscha. Kurt Fickert

Uscha. Gottlob Braun   Uscha. Werner Müler   Uscha. Pusch   Uscha. Rttf. Manfred Blumberg

"Ostwind" Anti-Aircraft Platoon: Oscha. Kastelik

Uscha. Dietrich   Uscha. August Rätzer   Rttf.   Rttf.

Strm. Martin Beutelspacher
Strm. Willi Gerstner
Strm. Anton Hriberscheg
Strm. Horst Kahlfeld

ANTI-AIRCRAFT PLATOON:
Strm. Valentin Roth
Rttf. Hans Gaiser
Kan. Rolf Bergmann
Rttf. Hans-Adalbert Gürke
Rttf. Eduard Hofbauer
Rttf. Ewald Mletzko
Rttf. Gustav Look
Uscha. Walter Frisch
Rttf. Viktor Bolduan

Senior NCO:
Hscha. Fritz Müller

Motor Transport Sergeant:
Oscha. Heinz Pfeil

Workshop Company, 501st SS Panzer Battalion, 16/12/1944

Company Commander: Ostuf. Gottfried Klein

Workshop Platoon: Ostuf. Oskar Gläser

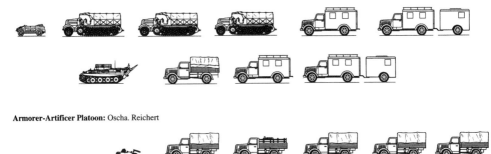

Recovery Platoon: Ostuf. Reinhold Wichert

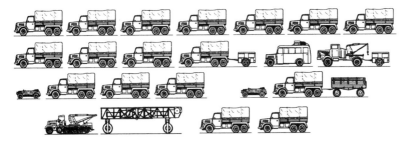

Armorer-Artificer Platoon: Oscha. Reichert

Uscha. Willi Seibert
Rttf.. Oskar Ganz
Uscha. Werner Freytag
Rttf. Franz Gilly
Oscha. Benno Bartel
Uscha. Jupp Schmitz
Uscha. Heinrich Roth
Strm. Otto Büchner
Strm. Heinz Feldstedt
Schtz. Franz Janski

Strm. Willi Kalender
Strm. Robert Oswald
Uscha. Heinz Fiebig
Uscha. Erwin Reisch
Oscha. Lehman
Strm. Fehrmann
Uscha. Schulz
Strm. Pitt Roland
Rttf. Langholz

Rttf. Ludwig Schulz
Rttf. Walter Rudolf
Oscha. Sepp Hafner
Strm. Paul Kleinschmidt
Strm. Paul Müller

Senior NCO: Hscha. Seidel
Account & Pay NCO: Oscha. Walter Havemann
Motor Transport Sergeant: Oscha. Michael Heimes

An aerial photograph depicting Wittmann's attack zone and his Tigers on 8 August 1944. On the left is N 158 from Falaise to Caen, beside which Wittmann and his tanks attacked toward the northeast. The white circles indicate the positions of the five knocked-out Tigers. The white spots are caused by the numerous bomb craters.

English troops on a knocked-out Tiger, which shows evidence of numerous hits. In the background is a Panther.

These three photos
show Tiger 334 of the
101st SS Panzer
Battalion's 3rd Company
after it was knocked out
and fell into the hands
of the English.

In August 1944 the 1st Company, 101st SS Panzer Battalion returned to France, now equipped with the Tiger II battle tank, the King Tiger. These two are King Tiger 101 and King Tiger 104.

King Tiger 104. This was the tank of SS-Oberscharführer Sepp Franzl, leader of the Company Headquarters Squad, 1st Company, 101st SS Panzer Battalion. The tank survives today in Shrivenham.

On 14 August 1944 the Tiger of the commander of the Tiger Battalion's 2nd
Company, SS-Obersturmführer Helmut "Bubi" Wendorff (upper left) was
knocked out, killing Wendorff, radio operator SS-Sturmmann Fred Zimmerman
(bottom), and loader SS-Sturmmann Peter Mayer. Gunner SS-Rottenführer
Walter Lau (upper right) was seriously wounded and captured by the English.
Only driver SS-Unterscharführer Franz Elmer was able to free himself from the
burning tank.

Tiger 104.

King Tiger of the 1st Company in the Vernon area at the end of August 1944.

Tiger 111, knocked out or broken down, in late August 1944.

King Tiger 113 in the Avenue Foch in Jemappes near Mons, Belgium. It was abandoned on 2/9/1944.

After Wittmann's death, Battalion Medical Officer, SS-Hauptsturmführer Dr. Wolfgang Rabe took over command of the battalion. On 14 November 1944 he became the first member of the battalion to be decorated with the German Cross in Gold.

SS-Hauptsturmführer Dr. Wolfgang Rabe.

Driver's and radio operator's positions in the Tiger II.

SS-Untersturmführer Fritz Stamm's Tiger II was knocked out near Fontenay-St.-Père on 26/8/1944. A member of the 1st Company, Stamm was killed along with his loader, gunner and radio operator.

A Canadian "presents" a prisoner from the Hitlerjugend Division. Barely eighteen years old, the young German shows obvious signs of mistreatment during interrogation.

Knocked-out Tiger II in France.

SS-Junker Leopold Aumüller, 3rd Company.

SS-Unterscharführer Fritz Belbe, radio operator in the 1st company.

SS-Standartenjunker Franz Staudegger, Knight's Cross wearer, section leader 1st Company.

SS-Untersturmführer
Eduard Kalinowsky
(seen here while still an
SS-Unterscharführer)
became battalion
adjutant in June 1944.

SS-Oberscharführer Paul Klose, tank commander in the 501st SS Panzer
Battalion's 2nd Company, was previously a platoon commander in the 8th
Company, 1st SS Panzer-Grenadier Regiment Leibstandarte.

SS-Obersturmführer Paul Vogt, commander of the Headquarters and Supply Company from September 1943 until the end of the war.

SS-Hauptsturmführer Gottfried Klein, commander of the Workshop Company from December 1943.

SS-Untersturmführer Hubert Hartmann, Technical Officer in Charge of Ordinance from Autumn 1944 (seen here as an SS-Standartenoberjunker).

SS-Oberscharführer Alfred
Laser, Motor Transport
Sergeant, Headquarters
Company.

SS-Sturmmann Siegfried
Walther, Maintenance Echelon
3rd Company.

SS-Sturmmann August-
Wilhelm "Büding" Belbe,
loader in the 3rd Company.

SS-Untersturmführer Walter Brauer, Pioneer Platoon.

SS-Hauptscharführer Martin Appelt, Armored Reconnaissance Platoon.

SS-Oberscharführer Kurt Fickert, Anti-aircraft Platoon.

SS-Obersturmführer Georg
Bartel, Technical Officer in
Charge of Motor Vehicles.

SS-Untersturmführer Heinz
Belbe, special duties officer in
the battalion staff.

SS-Obersturmführer Jürgen
Wessel, commander of the
1st Company.

SS-Untersturmführer Rolf
Henniges, 1st Platoon.

SS-Untersturmführer Heinz
Buchner, IInd Platoon.

SS-Oberscharführer Jürgen
Brandt IIIrd Platoon.

SS-Unterscharführer
Eduard Stadler.

SS-Untersturmführer Georg
Hantusch, platoon commander
(seen here while still an SS-
Unterscharführer).

SS-Unterscharführer Ludwig
Eser, (seen here while still an
SS-Rottenführer).

SS-Hauptsturmführer Wilhelm Spitz, commander of the 4th (Light) Company, 501st SS Panzer Battalion.

SS-Obersturmführer Oskar Glaeser, commander of the Workshop Company's Workshop Platoon (seen here as an SS-Unterscharführer).

SS-Hauptsturmführer Alfred Veller, administration officer (seen here while still an SS-Scharführer).

The Ardennes Offensive, 16 December 1944–24 January 1945

On 3 December 1944 SS-Hauptsturmführer Birnschein, the future commander of the 3rd Company, joined the company at the battalion's new quartering area of Weilerswist. Heinz Birnschein was an East Prussian who was born in Lyck on 9 January 1918. He joined the SS-Verfügungstruppe in 1936, and in January 1940, after attending the Junkerschule, became a member of the reconnaissance battalion of the SS-Verfügungs-Division. He was decorated with the Iron Cross, Second Class for his actions in the Western Campaign. In December 1940 he joined the Wiking Division's reconnaissance battalion and took part in the Eastern Campaign. Birnschein received the Iron Cross, First Class on 6 October 1941 and on 9 November was promoted to SS-Obersturmführer. After training for the armored forces, in October 1942 Birnschein joined the SS Panzer Battalion Wiking, which in March 1943 was expanded into a regiment. He served on the Eastern Front until March 1944, holding the rank of SS-Hauptsturmführer since 9 November 1943, and then transferred to the 103rd SS Heavy Panzer Battalion. The latter had been formed for the IIIrd (Germanic) SS Panzer Corps and in summer 1944 was taken over by SS-Obersturmbannführer Leiner, who had been the commander of the 101st SS Panzer Battalion until February 1944. Birnschein commanded the 1st Company.

Birnschein and the commander of the 2nd Company, SS-Obersturmführer Kuno Ther, filed complaints against the battalion commander. There was a hearing and Leiner was relieved. Following an old tradition, Birnschein and there were also transferred and on 3 December 1944 joined the 501st SS Panzer Battalion. As there was no company commander position available to Ther, he was sent to the officer reserve and in early 1945 took over the Tiger company (Tiger I) of the 3rd SS Panzer Division Totenkopf. Birnschein had little time to acclimatize himself to his new unit. The men of the Tiger battalion as yet knew nothing of the coming offensive. To make up for the shortfall of tanks, the battalion was allocated twelve of the 509th Panzer Battalion's King Tigers.

The plan for the Ardennes offensive, indeed the very concept of an attack in the west, originated with Hitler himself. It foresaw a rapid advance through the American positions between Hellenthal and Ormont by the Ist SS Panzer Corps Leibstandarte. The 1st SS Panzer Division Leibstandarte was to attack on the left wing and the 12th SS Panzer Division Hitlerjugend on the right and the two divisions were to reach the Maas in two to four days. Bridgeheads were to be established between Liege and Huy and held until the arrival of the IInd SS Panzer Corps. The two divisions of the Ist SS Panzer Corps were to advance west as quickly as possible, ignoring their undefended flanks. Advance roads were assigned to the SS Divisions Leibstandarte and Hitlerjugend. Leibstandarte was to use Roads D and E, Hitlerjugend Roads A, B and C. The nature and condition of these roads varied greatly, however, and they were generally unsuitable for use by tanks. This region offered no through roads in the necessary east-west direction, though such were available in a north-south direction.

All preparations were made under conditions of utmost secrecy. The 501st SS Panzer Battalion was at full strength except for the 4th Light Company. Each panzer company possessed fourteen Tigers (three platoons of four tanks, plus two for the company commander and the leader of the company headquarters squad).

The battalion moved into the assembly area on both sides of the Zingsheim-Engelgau road during the night of 12–13 December 1944. SS-Obersturmbannführer von Westernhagen and his staff were located in Tondorf. All movements by day were forbidden, all cooking was done at night. Tension among the men grew, and rumors circulated in ever more adventurous versions. One thing was certain though: they were about to embark on a major offensive which was to be launched against the Americans with the maximum of men and materiel. Heinz von Westernhagen had already been informed on 11 December that he and his battalion were being incorporated into Panzergruppe Peiper. SS-Obersturmbannführer Jochen Peiper had only a mixed battalion in his panzer regiment, consisting of two companies of Panzer IVs and Panzer Vs, together with the 9th Panzer-Pioneer Company and the 10th Panzer-Flak Company. This mixed Ist Battalion was commanded by Knight's Cross wearer SS-Sturmbannführer Poetschke. The 501st SS Panzer Battalion was therefore incorporated into the panzer regiment of the Leibstandarte as its IInd Battalion. Peiper and von Westernhagen knew each other from the Eastern Front and thought highly of each another. The 501st (Heavy) SS Panzer Battalion was thus no longer a corps unit, available for use at developing points of main effort, but was to fight as an integral part of the panzer regiment. As point group, the role of Panzergruppe Peiper was to force the breakthrough; consequently, much was expected of the formation. Peiper had the following units under his command:

1st Panzer Regiment	Ostubaf. Peiper	
I/SS Rgt. 1 ("mixed battalion")	Sturmbannfuhrer Poetschke	
1/SS Pz. Rgt. 1	Ostuf. Kremser	Pz. V
2/SS Pz. Rgt. 1	Ostuf. Christ	Pz. V
6/SS Pz. Rgt. 1	Ostuf. Junker	Pz. IV
7/SS Pz. Rgt. 1	Hstuf. Klingelhöfer	Pz. IV
9 (Pi)/SS Pz. Rgt. 1	Ostuf. Rumpf	APC
10 (Flak)/SS Pz. Rgt. 1	Ostuf. Vögler	Pz. IV
501st SS Panzer Battalion	Ostubaf. von Westernhagen	
1/SS Pz. Btl. 501	Ostuf. Wessel	Pz. VI
2/SS Pz. Btl. 501	Hstuf. Möbius	Pz. VI
3/SS Pz. Btl. 501	Hstuf. Birnschein	Pz. VI
III (Armored) Btl. /SS Pz. Gren. Rgt. 2	Hstuf. Diefenthal	
9 (Armored) /SS Pz. Gren. Rgt. 2	Ustuf. Leike	APC
10 (Armored) /SS Pz. Gren. Rgt. 2	Ostuf. Preuß	APC
11 (Armored) /SS Pz. Gren. Rgt. 2	Ostuf. Tomhardt	APC
12 (Hvy. Armored) /SS Pz. Gren. Rgt. 2	Ustuf. Thiele	APC
13 (IG) /SS Pz. Gren. Rgt. 2	Ostuf. Koch	
3 (Armored) /SS Pz. Pi. Btl. 1	Ostuf. Sievers	APC
I (Armored) /SS Pz. Art. Rgt. 1	Hstuf. Kalischko	
1 (Armored) /SS Pz. Art. Rgt. 1	Ostuf. Neugebauer	
2 (Armored) /SS Pz. Art. Rgt. 1	Ostuf. Werner	
3 (Armored) /SS Pz. Art. Rgt. 1	Ostuf. Freist	
Luftwaffe Flak Battalion 84	Major von Sacken	

The other elements of the 1st SS Panzer Division were combined into battle groups commanded by Hansen, Sandig and Knittel. The order of march was laid down at the same time the battle groups were formed. Peiper's armored group was allocated Advance Road D. As the sixty-eight tonne Tigers could reach a speed of only thirty-eight kilometers per hour, they formed the rearguard in the order of march together with the flak and the artillery.

By 14 December 1944 all elements of the Leibstandarte had gathered in their assembly areas. At 11.00 hours the regimental commanders were ordered to the division command post in Tondorf, where SS-Oberführer Mohnke disclosed to them the verbal order for the coming attack. In summary, the Leibstandarte was given the following tasks: Panzergruppe Peiper will drive through the breach smashed in the American front near Losheim by the 12th Volksgrenadier Division and, advancing by way of Trois-Pont and Werbomont, reach the Maas between Liege and Huy. There it will establish bridgeheads from which a further advance, reinforced by the following forces, can be made on Antwerp. The group under SS-Obersturmbannführer Sandig will follow Peiper in expectation of further tasks. After the breakthrough by the 3rd Parachute Division, the group of forces under SS-Obersturmbannführer Hansen will advance into the enemy rear and likewise reach the Maas via Advance Road E (Heppenbach, Amel, Recht) and establish bridgeheads near Huy. The Knittel Group with the reinforced reconnaissance battalion will follow Hansen and join the group which may be expected to break through the soonest. Its mission is to seize and hold the Maas crossings.

On the afternoon of 14 December 1944, in his command post in the Blankenheimer Wald forester's house, Peiper briefed the battalion and company commanders on the exact plan of attack. There from the 501st SS Panzer Battalion were SS-Obersturmbannführer von Westernhagen, SS-Obersturmführer Wessel, SS-Hauptsturmführer Möbius and SS-Hauptsturmführer Birnschein. Peiper arranged his armored battle group taking into consideration the state of the terrain and the anticipated road conditions. Later, during the Malmedy Trial, there was much speculation regarding the composition of the Panzergruppe in general and of the armored spearhead in particular. The Tigers received orders to march at the rear from the beginning. They were to take their place in the march column in the following sequence: 2nd Company, Headquarters, 3rd Company, 1st Company. For them too speed was the prime necessity.

On 15 December 1944 the unit commanders met once again at Peiper's command post to discuss final details of the coming offensive. When SS-Obersturmbannführer von Westernhagen subsequently returned to his battalion he summoned all the company commanders and went over the plan of attack with them. For the first time the company commanders received detailed information concerning the attack; this was also supposed to be the final briefing of the company commanders.

The Ist (Mixed) Battalion, 1st SS Panzer Regiment was to do the fighting in the course of the penetration of the Ardennes. After leaving the hilly section of the offensive zone the 501st SS Panzer Battalion, which

MARCH ORDER OF THE ARMORED BATTLE GROUP PEIPER
NEAR ENGELSDORF

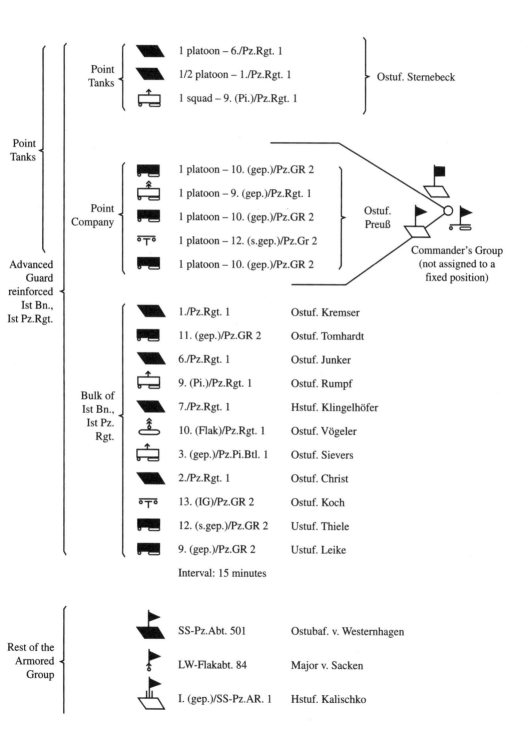

Point Tanks

1 platoon – 6./Pz.Rgt. 1
1/2 platoon – 1./Pz.Rgt. 1
1 squad – 9. (Pi.)/Pz.Rgt. 1

Ostuf. Sternebeck

Point Tanks / **Advanced Guard reinforced Ist Bn., Ist Pz.Rgt.**

Point Company

1 platoon – 10. (gep.)/Pz.GR 2
1 platoon – 9. (gep.)/Pz.Rgt. 1
1 platoon – 10. (gep.)/Pz.GR 2
1 platoon – 12. (s.gep.)/Pz.Gr 2
1 platoon – 10. (gep.)/Pz.GR 2

Ostuf. Preuß

Commander's Group
(not assigned to a fixed position)

Bulk of Ist Bn., Ist Pz. Rgt.

1./Pz.Rgt. 1	Ostuf. Kremser
11. (gep.)/Pz.GR 2	Ostuf. Tomhardt
6./Pz.Rgt. 1	Ostuf. Junker
9. (Pi.)/Pz.Rgt. 1	Ostuf. Rumpf
7./Pz.Rgt. 1	Hstuf. Klingelhöfer
10. (Flak)/Pz.Rgt. 1	Ostuf. Vögeler
3. (gep.)/Pz.Pi.Btl. 1	Ostuf. Sievers
2./Pz.Rgt. 1	Ostuf. Christ
13. (IG)/Pz.GR 2	Ostuf. Koch
12. (s.gep.)/Pz.GR 2	Ustuf. Thiele
9. (gep.)/Pz.GR 2	Ustuf. Leike

Interval: 15 minutes

Rest of the Armored Group

SS-Pz.Abt. 501	Ostubaf. v. Westernhagen
LW-Flakabt. 84	Major v. Sacken
I. (gep.)/SS-Pz.AR. 1	Hstuf. Kalischko

until then had been at the rear, was to be moved forward and spearhead the breakthrough to the Maas. In the evening the company commanders briefed their platoon leaders, who in turn informed the tank commanders of the attack. The crews were told of a German commando operation and of the possibility that they might encounter friendly troops in American uniforms and vehicles on the other side of the lines. A hand signal was arranged for purposes of identification. The crews were to take two day's rations with them. Filled with expectation and tension, the companies of the Tiger Battalion made ready. After the weeks of retreat out of France and the reorganization of the battalion they were finally going to take the offensive again. SS-Oberstgruppenführer Sepp Dietrich issued an order of the day to the soldiers of his army:

"Sixth Panzer Army, the Commander in Chief, Army Headquarters, December 1944: Soldiers of the Sixth Panzer Army! We face one of the great decisions of the war. The Führer has committed us at an especially important place. Our mission is to advance across the Maas quickly, looking neither to the left nor right. Together with other units of the army and air force, we will destroy the enemy forces standing on German soil. The homeland is working day and night for us, protecting it is our supreme duty. I expect every soldier to give his utmost while fully exploiting the engine, in order to be the first to reach the Maas. We intend to be the first German armored unit to cross the Maas. signed Sepp Dietrich, Generaloberst der Waffen-SS."

While the units of Panzergruppe Peiper arranged themselves in the planned attack formation during the bitterly cold night of 16 December 1944, the Tiger companies initially stayed behind in their assembly areas. All elements not needed for combat took their place at the end of the march column as ordered. This included all train elements, including all the kitchens, but excluding the maintenance echelons. Only fuel, munitions and messenger vehicles had the right of way to the combat elements. At 02.00 hours the Ist SS Panzer Corps reported to Sixth SS Panzer Army that preparations were complete. The leaders of the waiting units now received the order of the day from the Commander in Chief West: "Soldiers of the Western Front! Your great hour has come! Powerful attack armies have today set out against the enemy. I need not say any more to you. You all feel it: it's all or nothing! Carry in you the sacred commitment, to give everything and to do the superhuman for our Fatherland and our Führer! The Commander in Chief West, signed von Rundstedt, Genera Fieldmarschall."

16 December 1944 was a cold, misty winter day, whose snow and rain prevented the Allied air forces from taking off. The artillery barrage that

opened the Ardennes offensive began at 05.30 hours. Not Peiper's panzers, but the 27th and 48th Grenadier Regiments of the 12th Volksgrenadier Division had the task of tearing apart the American front between Losheim and Losheimergraben in order to open Advance Road D for Panzergruppe Peiper. The struggle to break through took more time than expected. By midday the 12th Volksgrenadier Division had taken Losheim, but the 27th Grenadier Regiment was bogged down in heavy fighting near Buchholz Station (Losheimergraben). Panzergruppe Peiper was finally able to move out at 16.30 hours. At the end of the march column the Tigers did not begin their advance until evening. The heavy tanks rolled through Tondorf and then down narrow roads in the direction of Losheim. Leading the 1st Company, which brought up the rear, were the platoon commanders and the company commander. Near Losheim there was almost an exchange of fire with some members of Skorzeny's 150th Panzer Brigade; however, they were recognized just in time.

The spearhead of the 501st SS Panzer Battalion made contact with the Ist Battalion, Panzer Regiment Leibstandarte in Losheim at approximately 22.00. Toward midnight Peiper and his spearhead reached Lanzerath, where the 9th Parachute Regiment was placed under his command. Some of the paratroopers climbed onto the tanks and so accompanied the advance. Parachute troops also rode on the Tigers. They reached Honsfeld during the night. Earlier Peiper had surprised an American reconnaissance battalion there as it slept; the paratroopers mopped up in the village while Peiper continued to advance toward Büllingen. By that time the Tiger battalion had already lost a number of its tanks due to mechanical breakdown, the most common problem involving the final drive. The roads were in poor condition, narrow, and ground into a muddy mess by the tanks and armored troop carriers that had already passed by. The tank drivers had to do precision work on the slippery subsoil.

In Honsfeld one of the panzer regiment's Wirbelwind anti-aircraft tanks was knocked out in front of a Tiger. Riding on the Tiger were some men of the 14th (Anti-tank) Company, 9th Parachute Regiment; they quickly jumped for cover when the Tiger, too, came under fire from American anti-tank guns positioned at the cemetery. The Tiger drove toward the anti-tank guns, knocked down a wall and destroyed two of them. The Tiger was itself hit four times but suffered no damage. The paratroopers discovered an abandoned American supply dump and Obergefreiter Sepp Reiner passed out cigarettes to several Tiger crews as the tanks rolled past. His "own" tank crew, commanded by a youthful Untersturmführer ("all excellent chaps," as Reiner later recalled) was also supplied with cigarettes. The paratroopers then got back aboard the Tigers and rode as far as the outskirts of Schoppen, where they were separated from the tanks by artillery fire.

In the late morning hours of 17 December the Tigers passed through Büllingen, where Peiper's tanks had previously refuelled from an American fuel dump while under artillery fire. The Tigers struggled forward over hopelessly muddy and in some cases snow-covered roads, passing Schoppen, Faymondville, Ondenval and Thirimont. They had yet to make contact with the enemy. On the morning of 18th December the 1st Company was still in the Thirimont area, where the men had spent the night in a field to the right of the road. Suddenly, eight four-engined bombers dropped down and showered the tanks with bombs. While the tank crews suffered no casualties, there were several killed and wounded among the parachute troops. The tanks had sustained no damage and the 1st Company resumed its advance. By this time the units of the Tiger battalion had already become separated, as considerable gaps had developed in the march formation. It proved impossible to close these gaps as the advance went on. Several tanks of the 1st Company set out from Thirimont over secondary roads in a southwesterly direction straight toward Engelsdorf. The bulk of the battalion followed Peiper, however, and took the route past the Baugnez crossroads, which was later to gain notoriety.

At about noon on 17 December 1944 an American supply column rolling in the direction of Engelsdorf had been fired on by German tanks. The crews of the trucks, which belonged to an artillery observation battery (285th Field Artillery Observation Battalion), subsequently jumped down from their vehicles and surrendered. Since the armored spearhead had no time to lose, it drove past the Americans standing at the side of the road toward Engelsdorf. The prisoners were left unguarded. Some of the Americans picked up their weapons again. From a distance the next group of German tanks decided that the group was hostile and opened fire, resulting in more casualties. When the armored group reached the prisoners several attempted to flee. Several shots were fired at them to make them stop. From the total number of victims the Americans produced the "Malmedy massacre." A show trial later staged against seventy-two members of Panzergruppe Peiper, including the commanding generals of the army and corps, served the American victors in their plan to brand everyone who served in the Waffen-SS as a criminal.

The 1st Company reached Engelsdorf at 10.30 hours and stopped to rest in front of the Hôtel du Moulin. Sitting in front of the building was the Panther of SS-Untersturmführer Arndt Fischer, SS-Sturmbannführer Poetschke's adjutant. It had been knocked out the day before. American

General Timberlake and the staff of the 49th Anti-aircraft Brigade escaped from the hotel shortly before the arrival of Peiper's spearhead. At that time the Tigers of the 2nd and 3rd Company's, accompanied by the battalion commander, were driving through Stavelot under American defensive fire. Driving in the rear, the Tigers of the 3rd Company returned fire at lone riflemen visible in the windows of houses. By this time SS-Hauptsturm-führer Birnschein had already moved to another Tiger as his tank had bro-ken down.

The 1st Company moved out again at about noon. Following the nar-row roads, which more closely resembled country lanes, it reached the vil-lage of Vaulx Richard, high above Stavelot, via Lodomez. The Tigers had to clear the road to allow elements of the armored reconnaissance battal-ion to pass. Isolated artillery rounds fell now and then. The Tigers soon resumed their march. Stavelot was visible below to the right, deep in the valley of the Amblève. A narrow, precipitous road led down into the valley, bordered on its right side by a sheer wall of rock. The drivers had to exer-cise extreme caution in moving their almost seventy-tonne tanks over the slippery surface, as the danger of skidding off the road was great.

The winding road finally led to the first houses of the city and then made a sharp right turn to the Amblève bridge. The company com-mander, SS-Obersturmführer Wessel, was driving point. His crew consisted of driver SS-Unterscharführer Walter Bingert, radio operator SS-Unter-scharführer Fritz Belbe, gunner SS-Unterscharführer Georg Przibylla and loader SS-Sturmmann Oskar Batsch. Following Wessel were three other Tigers, including those commanded by the officers of the IIIrd Platoon, SS-Oberscharführer Brandt (Tiger 131) and SS-Oberscharführer Wendt (133). While crossing the Amblève bridge the tanks were surprised by fighter-bombers. The running gear of Brandt's tank was hit and he halted thirty meters from the bridge to make repairs. The other Tigers continued into the interior of the city.

SS-Obersturmführer Wessel described the action: "I was driving point myself. Was hit just short of the Amblève bridge, cannon unserviceable. Nevertheless rolled across the bridge at high speed, soon reached a rec-tangular marketplace and there was hit twice in front by anti-tank fire. I backed the tank up and in doing so struck the wall of a house, which fell on the tank. My crew and I escaped through the belly hatch, committed the following tank of my company, SS-Oberscharführer Brandt, against the enemy anti-tank guns and climbed into the nearest tank. With this tank I drove through Stavelot at high speed in an effort to make contact ahead; however my company was unable to follow and I could not go back as the

Americans had reinforced their forces in the town. The company also later failed to make contact with Battle Group Peiper."

The source of the anti-tank fire is still uncertain. Wessel's radio operator, SS-Unterscharführer Belbe, recalled seeing a flash from a window; the projectile failed to penetrate the tank's frontal armor. It may have been a bazooka. Wessel and his Tiger 105 sat in the Rue Haut Rivage No. 9; light artillery fire and sporadic rifle fire could be heard. The current atmosphere was nothing like the furious defensive fire that had met the tanks of Battle Group Peiper in the morning.

SS-Oberscharführer Werner Wendt recalled: "Wessel climbed into the second tank and drove down the road, which forked before the marketplace, in the direction of Trois-Ponts. Brandt was sitting about thirty meters from the bridge. Because of the narrow street I could not get by him with my 3.75-meter-wide tank, so we helped him repair the track. By now it had become dark. As we had lost all contact ahead and behind, we decided to wait for daylight. Toward midnight an anti-aircraft gun raced past us. Brandt and I spent the entire night in Stavelot. Several paratroopers kept us company, so we had a little security. But all remained quiet."

Stavelot had been occupied by the 117th Regiment of the American 30th Infantry Division, which was joined by elements of the 120th Regiment during the night. The Tigers of Brandt and Wendt were not the only ones to have lost contact with the battalion, however. SS-Hauptscharführer Rolf von Westernhagen, commander of the 3rd Company's Turd Platoon, had also lost contact with his company. He reached the steep road to Stavelot alone in his Tiger 331.

After completing the perilous journey to the valley floor he approached the outskirts of the city. Suddenly the Tiger came under furious defensive fire from the first houses. The six paratroopers riding on the tank immediately jumped down and advanced on the enemy soldiers in the houses. There was a brief flurry of hand grenades and the threat was eliminated. SS-Hauptscharführer von Westernhagen continued on his way to Stavelot but shortly afterward was forced to halt by a final drive failure. Slowly he backed the tank up the climbing road in reverse gear until he reached a farm outside the city. On the way several Luftwaffe quadruple flak passed him heading in the direction of Stavelot. Near the farm von Westernhagen came upon two more Tigers which had broken down with similar problems. Together the crews set about to make repairs to the tanks. In their position the men were exposed to American artillery fire, which, as von Westernhagen recalls, was directed by a Belgian civilian from a church steeple. Continuing the advance was out of the question for the time being, especially since the paratroopers had meanwhile left the Tigers.

At this time Kampfgruppe Hansen withdrew from Stavelot toward Francorchamps and Malmedy. At 15.00 Stavelot was struck by a bombing raid and subsequently units of the US 30th Infantry Division infiltrated into the city from the north and northwest as far as the city center and went over to the defensive there.

The 3rd Company lost a Tiger in Stavelot; it was knocked out from behind by an anti-tank gun. A second of the company's Tigers was hit in the turret, which was then unable to rotate. The crew stayed in the tank, however, and destroyed an American tank from a range of one hundred meters. Not all the elements of the Tiger battalion were left so far behind, however. Late on the morning of that 18 December, SS-Hauptsturmführer Möbius, whose tank had also broken down, forcing him to transfer to the Tiger of the company headquarters squad leader, reached Panzergruppe Peiper in La Gleize with his 2nd Company via Stavelot, Trois-Ponts and Coo. With him was the command group with SS-Obersturmbannführer von Westernhagen and SS-Untersturmführer Kalinowsky.

SS-Sturmmann Hubert Heil, radio operator in the Tiger of SS-Obersturmführer Helmut Dollinger, commander of the 2nd Company's Ist Platoon, remembered the difficulties encountered on the advance: "For our heavy tanks the action in the Ardennes could not be compared with action on the Eastern Front. There was no open battlefield for us. Over our heads flew the V 1 and V 2; they came to be known as 'the terror of the Eifel' for in some cases they came down too soon, squandering their effect as wonder weapons. Without winter clothing it was very cold for us in the tanks and we suffered even more than in the winter of 1943/44 in the Soviet Union. Our unit also received insufficient fuel. Such shortcomings caused the rapid advance to falter.

The Tigers of the 2nd Company rolled through La Gleize in the direction of Cheneux on their way to Werbomont. At approximately 13.00 hours a short-lived improvement in the weather resulted in the immediate appearance of American aircraft. Sixteen Thunderbolts dove on Panzergruppe Peiper's two-kilometer-long march column. The head of the column was completely exposed on the narrow road in front of Cheneux. In the ceaseless attacks that followed, three Panthers and five armored troop carriers were so badly hit that they were lost to the subsequent advance. The tank crews sat out the attacks under their tanks, many also stayed inside their vehicles. Furious defensive fire put up by the quadruple guns of two anti-aircraft tanks of the 10th (Flak) Company, 1st SS Panzer Regiment prevented the enemy pilots from making accurate firing passes; nevertheless the attack lasted approximately two hours. The fighter-bombers repeatedly hammered away at the tanks with their machine-guns. SS-Obersturmbannführer von Westernhagen was fortunate enough to escape injury himself, but his adjutant, SS-Untersturmführer Kalinowsky, was wounded in the right arm by bullet fragments.

One fighter-bomber was shot down. The advance had suffered another delay of several hours. The wounded were cared for immediately and the damaged vehicles were pushed aside. At approximately 18.00, after passing Rahier, the armored spearhead reached the main Trois-Ponts-Werbomont road south of Froidville. It was supposed to take the bridge over the Lienne near Neucy; however, the bridge was blown up just as the tanks reached the point where the road branched off to Chauveheid. It was now approximately 22.00 hours. Peiper immediately dispatched patrols to locate crossings over the Lienne suitable for tanks. While engaged in one of these scouting missions, the 10th (Armored) Company, 2nd SS Panzer-Grenadier Regiment under SS-Obersturmführer Preuß walked into an ambush laid by the 119th Regiment of the American 30th Infantry Division (Major McGown) near Outry and took heavy losses. After these unsuccessful reconnaissance efforts Peiper decided to lead his armored group to La Gleize and wait out the night there. He intended to resume his attack in the direction of the Meuse by way of Stoumont the next day.

Meanwhile SS-Hauptsturmführer Birnschein and several of his Tigers of the 3rd Company reached Panzergruppe Peiper in La Gleize. SS-Obersturmführer Wessel, too, reached the small village in the evening and reported to von Westernhagen. The battalion commander ordered him to remain in La Gleize and not to return to his company. Von Westernhagen was happy to have every Tiger that hadn't broken down.

During the return to La Gleize, SS-Unterscharführer Wortmann, commanding one of the two remaining Wirbelwind anti-aircraft tanks of the 10th (Flak) Company, 1st SS Panzer Regiment, spent the night in back of Cheneux with engine trouble: "We drove back in the direction of La Gleize. It was very foggy that night and we literally couldn't see a thing. We had already driven through the village of Rahier again and also the small village of Cheneux. We soon must come to the large viaduct again. Suddenly, part way through a left-hand turn, our tank quit. What was happening? Even my experienced driver Erich Miechen was left speechless. All the other tanks and vehicles overtook us. We were left all alone. The workshop tank already had another in tow and promised to pick us up later! Our situation became uncomfortable as time passed. We sat alone in the dark and waited. Morning was breaking when suddenly we heard the sound of tanks behind us. What should we do? After all we were sitting there like a target on a firing range!

Our radio operator Günther Sträter removed the machine-gun. My crew took the gun and moved into position behind the huge arched pillar of the viaduct. The sound of tanks had meanwhile grown louder and I was sure that they must emerge from behind the last houses of Cheneux at any minute. As far as we were concerned they had to be Americans, because everyone else had passed us. Then the first appeared from behind the houses, with the second right behind it, then some distance behind the third and the fourth. They were moving slowly, almost at a walking pace, as if they were being extremely cautious themselves. The distance to our tank dwindled steadily. Then I recognized one of the commanders: it was Hauptsturmführer Möbius. Like our armored column, these King Tigers had driven steadily from the first day of the attack on. Now their fuel was as good as gone. They had emptied the tanks of two panzers and thus supplied the others. So now one had the other in tow!" SS-Hauptsturmführer Möbius had probably got these Tigers moving during the night in the manner described by Wortmann and so brought them to La Gleize.

The morning of 19 December 1944 dawned foggy. Peiper assembled his tanks for the attack on Stoumont. The Americans had bolstered their forces in the town considerably during the night. The 119th Regiment had moved to the east end of town, the tanks of the 740th Armored Battalion were in position, and elements of the 82nd Airborne Division were on the way. The German attack began at 09.00 hours. The tanks advanced in inverted wedge formation to just short of the east end of Stoumont. Met by defensive fire from tanks and anti-tank guns, the attack faltered. As well the attackers began taking flanking fire from the edge of a wood to the right of the road. Armed with a Panzerfaust, SS-Sturmbannführer Poetschke fought in the front lines with the paratroopers. American resistance was worn down after two hours of heavy fighting; eleven Sherman tanks were destroyed and a number of anti-tank guns knocked out and run over. Many Americans surrendered in Stoumont, others fled to the west. The tanks advanced to Stoumont Station, which was located three kilometers further on near Targnon. When the fighting was over the shortage of ammunition and fuel slowly began to make itself felt among the tanks engaged in the action. No supplies could reach Panzergruppe Peiper over the former advance road as the enemy had reoccupied Stavelot. There were already signs that the unit that had advanced the farthest was going to be cut off. The situation became critical for Peiper. None of the Tigers had been committed to the attack on Stoumont. Peiper had his point units go over to the defensive where they stood. At approximately 14.00 hours Peiper issued instructions to the Ist Battalion, 1st SS Panzer Regiment to hold its positions near the town and station of Stoumont; the Tiger battalion was to secure La Gleize to the north and northwest against enemy attack. In La Gleize there was a total of six Tigers from the entire battalion plus the command group.

Several tanks of the 6th and 7th Companies, 1st SS Panzer Regiment, armored troop carriers of the 3rd (Armored) Company, 1st SS Panzer-Pioneer Battalion and some parachute troops had remained behind in Wanne on 18 December due to lack of fuel. After receiving supplies, on 19 December 1944 they attacked Stavelot from the south through Wanneranval; however the attack was blocked by the massed American resistance in Stavelot. Tiger 222 of SS-Oberscharführer Kurt Sowa participated in the Battle of Stavelot that day. He had previously lost his way and drove alone through Amel to Deidenberg. The lone tank received an enthusiastic welcome from the village children. The men of the crew and the paratroopers riding on the tank received food and they in turn gave the children chocolate and sweets.

After a brief stop Sowa proceeded via Kaiserbarracke and Engelsdorf to Stavelot. He arrived there in the afternoon and intervened in the fighting in front of the approach to the bridge. Several other Tigers that had broken down en route also reached the outskirts of Stavelot. One of these tanks was commanded by SS-Hauptscharführer Lötzsch, who engaged the enemy by firing at muzzle flashes visible on the opposite bank of the Amblève. In the afternoon SS-Oberführer Mohnke joined the Tigers engaged in front of Stavelot. One other Tiger continued to engage targets in Stavelot for some time even though it was immobilized. At about 22.00 hours the bridge was blown by the Americans.

What had happened to the two Tigers of SS-Oberscharführer Brandt and SS-Oberscharführer Wendt that had been stranded in Stavelot the day before? On the morning of 19 December at 07.30 hours, the two tanks moved off, drove through Stavelot and turned onto the west road, which led to Trois-Ponts. Approximately two kilometers beyond the city they came upon the reconnaissance battalion's command post near Coreux. Even the battalion commander, SS-Sturmbannführer Knittel, was unable to tell the two tank commanders anything definite about the situation. He had no idea where their 1st Company was. Brandt and Wendt at first waited with Knittel to see what would happen. At approximately 10.00 the two tank commanders were instructed to reconnoiter to Stavelot together with the reconnaissance battalion's 2nd Company under SS-Obersturmführer Coblenz. The group moved out and reached the outskirts of the city unopposed. Wendt spotted mines lying on the ground and backed his

Tiger away, coming under small arms and later tank fire. Wendt returned to Coreux after an hour and was deployed by SS-Sturmbannführer Knittel to guard the command post. He positioned the Tiger about thirty meters in front of the command post facing Stavelot. On Knittel's orders SS-Oberscharführer Brandt drove to Trois-Ponts to guard the viaduct there. He positioned his Tiger one hundred meters west of the Petit Spai bridge. Attacks on Stavelot in the afternoon by the Ist Battalion, 2nd SS Panzer-Grenadier Regiment resulted in the gaining of a bridgehead across the Amblève bridge; however, the panzer-grenadiers were isolated there as no heavy weapons or other reinforcements followed up. The old Amblève bridge was blown by the enemy, and the panzer-grenadiers lay under American artillery fire, pinned down and completely unable to move.

In Stoumont Peiper's battle group was attacked persistently by American tanks. As the long, open flank between Stoumont and the station was difficult to defend, Peiper decided to withdraw the elements at the station to the west end of Stoumont. In the evening the Panzergruppe held positions near La Gleize facing southwest, at the arterial road to Spa abeam Borgoumont facing northwest, in the Bois de Bassenge facing north, and at the road to La Reid facing northeast. The defenses at the east end of Stoumont faced west and southwest, while pickets were positioned at the outskirts of Cheneux facing south. Peiper's command post was situated in the manor house near Castle Froid-Cour. SS-Obersturmbannführer von Westernhagen sent a patrol north in the direction of Borgoumont which reported no contact with the enemy. Tiger 334 took up position on the road leading from La Gleize to Borgoumont.

On 20 December 1944 Battle Group Peiper was attacked from all sides from morning on. The Americans had moved in further reinforcements during the night and these now joined in the fighting. La Gleize, Stoumont and Cheneux lay under nonstop artillery fire, and tanks attacked from the forest north of the La Gleize-Stoumont road in an effort to break open the German barrier at the west exit from Stoumont from behind. Elements of the Ist Battalion, 1st SS Panzer Regiment repulsed the attack and inflicted heavy losses on the Americans. Major Hal McCown, a battalion commander in the US 117th Regiment, was taken prisoner. The "Sankt Eduard" sanatorium was vital to the defense of Stoumont. SS-Obersturmführer Sievers, the commander of the 3rd (Armored) Company, 1st SS Pionier Battalion, and his men fought for their lives there. Tanks, anti-tank guns and artillery softened up the building. The Americans entered the ground floor but were driven out again by the defenders in bitter hand-to-hand fighting. SS-Rottenführer Rolf Ehrhardt, driver of the commander of the 7th Company, 1st

SS Panzer Regiment, was one of a small group which marched in the direction of Coo the day before.

"Then we set off at first light. Before the viaduct on the road to Coo an armored troop carrier with an operations officer of the division headquarters came toward us. He stopped us and reported that somewhat farther ahead the road was blocked by American tanks. We withdrew to the mill and guarded the road to Coo. This task was legalized from above immediately afterward. A King Tiger under the command of Untersturmführer Hantusch, as well as a small unit of the reconnaissance battalion with an armored car (Puma eight-wheeled car with 75 mm KwK short) and a Panzerschreck (bazooka) platoon formed Blocking Group 'Mill' in the course of the day. My Panzer IV was behind the arbor, the King Tiger in a coach house in the yard, the Puma between trees along the road. All guns were trained on a bend in the road where an attacker must come into view. We had undoubtedly prepared a hot reception for the Americans; however, in the event of a concentric attack we couldn't have held out long. A retreat over the open road wouldn't have exactly been life insurance in any case.

The expected attack did not materialize and the 19th and 20th of December passed tolerably, even if not boring. I reconnoitered on foot several times, especially over the slope in the direction of Werimont. At times there was heavy fog and we had to depend more on our ears than our eyes. Engine noise from the Coos-Francorchamps road kept us at a constant state of alert readiness. Once, when the sound of powerful engines idling indicated the presence of tanks nearby, I undertook a lone scouting mission. I spotted six American tanks. The range was too great for the Panzerfaust, but not too great for the American machine-gunner. Bullets suddenly flew about my ears and it took an olympic-class hurdle over a barb wire fence to save me. Over generations industrious farmers had picked rock from the fields, gathered them together and used them to put up walls. It was thanks to their hard work that that Ami didn't get me. After an anxious quarter of an hour the tanks, and with them probably my special friend, drove away in the direction of Coo.

Personally I didn't like the inactivity in the 'mill' blocking position, as it might eventually prove to be the calm before the storm. So I kept moving constantly. My particular attention was focused on the road above the mill and beyond the stream. For a time I sat in the roof hatch with the binoculars, then I felt the urge to return to the slope. The mill was a big house with its bottom floor at street level, and in the basement there was a large kitchen. From there a door led into the courtyard in an easterly direction to the Rognay Brook. As the mill was in a blind spot we were scarcely fired on there and the building was undamaged. We made use of the kitchen range to prepare several portions of roast potatoes. The house and kitchen were so busy that they resembled an anthill most of the time.

Suddenly, without warning, bursts of fire from a (probably) 16 mm machine-gun poured into this throng. Unnoticed by us, an American patrol had worked its way along the stream to within close range, approximately thirty meters, of the house. The panic that broke out in the kitchen was indescribable. Some of the men tried to get up the stairs. The door to the stairs opened inward, however, and it simply could not be opened because it was blocked by men seeking cover in that corner. I had thrown myself under the window with six or eight comrades, for the massive natural stone walls offered us good protection.

How long the firing lasted I cannot say. It seemed like hours to us, although it certainly wasn't any longer than two or three minutes. Instead of waiting for the hand grenades which in such cases must come through the window sooner or later, I and an Unterscharführer of the reconnaissance battalion who was lying beside decided to break out. But then the firing stopped as suddenly as it had begun. The Puma had put an end to the nightmare.

Miraculously no one was killed or wounded. One comrade had an insignificant fragment injury. The stout walls and the cover in the blind spot were our salvation. Astonishingly, the Amis also succeeded in withdrawing without loss—truly a miracle given the firepower of the Puma.

In the afternoon I returned to my post in the roof hatch. Meanwhile the fog had lifted and I could see the road well. Then I spotted an American armored column of thirty to thirty-five vehicles, two thirds of them tanks, coming from the direction of Francorchamps. They were driving slowly in march order. I immediately went to Hauptsturmführer Klingelhöfer with a plan: 'Our Panzer IV will remain left of the mill, the King Tiger right. When a sufficient number of vehicles have driven through the wood, the Tiger will take out the point tank, we the last tank within reach. After that we'll decimate the column from both sides to the center. The Amis will be unable to deploy as the road is too narrow. The element of surprise is with us, the terrain profile is favorable. If things get tricky we need only drive in the direction of the slope or behind the mill.'

The plan was rejected by the Tiger commander, however, with the following justification: 'Fire uphill? I'm not tired of living. I have only three centimeters of armor on top'."

Communications between SS-Obersturmbannführer Peiper and division were spotty. He had been forced on to the defensive for good. The

Americans kept up their assault-team-style attacks on the town held by Panzergruppe Peiper with undiminished fury. There was house-to-house and hand-to-hand fighting in Stoumont and Cheneux, which demanded the utmost of the panzer-grenadiers. For the Tigers in La Gleize, these were the first combat operations in which they took part. Until now they had had to struggle more with technical problems and the difficult road conditions. There was no classic panzer assault, for a deployed advance had so far not been possible. SS-Hauptsturmführer Birnschein confirmed this and wrote: "We, meaning my 3rd Company, did not participate in any heavy fighting prior to La Gleize. Two to four of my company's Tigers were in La Gleize and had been employed in a security role. The other Tigers had been stranded during the march by mechanical breakdowns."

West of Stavelot that day were the Tigers of Brandt and Wendt. At 09.00, together with the reconnaissance battalion's 2nd Company, they attacked again in the direction of the city, with the goal of driving through Stavelot and reaching the blown Amblève bridge. After moving off the group came under heavy artillery fire; as well fighter-bombers dived on the reconnaissance battalion, bombing and strafing. Although the first houses were taken, the attack failed. At noon the two Tigers returned to the screening positions they had held earlier. Kampfgruppe Knittel was subsequently attacked along the road to Trois-Ponts by an American assault group with forty tanks. Several anti-tank guns and SS-Oberscharführer Brandt's Tiger fought a defensive battle abreast the Amblève bridge near Petit Spai (three kilometers west of Stavelot). Six enemy tanks were destroyed from close range, one by Brandt. The rest turned tail and fled.

Tiger 222 of SS-Oberscharführer Sowa was knocked out just short of the approach to the bridge in Stavelot on that day. As the Tiger showed no signs of catching fire, the crew, who were unhurt, remained inside the tank and did not leave it until later. In Stavelot, Belgian guerrilla snipers were becoming more active. A Tiger positioned near the bridge was kept under constant fire from the opposite rooftops, preventing the crew from leaving the tank. They were forced to back the Tiger into a shed to find cover. SS-Untersturmführer Heinz Belbe, an officer in the staff of the 501st SS Panzer Battalion, was stopped in front of Stavelot by artillery fire. The driver of his Schwimmwagen was badly wounded. Belbe jumped from the vehicle and was about to pull the driver to safety, when another shell fell in front of them. The explosion killed the driver instantly and blew off one of Belbe's feet. Belbe was rescued by another unit and taken immediately to Germany. As a result he was listed missing by the battalion. The 501st SS Panzer Battalion's situation was becoming increasingly critical. Acquisition of replacement parts was proving to be as difficult as obtaining fuel.

SS-Sturmmann Kufner described the situation: "I was a tank radio technician in the 3rd Company. It was my job to service all of the company's radio and intercom systems and eventually repair them, or in the case of more major problems, replace them with new systems. In addition I was called on to do other jobs. One night (17–18 or 18–19 December) I had to drive back to Germany, to Stadtkyll-Blankenheim, with the armorer-artificer's driver in the tracked vehicle (three-and-a-half tonner) to pick up replacement parts for stranded tanks. The way back to Germany was difficult. We drove from the front through Bütgenbach in the direction of Büllingen. Twenty kilometers from Büllingen it was quiet; however, there was fighting in the forests around Büllingen. The infantry was locked in battle with the Americans still holding out in the forests. During the night the Amis felled trees onto the road.

In Büllingen the houses were burning. The town and the streets were under constant artillery fire. At the entrance to Büllingen there was an aid station with many wounded who could not be evacuated. The doctors asked us to take some of the wounded with us on account of the lack of transport. We took some hay from a barn and bedded down two seriously wounded on the open vehicle; two less seriously wounded sat on the front fenders. We lost our way soon after Büllingen and stopped under a railway viaduct. We saw lights and trucks two-hundred meters away. It turned out that they were Ami vehicles; the keys were in the ignitions and the hoods were warm. Nevertheless, they took to their heels, probably on account of the rattling of our tracks. We turned around quickly and drove in the proper direction to Germany. With us was the motor transport sergeant, Oberscharführer Tramm, in a VW Schwimmwagen. Following our return we took up quarters in the village of Bellevaux; the train with the Senior NCO had already moved in there. There were none of our company's Tiger tanks in the village itself." Eight dead from the 3rd Company were buried in Bellevaux, including radio operator SS-Sturmmann Mitscherlich, who died in hospital in Wanne on 31 December 1944.

THE CUT-OFF: PANZERGRUPPE PEIPER ON 21 DECEMBER 1944

The situation in which the cut-off Panzergruppe Peiper found itself was growing more difficult from day to day. In the dreary, foggy dawn the Americans continued their attacks with undiminished fury; Cheneux was lost. Heavy artillery fire fell on the towns held by Peiper's battle group. The Tigers, too, were on the defensive everywhere. SS-Sturmbannführer Poetschke's adjutant, SS-Untersturmführer Rolf Reiser, described the situation of the armored forces: "Like the day before, they attacked in the sector north of the La Gleize-Stoumont road with masses of tanks and infantry in an attempt to sever the road and break open our defensive position in Stoumont from the rear. These attacks were repulsed by several Panthers of the 1st and 2nd Companies, 1st SS Panzer Regiment and grenadiers of the IIIrd (Armored) Battalion, 2nd SS Panzer-Grenadier Regiment. Our command post on the south side of the La Gleize-Stoumont road lay under direct fire. As a precaution SS-Sturmbannführer Poetschke gave orders to prepare to move to Château Stoumont, Froid-Cour. This did not come about, however, for the enemy now attacked from the south, from the Cheneux sector, with superior forces. He simultaneously intensified his artillery fire on Stoumont and Château Froid- Cour. Our defense was severely hampered by the lack of fuel and ammunition. We could scarcely still allow the tanks to move, and the armor-piercing ammunition was husbanded. Every shot with an armor-piercing round had to be a certain hit. In the middle of this difficult, hard-fought battle we received orders from SS-Obersturmbannführer Peiper to abandon Stoumont and Château Froid-Cour in the evening."

SS-Obersturmbannführer von Westernhagen sent SS-Hauptsturmführer Birnschein to Stoumont by motorcycle to maintain contact with the group of forces fighting there. Just short of the village the motorcycle came under small arms fire and Birnschein was wounded in the jaw and both legs. He returned alone and reached his commanding officer in La Gleize. The group at the mill, which included SS-Untersturmführer Hantusch of the 2nd Company, was also pulled back to La Gleize. Rolf Ehrhardt continues his account: "We left the cozy mill on the morning of 21 December and reached the village and the Werimont farm unharmed. There SS-Hauptsturmführer Klingelhöfer assumed command of sector 'East.' Our command post was set up in the cellar of one of the farm outbuildings. The main building had burned down to its foundations. There were several cows were running around the area constantly breaking the field telephone lines, unfortunately for the trouble-shooters. The natural-stone cellar was quite secure against artillery fire but very cool. Our Panzer IV command tank took shelter in a shed which was attached to the outbuilding. That was the end of the line for it too.

My fellow crewmen, radio operator Helmut Rentsch, gunner Engelbert Brock and loader Peter Mühlbach, spent their time in the tank, while I camped out in the cellar with SS-Hauptsturmführer Klingelhöfer. Other permanent residents were the commanding officer of the flak battalion, Major von Sacken, telephone operators and medics. We always had other guests in the cellar, especially the tank crews, who could stretch their tired limbs for a while. There, too, I was constantly on the move, as a runner to

Peiper's command post or to other units in the sector. In the evening we brought Hantusch's Tiger from the mill. All that was left there was a patrol from the reconnaissance battalion, which stayed in contact with us by field telephone. Present at the farm now were the Tiger tanks of Untersturm-führer Hantusch and Obersturmführer Dollinger (his Tiger still sits in La Gleize today), a Panther commanded by Unterscharführer Friedrichs, another Panther and several more armored vehicles. We had received no hot food since 13 December. We had been given march rations for three days. None of us had been full for days, many hadn't had anything at all to eat for a long time. Some sugar cubes and several frozen apples from the upper rooms of the farm were our nourishment for several days. True, my crew still had a crust of bread; however, the company commander and I didn't ask them for it, for there wasn't enough to divide. The same went for sleep. It was out of the question. Only once or twice from the beginning of the attack until after the breakout did I sleep for more than an hour. Of course one closed his eyes whenever possible and slept briefly in the most impossible situations and positions. Everyone, whether common soldier or commander, had long since exceeded the limit of his ability to go on. The faces were drawn, unshaven and unwashed, the eyes inflamed, everyone had caught cold. Many of the men had wounds. Their condition was heart-wrenching and everyone knew that the final increase in burden was yet to come. Actually I can't properly describe my own condition. A good consti-tution and iron energy, the awareness that the outcome depended on everyone, and the realization that others had it worse, helped me. My greatest difficulties were swollen feet in tight shoes. The instinct to survive was never greater than in those hardest and probably also most hopeless days of my life."

Peiper evacuated Stoumont and Cheneux in the early evening hours of 21 December 1944 and withdrew his entire battle group to the small village of La Gleize. La Gleize thus became the center point of the pocket. In addi-tion to SS-Obersturmbannführer von Westernhagen, those present in La Gleize from the 501st SS Panzer Battalion were the commanders of the 1st, 2nd and 3rd Companies, Wessel, Möbius and Birnschein, and all the pla-toon commanders of the 2nd Company, Dollinger, Hantusch and Hahn, each with their crews. During the night of 22 December 1944 Peiper learned by radio that the relief attack by SS-Obersturmbannführer Max Hansen down the Trois-Ponts-Coos road had failed. Peiper's group was sup-posed to receive an air-drop of supplies on the night of 23 December.

West of Stavelot Kampfgruppe Hansen was supposed to advance toward the north. On Mohnke's order a Panzerjäger IV of the 1st SS Anti-tank Battalion (formerly the assault gun battalion) crossed the bridge near Petit Spai; it fell through and plunged into the Amblève. The only occupant of the vehicle was the driver and he was rescued. Pioneers began building a new bridge, but this was washed away just prior to its completion. Further work was hindered by nonstop artillery fire. The nearby covering force, reinforced by SS-Oberscharführer Brandt and his Tiger, had been cut off since morning by elements of the 505th Regiment of the 82nd Airborne Division which had advanced east from Trois-Ponts. Not until Kampfgruppe Hansen's attack was the desired relief achieved. Hansen's 1st Battalion crossed the Amblève near Petit Spai to support the reconnaissance battalion. The IInd Battalion, 1st SS Panzer-Grenadier Regiment remained in covering positions above the Salm at the Bois des Echevins and south of Spireux. The IIIrd Battalion, 1st SS Panzer-Grenadier Regiment established contact with the reconnaissance battalion opposite the sanatorium near Petit Spai.

The artillery fire on La Gleize persisted throughout the night of 22 December 1944 and in the morning it intensified to drum fire. The Panzergruppe was squeezed into a tiny area with its tanks and vehicles. Some of the crews were in their tanks, ready to meet surprise attacks by the Americans immediately. There were a total of six Tigers in La Gleize. SS-Untersturmführer Rolf Reiser recalls that cold and misty December day: "After a somewhat quiet night, the enemy hadn't attacked and we had long since become used to the continuous artillery fire, in the morning there followed a steadily intensifying barrage. Communication with the officers in the defensive positions was only still possible by runner. The runners performed indescribable feats that day in the face of murderous artillery fire and in direct sight of the enemy. At 14.00 hours the Americans stopped the barrage fire and launched attacks on all the approach roads with tanks and infantry. All hell had broken loose! Obersturmbannführer Peiper ordered: 'Everyone out to the defense!' We left the command post. Armed with submachine-guns, rifles and Panzerfaust anti-tank weapons, members of tank crews, runners and radio operators went into position in the ruined houses and waited for the enemy. Beside me a sniper kneeled in a niche in the shattered wall of a house and took target practice on the American infantry as they advanced through the ditches. The numerical superiority of the American tanks enabled them to advance down the road from Stoumont and Borgoumont as far as the first houses. After a counterattack and fighting in houses that lasted hours, we were once again able to repel all attacks. With the coming of darkness the enemy broke off the attack and withdrew. Prisoners and wounded from both sides were brought into the few cellars and patched up."

During the described advance by the Americans Tiger 334 destroyed a Sherman near Borgoumont before it was itself put out of action. The crews of Dollinger's and Hantusch's Tigers, which were on the Wérimont farm in the east part of La Gleize, also experienced this attack. Rolf Ehrhardt recalled: "The commanding forward slope position around the farm gave the Americans little encouragement to employ their infantry there. Combat was thus at longer ranges. American tanks often drove up on the opposite slope, on the Coos-Francorchamps road; however, they remained in cover so that they couldn't be reached by the guns of our Tigers. At a range of over a thousand meters they calmly blazed away at us with no danger to themselves. They picked off our infantry from their holes one by one, and especially the men of the army flak, who had dug in with their 20 mm guns in a ground role. Unlike us, they had absolutely no need to conserve ammunition. I can't estimate the resulting casualties, but they were very high. We could only look on, powerless and frustrated.

Then, finally, the situation changed. A number of Shermans drove up on the road on the facing slope. The gun of our Panzer IV was of little significance due to the great range. The extra-long 88 mm guns of the two King Tigers and the 75 mm guns of the Panthers would have an easy time with the Shermans, which were definitely inferior at that range. Was it a feeling of revenge? Yes, but there was certainly also the desire to finally see a success of one's own. The American unit was spotted in good time and they let it approach to a favorable firing position. Now the firefight could begin. After the first shot by one of the Tigers missed, the Shermans unexpectedly made an about face and opened up with a rapid fire. This caused me to flee into the cellar from my observation post on the second floor. From there we followed the battle by sound. American shells whizzed through the house. The cellar was overfilled with men waiting for a lull in the firing to count the knocked-out Shermans. Mortar and bits of stone fell gently from the cellar roof. The discharges from the super guns of our Tigers were easily distinguishable from the impacting enemy shells. In our minds every shot by an eighty-eight was a hit.

Suddenly the Tiger commander Hantusch burst into the cellar, both hands pressed to his head, and shouted: 'That was Hantusch's last roar!' His Tiger had taken several hits which so shook the sensitive weapons system that the electrical firing mechanism was knocked out. A further hit on the cupola injured Hantusch slightly in the head and he was forced to abandon the smoking tank, which might have gone up in flames at any minute. Minutes later a second Tiger commander, Obersturmführer Dollinger, bleeding heavily from his head, came into the cellar without saying a word. After a dressing had been applied he related that the smoke from firing had made target observation and accurate firing impossible. The rain of enemy shells prevented any chance for a hit. The numerical superiority of eight to ten Shermans and their nonstop rapid fire negated the superior weapons of our tanks. Dollinger's Tiger also took a hit which 'amputated' the front third of its gun. We were all severely depressed and realized that everything was reversed and turning against us in this awful hole. Our highest trump card had failed when we needed it most. What good it would have done those desperate men to experience a success, even one with no tactical value. And so a despondency became noticeable which previously hadn't been so openly discernable. The daily losses, the absence of all the necessary things and the failed air drop spread discouragement. What would the next day bring?"

The commander of the 2nd Company, SS-Hauptsturmführer Rolf Möbius, sat with his Tiger in a garden in La Gleize. He spotted an American tank at a distance of 2,400 meters and ordered his gunner to open fire from that range. Even at that range the second shot was a direct hit. At about 17.00 the fighting began to die down gradually, darkness began to fall. Unlike previous days, however, the sky was clear, which gave the men hope for the coming night. The roar of aircraft engines was heard at about 20.00 and two Ju 52s appeared with the promised supplies. Due to the small size of the target area in La Gleize and the effects of the enemy anti-aircraft fire, the majority of the supply canisters fell in no-man's land, coming down south of La Gleize on the slope which fell away to the Amblève. Few fell into the hands of Peiper's men and efforts to recover the others failed. The situation of the defenders of the pocket became ever more difficult, the outlook for supply was hopeless.

During the night pioneers began building a makeshift bridge west of Stavelot. In the morning the Ist Battalion, 1st SS Panzer-Grenadier Regiment attacked north from the line Rénardmont-Ster, while the IIIrd Battalion set out to advance through Petit Spai to Coreux in order to reach La Gleize via Coo. While the Ist Battalion's attack did not get far, the IIIrd Battalion reached Petit Coo, where it was attacked from the east and west and forced to halt. Faced with this news, SS-Obersturmbannführer Hansen reached the difficult decision to call off the attack and go over to the defensive.

SS-Sturmmannführer Knittel gave Oberscharführer Wendt the task of blasting free soldiers of the reconnaissance battalion surrounded at the west end of Stavelot. The surrounded men were in the cellar of a house whose upper floors were occupied by the Americans. There was heavy fighting in the interior of the house. Knittel explained the exact location of the house to Wendt, after which Tiger 133 moved off. Let us read the commander's own statements concerning the action: "I drove in the direction of Stavelot and placed a high-explosive shell near the house that was described to me in order to draw out the enemy. I watched for a while, saw nothing and drove back to the command post. I reported what had happened to Sturmbannführer Knittel. He passed me the telephone and said, 'Speak to the men yourself.' There was still a telephone line to our comrades. The situation in the house had not changed. I once again set out for Stavelot, intending once again to try my best. Fifty meters from the entrance to the town my driver suddenly turned the tank, the intercom was no longer working. At full speed my driver raced back past the command post in the direction of the Petit Spai bridge. We landed in the ditch about one hundred meters in front of it. Only then did I realize the cause of the sudden about face by my driver. We had taken a hit in the turret ring, where the turret is mounted on the hull. The upper hull armor is five centimeters thick there. The shell was deflected downwards into the hull, tearing off the driver's hatch. The radio operator, Panzerschütze Hans Keck, was killed. Shrapnel damaged the transmission. As steering and shifting are hydraulic, fluid pressure fell rapidly, hydraulic fluid ran out and the tank went out of control. The Tiger was completely immobilized, but we could still shoot."

Peiper learned from one of the last radioed orders to reach him in La Gleize that Hansen's relief attempt had failed. The men of the Panzergruppe were sitting 'like a mouse in a trap," as Heinz von Westernhagen drastically, but accurately, characterized the situation. There was a conference in Peiper's command post, a massive cellar room; he, Poetschke, Diefenthal and von Westernhagen had a frank discussion concerning the hopeless situation. They were unanimous in their assessment of their own chances. Peiper radioed the division for permission to break out. Apparently several transmissions failed to reach the division, as no acknowledgement was forthcoming. Peiper recalled that a radio message arrived from the division that day with the following advisory: "Six operational King Tigers at the east entrance to Stavelot. Where shall we send them?"—"By air to La Gleize' was my answer." Night fell over the exhausted men in La Gleize; light snow began falling.

Compared to the days that had preceded it, 23 December 1944 passed quietly. Apart from the phosphorous shells fired by the American artillery, the defenders had no difficult attacks to tight off that day. The fighting of the previous days had destroyed much of the village, only the massive cellar rooms offered protection against the impacting shells. Like the rest of the tanks in the pocket, the Tigers had neither fuel nor ammunition. The food supply finally ran out. Toward midday SS-Oberführer Mohnke gave the order for the breakout. Following initial reservations on the part of the Sixth SS Panzer Army, the Ist SS Panzer Corps was informed that the decision lay with the division. Peiper was informed of the location of the 1st SS Panzer-Grenadier Regiment's main line of resistance by radio. In La Gleize preparations for the breakout began. Peiper issued his final instructions at a command briefing held in the afternoon. The hopes of the men now rested on Peiper, they all trusted him implicitly.

Rolf Ehrhardt frequently made the trip from the Wèrimont farm to Peiper's command post: "I made the trek to Peiper's command post approximately twenty to thirty times in those days leading up to 23 December. An American anti-tank gun had ranged in on the lowest-lying part of the route and it sent me into the dirt more often than I liked. With time I saw through the Amis' trick and all went well. Now a few words about the armored group's 'main command post' in La Gleize. Not far from the church, in a house on the right side of the street, from whose rear windows one must have been able to see the villages of Roanne and Borgoumont to the north, was 'Command Post Peiper.' The vaulted cellar had been built with the usual natural stone and wasn't very spacious. Its one special feature was a very large table which consisted of a slab of stone as thick as a man's fist. In this room was where Obersturmbannführer Peiper was to be found when he wasn't out somewhere with his men. In the final days of the action at La Gleize I was in the cellar several times, during conferences as escort to Hauptsturmführer Klingelhöfer and even more often as a messenger or receiver of orders. The radio station was in the cellar of a house on the way to the farm. All that was installed in the command post was a field telephone.

When the cellar first came into use, I set up a small cast iron stove at Peiper's request. It worked splendidly in spite of the improvised draft with several stovepipes stuck through the tiny cellar window. Peiper thanked me and took the opportunity to ask about my later career plans. I said, 'Perhaps TFO.' It was of course a joke. In the forces the Engineering Officer Motor Vehicles was called the TFK (Technischer Führer Kraftfahrwesen). Peiper laughed heartily at my version, TFO (Technical Officer Stoves). Sadly my sorry piece of work had one uncomfortable drawback. As soon as the first smoke left the pipes it was spotted by the Amis, who fired on the house with howitzers or mortars. Perhaps the poor fellows were freezing just like us and were jealous? My effort could therefore only lend some warmth to the cellar during the night.

The command post resembled a busy railway station. Messengers and officers came and went almost nonstop. Their faces were not just stress-filled, but very serious and hard as well. Peiper was calmness personified. He scarcely ever betrayed an emotion. I saw his face up close when he was told that an infantry officer to whom he was very close had been killed. The mouth narrowed, as much as that was possible. His eyes became slits, he clenched his fists as if he wanted to break something, but only for a few seconds. Then the tension melted and he was as always. He asked his questions in a businesslike fashion, gave orders. No swearing, no harsh words. That was Peiper, who even in the hopeless phase in La Gleize gave every last one of his men support and security, as he had throughout his entire career, in a way that few other officers in the forces could.

I met another interesting personality in the cellar. I happened to be present when American Lieutenant-Colonel McGown, staff officer of the US 30th Infantry Division, was led into the command post as a prisoner by Oberscharführer Max Bergmann. The tall officer had to stand stooped over in the low cellar door when he introduced himself with a casual-correct salute. Peiper stood up from the table and extended McGown his hand. I understood nothing of the ensuing discussion, because it was conducted in English, but I instinctively felt that here were two personalities who had much in common in attitude, correctness, education and way of thinking. The correctness of this impression was confirmed in 1946 by McGown's appearance at the Malmedy Trial."

The battalion adjutant, SS-Untersturmführer Kalinowsky, also talked to Lieutenant-Colonel McGown. The adjutant and the American lieutenant-colonel understood one another. McGown told him that he wanted to invite all the German officers from La Gleize to visit him at his farm in the USA after the war. SS-Sturmmann Hubert Heil, the radio operator from Dollinger's Tiger 213, met McGown in Peiper's cellar while delivering a message. Jochen Peiper concluded an agreement with him that all captured Americans should be given their freedom after the successful breakout; in return the German wounded were to be handed over to the Leibstandarte by the Americans. Both officers signed a document to that effect. Peiper described the American as ". . . a front-line soldier among front-line soldiers. We talked less about ideologies and more about the tragedy and folly that people like us had to fight against each other. In this particular case I convinced McGown that we still had the situation under control and that we had just been recalled. He smiled and said, 'All right colonel, I've always looked forward to a ride in a King Tiger!' Little did he know that he would have to go on foot."

All weapons and equipment that could be carried were to be divided among the men of the battle group. The vehicles and tanks were wrecked, not blown up, as is often claimed. That would have tipped off the Americans to the planned breakout. Throughout the afternoon the men in La Gleize had to repulse several more attacks made with armor support. Tanks which broke into the northeast part of the village were destroyed from close range by panzer-grenadiers of the armored troop carrier battalion. As of 22 December the days in La Gleize were counted as infantry close combat days for the men of the Tiger battalion, while 17–21 December were confirmed as tank combat days. There was no slackening of the artillery fire, but the men had long since grown used to it. In the evening the planned breakout was discussed at length in Peiper's cellar and the last details were finalized. The route was to follow the road south in the direction of Basse-Bodeux through Trois-Ponts. The breakout was scheduled to begin at 02.00 hours on 24 December. The password was "Merry Christmas."

One of the officers participating in Operation Greif by Skorzeny's 150th Panzer Brigade, a navy Oberleutnant, was ordered to scout a crossing over the Amblève and possible American pickets in that sector. He and his two men returned after dark and reported that the railway viaduct and the somewhat lower old wooden bridge over the Amblève might be suitable for the breakout. An American security detachment situated in a linesman's cabin between the viaduct and the tunnel lying to the east would have to be eliminated first. This mission, too, was taken care of by the men of the 150th Panzer Brigade.

In Engelsdorf were some elements of the 501st SS Panzer Battalion, among them SS-Unterscharführer Erwin Reisch of the workshop company: "In Engelsdorf we completed an engine change on a Tiger at the entrance to the village in spite of harassing fire from the enemy. On Christmas Eve Sepp Hafner and SS-Obersturmführer Reinhold Wichert arrived with a maintenance section in captured vehicles; they also delivered the Führer Christmas cakes. The group of vehicles was hit by the nocturnal harassing fire and an oxygen bottle was blown into the burning house where the cakes were stored. The cakes were saved and in spite of everything there was still a booze-up that night."

SS-Sturmmann Eduard Kastl,
Workshop Company. Missing
since August 1944.

SS-Rottenführer Rudolf
Vornberger, 3rd Company,
missing since February 1945.

SS-Sturmmann Otto Büchner,
Workshop Company, missing
in the Ardennes since January
1945.

SS-Sturmmann Willi Kalender, Workshop Company, missing since January 1945.

SS-Panzerschütz Konrad Sollfrank, Headquarters Company, missing since March 1945.

SS-Sturmmann Franz Gilly, Workshop Company.

SS-Unterscharführer Peter
Schnitzer, 1st Company Account
and Pay NCO, missing since
March 1945.

SS-Panzerschütze Gottfried
Salzmann, Headquarters
Company, missing since March
1945.

SS-Hauptscharführer Rolf von
Westernhagen, platoon
commander in the 3rd
Company, 501st SS Panzer
Battalion. Spent ten years in
Soviet captivity.

SS-Obersturmführer
Jürgen Wessel, 1st
Company.

SS-Obersturmbannführer
Hein von Westernhagen,
battalian commander.

SS-Hauptsturmführer
Heinz Birnschein,
3rd Company.

SS-Hauptsturmführer
Rolf Möbius, 2nd
Company.

On the morning of 16 December 1944 the Tigers of the 501st SS Panzer Battalion drove into their jump-off positions for the Ardennes Offensive. Here a Tiger in Tondorf.

Tiger 008, the adjutant's vehicle. The significance of the "G" on the bow plate beneath the machine-gun port is unknown.

A King Tiger of the 501st SS Panzer Battalion in the first days of the Ardennes offensive.

The King Tigers roll through Tondorf, 15 December 1944. The ground, which was thawed and soft on top and frozen hard underneath, made for hard work for the tank drivers.

Tiger 222 in Tondorf.

The same Tiger 222 near Kaiserbarracke with paratroopers of the 14th Company, 6th Parachute Regiment hitching a ride.

The crew of Tiger 222 received an enthusiastic welcome from the local children in Deidenheim, Belgium. At left a member of 222's crew has been given a refreshment.

Tiger 008 on the march. The tank commander has placed the anti-aircraft machine-gun on the ring of the turret cupola.

The driver of SS-Obersturmführer Wessel's tank lost control of the vehicle in Stavelot. The Tiger slid into house No. 8 on the sloping Rue Haute Rivage.

These photos show
Tiger 222 of the 2nd
Company, 501st SS
Panzer Battalion.

Near Kaiserbarracke with paratroopers Oberjäger Koos and Lentz and
Obergefreiten Löwe and Hess.

This photo and the left photo on the next page show the bridge in Stavelot; the last four Tigers of the battalion's 1st Company crossed on 18/12/1944. Later it proved impossible to cross in the face of the massed resistance of the Americans. SS-Oberscharführer Kurt Sowa's Tiger 222 was knocked out on the approach to the bridge on 20/12/1944. This Tiger can be seen in the center photo on the extreme left in front of the bridge as well as the two following photos.

In Deidenberg
on 18/12/1944.

Tiger 222.

Kurt Sowa's
Tiger 222.

THE BREAKOUT FROM LA GLEIZE

The breakout began during the night of 24 December 1944 at 02.00 hours. The wounded who could still walk were taken along. Of the approximately 3,000 men of Panzergruppe Peiper, 850 set out on this hopeful march to freedom. The members of the 501st SS Panzer Battalion did not participate in the breakout as a group. The breakout route took the men south as far as the viaduct, then they crossed the wooden bridge and entered the Bois des Stalons. The men tramped through the dense forest in knee-deep snow until they had left behind them the extended slope of Brume Hill. From there they saw the American artillery pounding the village, as it did every morning. The flashes of gunfire were clearly visible. The long column silently moved off again, each man lost in his own thoughts.

They were all held together by their determination to survive, and that goal overshadowed all the deprivations, the hunger and the icy cold. Rest breaks were called after longer stretches. Peiper walked down the column and spoke with the men, cheering them up and giving them courage. Once again he was leading by example. Elsewhere, during a brief rest, Heinz von Westernhagen sat exhausted on the ground, surrounded by several members of his battalion. They talked quietly about the journey yet to come. The battalion commander was confident that they could escape the American encirclement and reach their own lines again.

Patrols scouted the terrain ahead of the main column in order to avoid surprises. At 10.00 hours Brume was reported occupied by the enemy. Peiper subsequently led his group back to the north and then veered west near the large bend in the Amblève abreast of Grand Coo. The battle group thus made a circle, left Beaulou to the right and marched in its initial direction in order to skirt Brume with plenty of room to spare. The long march took the men through the extensive forests of the Bois Tourbaileux to the Waldweiler Henri-Moulin. Since the first signs of exhaustion were becoming evident, a longer rest stop was laid on in Henri-Moulin. Many didn't even know that it was Christmas Eve. The circumstances certainly weren't conducive to a Christmas-like mood.

The route was extremely taxing and was made even more difficult by the up and down nature of the terrain. With darkness falling, the group set off again in biting cold. While crossing the Trois-Ponts-Basse-Bodeux road they ran into an American roadblock guarded by tanks and infantry. The enemy immediately opened fire. There was a brief flurry of hand grenades and Panzerfaust rounds and the enemy was overcome. Aware that this encounter might have alerted other American units, the troops subsequently readied themselves to meet the enemy anywhere. The trek led through the forest on Mont Fosse into the high ground of Bergeval.

The mountain road leading there turned out to be held by the enemy. Once again a brief skirmish opened the way. Lieutenant-Colonel McGown used this unobserved moment to flee. He later came forward as a defense witness for those members of Panzergruppe Peiper on trial in Dachau; however, the American military tribunal gave no credence to his statements and instead accused him of cooperating with the enemy. Meanwhile the march group had begun to lose its cohesion in places. The group in which the two company commanders Wessel and Birnschein were marching tried to ambush an American transport column in a forest clearing. The attempt failed, however, and the trucks were able to flee in time.

Rolf Ehrhardt recalled this phase of the breakout: "Things went well until we neared the village of Bergeval. So far I had battled my own fatigue through constant activity. I had surely covered more than the normal distance, as I repeatedly shuttled some way up and down the column. In doing so I tried to help comrades who were on the point of falling asleep, encouraged them and used many well-meant lies. Everyone wanted to know how many more kilometers we had to go. In the second night, December 24–25—it may have been between 22.00 hours and midnight—an order was passed down summoning the senior ranking officers to the commander.

Dr. Neumeyer and Klingelhöfer also went to the conference. Time passed, I made my 'watch parade.' But then I slowly grew uneasy, for the conference was lasting much too long. I therefore set out for the head of the column. The tall forest ended in a glade. The men were scattered about this glade in rows and small groups, many slept or dozed. Crossing the glade I came to a spruce thicket and right in front of it was another group of sleeping men. Calling out softly, I entered the thicket. There was no answer—absolute quiet! Back to the sleeping men, I shook them awake roughly and asked where the others were.

In the pale moonlight I could see the dismay on their faces. Contact lost! The point gone! Peiper gone! The news made its way to the rear with unbelievable speed. At that moment I suddenly heard voices from the other side of the thicket. Shouts, the sound of a motor and two or three pistol shots. I cautiously entered the bushes and after a few minutes came to a paved road. On the other side, approximately 150 meters away, stood a house. That meant danger. As a result of the loss of contact with the point, the formerly very disciplined group had almost fallen into disorder. Naked fear was visible in many of the faces. If we met the Amis now we would be done for. I tried to find an officer to assume command and restore order. None felt interested. All the SS-Hauptsturm-führer, apart from the badly wounded and feverish Hauptsturm-führer Birnschein, were with the lost point. Requests for a map produced one. I was able to figure out roughly where we were and in which direction our lines might lie.

SS-Untersturmführer Koch of the 2nd Company, who so far had been walking at the rear of the column, seized the initiative. He led us through the thicket and across the road; we paused briefly to reassemble on the other side. Koch indicated the direction and the uncontrolled mob once again became a reasonable, disciplined group."

The long march went on through the snowy, ice-cold forests. The men heard the sound of American artillery fire and guessed that their own lines couldn't be much farther. The American front line ran beneath the ridge in the valley of the Salm. The men of the Panzergruppe climbed the slope, crossed the railway line in front of the Salm and broke through the American positions from behind. Then they reached the Salm, whose level had risen as a result of the snow that had come down. The men placed stones on the river bottom, over which the non-swimmers reached the other side. In other places it was possible simply to wade across the river. Birnschein and Wessel and their group reached the bank of the Salm in the twilight of 25 December. They were north of the main body of the march group. They cautiously crossed the river, the ice-cold water up to their hips. At dawn on Christmas Day Birnschein and Wessel reached the command post of SS-Obersturmbannführer Hansen (1st SS Panzer-Grenadier Regiment).

SS-Obersturmbannführer von Westernhagen and his group broke through the enemy lines at about midnight and reached the Salm. There they came under accurate machine-gun fire. At once von Westernhagen dove into the icy flood. The Salm was too deep to wade there and so the exhausted men had to swim ". . . a raging torrent under furious machine-gun fire," as von Westernhagen later recalled. The Obersturmbannführer personally dragged a wounded man with him, and in the morning hours he and his group, which he described as ". . . walking icicles . . .", reached the Leibstandarte Division's command post in Wanne. The men were finally able to get out of their soaking wet, ice-covered, filthy uniforms, and were given clean clothes and food by their comrades. Many fell into a deathlike sleep immediately afterward, others described their experiences of the past days in the pocket and on the march to freedom. Everyone badly needed sleep; Jochen Peiper wrote in retrospect: "During the entire offensive my people and I ate very little, slept even less and had no chance to shave. I venture to say that I went nine days with no sleep at all and that anyone who had taken along a second uniform would have been punished."

At about the same time on the morning of 25 December 1944 SS-Oberscharführer Wendt was ordered to the reconnaissance battalion's command post. From SS-Sturmbannführer Knittel he learned that the Amblève had to be crossed in a northerly direction by 09.00 hours as part of a straightening of the front. Wendt sent his loader, SS-Sturmmann Heinz Noß, to SS-Oberscharführer Brandt to deliver to him the order to withdraw.

When Noß reached "Captain" Brandt's Tiger 132 near the bridge in Petit Spai, the almost two-meter-tall Jürgen Brandt jumped down from the tank. It was completely quiet that morning. Noß was about to inform him about the order to withdraw when a single shell fell right in front of the men. Both were killed on the spot. SS-Unterscharführer Otterbein subsequently drove through the Amblève with Brandt's crew and after negotiating a steep slope arrived at the house that housed his unit's command post. They brought Brandt's body with them. Wendt and his driver prepared their immobilized tank for demolition by placing charges in the gun barrel and engine compartment. Then they crossed the Amblève and also made it to the command post. Though they were able to observe their Tiger for some time, from the distance they were unable to see any detonation. Tiger 133 had nevertheless been destroyed by the explosive charge; the force of the explosion blew off the turret. The next day the men rejoined their company.

Other tanks that had broken down also regained contact with their unit on 25 December 1944. SS-Oberscharführer Paul Klose of the Dollinger Platoon (2nd Company) had lost contact with his company days earlier. While en route he and his Tiger had become separated from the march unit on account of trans-mission trouble. He was later ordered to cover the 150th Panzer Brigade (Skorzeny) in front of Malmedy, where he sat quite alone, with no supporting infantry, on the road. Klose and his crew saw no little action.

The Tiger of SS-Unterscharführer Otto Blase rejoined the 3rd Company on Christmas Day. Blase had been stranded near Engelgau, short of Tondorf, by a mechanical breakdown on 16 December 1944. His driver was SS-Rottenführer Paul Rohweder. On 18 December SS-Hauptscharführer Rolf von Westernhagen arrived in the Engelsdorf area with several tanks that had broken down; from there he moved on to the Schlomerforter Mill. There he was reunited with his company commander. Soon after reaching the German lines SS-Hauptsturmführer Birnschein met the Senior NCO of the 3rd Company, SS-Hauptscharführer Hack, who had meanwhile brought back some of the broken-down tanks. The men from the pocket had little time to recover after rejoining their units. The battalion assembled in the Recht-Engelsdorf area after which it moved into a wood east of Vielsalm to carry out much-needed repairs.

SS-Obersturmbannführer von Westernhagen reviewed the recent fighting in a letter: "As always, this time we were once again in the worst mess.

We were the attack spearhead and were able to break through the American positions on the first day and drive deep into the hinterland. It was a wild chase with terrific shootouts—in the end, however, we were cut off and surrounded. For five days we sat like a mouse in a trap with no food and little ammunition, being pounded by the American artillery. Early on 24 December we decided to break out—it succeeded—we marched in the American rear for thirty hours, broke through their positions from behind on Christmas Eve, and swam a raging torrent under furious machine-gun fire. We crossed the river by summoning up all our remaining strength, but many brave soldiers died there because they hadn't the strength or their hearts failed. I dragged one wounded man with me, and on the morning of Christmas Day we reached our own lines, walking icicles. We were able to tweak the nose of the Americans and preserve 850 soldiers for the German Army; that is our pride. Now we are preparing ourselves for fresh deeds."

The 1st Company handed over its tanks complete to the 2nd and 3rd Companies, as it had before in Normandy, and left the battalion. Under SS-Hauptsturmführer Möbius the operational Tigers were combined into a battle group bearing his name. The 3rd Company was led by SS-Untersturmführer Amselgruber, as Birnschein was still feeling the affects of the wound suffered on 21 December 1944. Möbius had approximately fifteen tanks at his disposal. Tiger tanks 204 (Möbius), 213 (Dollinger), 221 (Hantusch), and three others had been lost in La Gleize. Tiger 334 was knocked out two kilometers north of La Gleize near Borgoumont.

The 1st Company commander's tank (105) remained in Stavelot. Tiger 222 of SS-Oberscharführer Sowa was knocked out in front of the bridge in Stavelot and another nearby. Tiger 332 broke down between Trois-Ponts and Coos, while 008, the signals officer's tank, was lost between Stavelot and Trois-Ponts. Furthermore, Tigers III (SS-Untersturm-führer Henniges) and 312 broke down. SS-Oberscharführer Wendt's 133 was blown up near the Petit Spai bridge. There is no concrete information concerning the sites of further losses.

BATTLE GROUP MÖBIUS IN ACTION NEAR BASTOGNE, 27 DECEMBER 1944–24 JANUARY 1945

On 28 December 1944 Army Group B ordered the accelerated transfer of the 1st SS Panzer Division so that it might attack and capture the important traffic junction of Bastogne together with the 3rd Panzer-Grenadier Division and the 167th Volksgrenadier Division. There are no reliable sources concerning the employment of Kampfgruppe Möbius. The Tigers probably took part in the attacks on Bastogne on 30 and 31 December 1944, which failed to achieve the desired success.

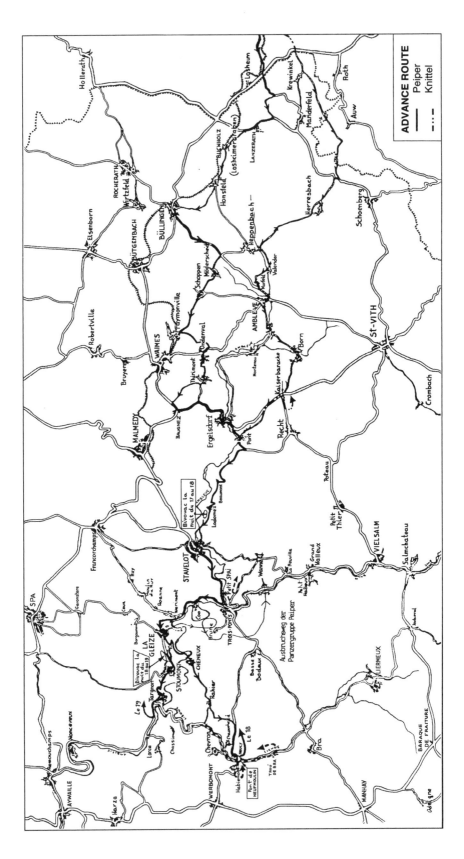

ADVANCE ROUTE

— Peiper

··· Knittel

At the beginning of January 1945 Obergefreiter Sepp Reiner of the 9th Parachute Regiment encountered eleven King Tigers in this area. One of the commanders recognized him from Honsfeld and asked how things had gone for him and his group of paratroopers. Reiner answered that only three men were left. When he asked what the Tigers were going to do, the crews, who appeared dejected and depressed, told him that they had to blow up their Tigers due to lack of fuel.

THE ARDENNES OFFENSIVE—A LOOK BACK

An attempt had been made to reach the Maas through the concentrated use of men and materiel. Why did this effort fail in spite of the powerful armored forces committed? The chosen area of attack, the Ardennes, consisted of a low mountain range with wooded hills and deeply-eroded river valleys. There was no room for the combat vehicles to take cover beside climbing or descending sections of the narrow, often twisting, roads. Furthermore, most of the roads ran in a north-south direction, while Panzergruppe Peiper was supposed to advance in an east-west direction. Consequently it was repeatedly forced to take to unpaved secondary roads. The more vehicles—especially armored troop carriers and tanks—that drove over these roads, the worse their condition became. The main problem, however, was the inadequate deliveries of supplies to the armored units. The vehicles were issued enough fuel for only 175 kilometers. Some crews of the Tiger battalion's 3rd Company carried drums of fuel on their tanks. Fuel from American stocks captured by Panzergruppe Peiper solved this problem for a few days at the beginning of the attack.

The panzer-grenadiers were unable to exploit the breakthrough by Panzergruppe Peiper, because they could not be moved forward quickly enough on account of transportation problems on the inadequate, clogged roads. As a result of the blocking of Stavelot by the Americans, no more German units were able to reach Peiper's armored group which had advanced far ahead. The Panzergruppe had to advance single-file on the narrow roads. This was to the advantage of the Americans and made it easier for them to defend. Several times bridges were blown up right in front of the armored spearhead, which forced Peiper to turn to alternate routes. Many tanks were lost before they ever saw action. Contact was severed to the following Battle Groups Knittel, Hansen and Sandig and the exposed Panzergruppe Peiper was cut off and encircled.

Six days after the start of the offensive the weather cleared and the enemy air force, which held air superiority above the Ardennes, bombed and strafed the armored group, attacked the trailing battle groups and significantly disrupted supply traffic. The German side was incapable of suppressing the oppressive Allied air superiority. From the very beginning Peiper's main problem consisted of finding suitable crossings over the Ambève, Salm and Lienne Rivers. Blown bridges repeatedly forced him to detour and use other routes. It became a race against time that he could not win. His losses could not be replaced, while the enemy grew stronger. His daring advance covered the open north flank of the Fifth Panzer Army, but in doing so he drew onto himself all the American forces brought in from the north.

Thanks to Peiper's unique personality, his determination to hold out and the courage of his soldiers, his surrounded armored group was able to escape the encirclement in a thirty-hour forced march and return to its division. Completely worn out and exhausted, the men reached their own lines on Christmas Day, bringing with them only what they could carry. Nevertheless, their courage and their morale remained unbroken. Looking back at La Gleize Jochen Peiper, who received the Swords, wrote: ". . . what a pitiful exhibition by three US divisions; they failed to destroy a small German battle group without fuel and ammunition, then the latter blew up all its materiel before it marched through the sleeping enemy, unafraid and unbroken."

BRIEF REFIT IN THE COLOGNE AREA, 2–24 JANUARY 1945

Following the Ardennes offensive the Leibstandarte, and with it the Tiger battalion, were pulled out of the front and transferred into the Cologne area. Several repaired Tiger IIs were delivered to the 2nd and 3rd Companies there, raising the battalion's strength to twenty-six Tigers. There were no changes in command positions in the companies and platoons. After recovering from his wound SS-Hauptsturmführer Birnschein once again assumed his post as commander of 3rd Company. The Senior NCO of the 2nd Company, SS-Hauptscharführer Konradt, had become a tank commander at the beginning of the year and his place had been taken by SS-Unterseharführer Mölly. These two now traded places again, Mölly once again becoming a tank commander. The 501st SS Panzer Battalion held a belated Christmas celebration on 2 January 1945. The men recuperated from the stress of recent past and wrote their first letters home.

SS-Untersturmführer Kalinowsky wrote: ". . . For eight days I've been out of the pocket in which we were encircled four days, having luckily reached the German lines after a thirty-hour march from the 24th to the 25th. We now have a chance to rest and thus also the opportunity to write . . . On 18 December I was wounded for the fourth time, bullet splinters from an English flier, which thank God only did minor damage to my neck and right upper arm. There were several difficult days when we fought our way through in the confined space of the crucible, but we made it, and we were given the best possible Christmas present. Healthwise I am well, apart from indigestion, and the coming days which we hope to spend in complete seclusion, will give us time to recuperate. The day before yesterday a V 1 which had missed its target came down three-hundred meters in front of the command post and shook our house somewhat. I can now understand why the Tommies and Americans are afraid of these things. Our Christmas celebration is being repeated tonight and I hope that the Tommies don't upset our plans."

While the panzer companies were only partially outfitted with new vehicles, the Tiger battalion flak received all new equipment. In actions on every front the flak had steadily evolved out of its original role, that of anti-aircraft defense, into a valuable infantry support weapon. An anti-aircraft system had to be developed for the fast-moving armored units which could keep up with the assault groups in order to provide the necessary support against infantry targets as well as a defense against attacking fighter-bombers. The Tiger battalion's existing flak, mounted on the eight-tonne prime mover, were completely unprotected. Development led to the installation of a four-barrelled 20 mm Vierlingsflak on the chassis of a Panzer IV, housed in a fully rotating hexagonal turret. Even though the turret was open on top, this anti-aircraft tank, or Flakpanzer, represented the best solution so far and was an immediate success. The Flakpanzer armed with the 20 mm Vierlingsflak 38 was known as the Wirbelwind, or "Whirlwind". Another anti-aircraft tank based on the Panzer IV chassis was the Ostwind, or "East Wind," which was armed with a single 37 mm Flak 36.

In November 1944, the existing Flak Platoon of the 501st SS Panzer Battalion, which was without guns, transferred from Wilhelmsdorf to Schwabhausen in Thuringia, where the NCOs and men took part in an armored flak course. The men spent Christmas on a moving train. On 27 December 1944 they arrived in Schloss Holte and transferred direct to Brüggen, near Cologne, where conversion training was to continue. The Flak Platoon thus played no part in the Ardennes offensive.

The former CO of the platoon, SS-Oberscharführer Kurt Fickert, assumed command of the newly-formed Wirbelwind platoon. Instead of its previous three anti-aircraft guns, the platoon now had four anti-aircraft tanks. The crew of the Flakpanzer consisted of five men with the vehicle commander also acting as gunner, as the four-barrelled Vierlingsflak required two loaders. Compared to the combination of four-barrelled flak and eight-tonne prime mover used in Normandy, the Flakpanzer possessed a much lower silhouette as the gun's substructure was enclosed within the hull. The gun crew was much better protected by steel plates than on the open prime mover. Mounted on the tank's turret ring, the gun turret consisted of steel plates sixteen millimeters thick. The four Wirbelwind anti-aircraft tanks were commanded by SS-Unterscharführer Braun, Werner Müller and Pusch, and SS-Rottenführer Blumberg. Also formed at that time was another flak platoon equipped with the Ostwind; placed in command of the platoon was SS-Oberscharführer Kastelik, who was new to the battalion. Four Ostwind anti-aircraft tanks increased the 4th Company's firepower considerably. The configuration of the 25mm armored sidewalls of this anti-aircraft tank allowed the 37 mm weapon to be depressed to the lowest possible barrel position while rotating through 360 degrees. Two of the Ostwind were commanded by Rottenführer who came over from the Luftwaffe, the others by SS-Unterscharführer Dietrich and Rätzer. The two flak platoon commanders had no tanks of their own, instead they operated from VW Schwimmwagen amphibious vehicles. As a result of these changes the battalion now had at its disposal two flak platoons equipped with a total of eight anti-aircraft tanks (28 barrels). The Armored Reconnaissance Platoon under SS-Hauptscharführer Appelt and the Pioneer Platoon under SS-Untersturmführer Brauer were also completely reequipped. The crews of the Tigers finally had a rest and were able to recover from their recent ordeal. The company commanders collected the reports on the killed and missing and notified the families.

On 13 January 1945 SS-Oberscharführer Jürgen Brandt of the 1st Company was decorated with the German Cross in Gold. The huge Holsteiner, who was generally referred to as "Captain", did not live to receive the decoration. He had been killed by a shell near the Petit-Spai bridge, west of Stavelot, on 25 December 1944. Brandt was one of the original members of the Leibstandarte Tiger company and had taken part in every action in the east and west, first as a tank commander and later as a platoon commander.

Brandt destroyed at least forty-seven enemy tanks in actions on all fronts. In his endorsement of the recommendation for the award of the German Cross in Gold to Brandt, SS-Hauptsturmführer Möbius wrote: "Oberscharführer Brandt has acquitted himself exceptionally well, be it in the Western Campaign of 1940, in the Eastern Campaign in 1941/42 and 1943, or on the invasion front, first as a gunner in the assault gun battalion of the Leibstandarte SS Adolf Hitler, later as a tank commander and platoon commander in the Tiger battalion of the Ist SS Panzer Corps. Brandt is a soldier who took part in almost every action and achieved decisive success." He was one of the old hands who, with his experience, was irreplaceable.

The men of the Tiger battalion followed the Wehrmacht communiques pensively. The general development of the military situation gave cause for serious concern. Men with relatives in Eastern Germany were relieved when they received news that their families had fled to the west. Reports of the crimes committed by the Red Army, which set foot on German soil in East Prussia in 1944, were too dreadful. The ethnic Germans had already lost their homes; many were left with no news concerning the fate of their relatives. The men of the Tiger battalion were in low spirits as they prepared for the coming action. The Soviets were at the gates of Königsberg, near Elbing and closing in on the Baltic coast; the Oder line between Stettin and Breslau was in great danger. The Soviets had only paused to catch their breath as they prepared for the assault on Berlin.

Tank of the 501st SS Panzer Battalion followed by two dispatch riders. At the side of the road captured Americans, members of the 99th Infantry Division.

In December 1944 the 4th Company, 501st SS Panzer Battalion was reequipped with two flak platoons. Here the "Wirbelwind" anti-aircraft tank, a four-barrelled 20mm flak on the chassis of a Panzer IV.

The "Ostwind", a 37mm flak on a Panzer IV chassis.

Abandoned King Tiger in back of Stavelot.

Tiger 008, disabled between Stavelot and Trois Ponts. The muzzle brakes are ventilated.

SS-Untersturmführer Hantusch's Tiger 221 on the grounds of the Werimont farm.

Tiger 334 stopped an American attack in Borgoumont on 22/12/1944. Here American troops are seen examining the Tiger, which was subsequently towed to the side of the road.

Two knocked-out Tigers of the 2nd Company.

Buildings on the Werimont farm, where Hantusch's Tiger and SS-Obersturmführer Döllinger's Tiger 213 were put out of action. A chance hit shot off half of 213's gun. Since 1951, Tiger 213 has been in the town center of La Gleize. It is seen here with its amputated cannon, which has since been replaced.

Tiger 204 of the 2nd Company, 501st SS Panzer Battalion being inspected by American troops.

The Americans carried out tests on this Tiger with their Bazooka anti-tank weapon on the Vielle-Voie Road in La Gleize, but were unable to penetrate the bow plate.

Knocked-out or abandoned Tiger in January 1945.

Tiger crew of the battalion's 2nd Company. *From left:* SS-Sturmmann Stark, SS-Unterscharführer Mankewitz, SS-Rottenführer Schenk, SS-Unterscharführer Grätzer and SS-Rottenführer Schmidt.

Tiger 133, which was blown up near the bridge at Petit Spai (the blown bridge may be seen on the right) on 25/12/1944.

A 3rd Company Tiger abandoned in the Ardennes.

In April 1945 SS-Untersturmführer Rolf Schamp returned to the 501st SS Panzer Battalion and became its last operations officer. He had earlier served as a gunner in the 13th Tiger Company from 1942 until the end of 1943 as an SS-Sturmmann.

The 501st SS Panzer Battalion had been part of Jochen Peiper's Leibstandarte Panzer Regiment since the Ardennes offensive. Peiper was decorated with the Knight's Cross with Oak Leaves and Swords on 11/1/1945.

On 13/1/1945 SS-Oberscharführer Jürgen "Captain" Brandt was awarded the German Cross in Gold for his accomplishments with the 2nd Company, 501st SS Panzer Battalion. Brandt was killed west of Stavelot 25/12/1944.

Tanks of the Leibstandarte at the Saviz Canal in Hungary in February 1945.

On 14/2/1945
SS-Untersturmführer
Thomas Amselgruber of
the 3rd Company, 501st
SS Panzer Battalion was
decorated with the
German Cross in Gold.

These two photos show members of the 4th Company, 501st SS Panzer Battalion shortly before the German surrender. Despondency and resignation are visible on their faces.

Bobby Warmbrunn as a prisoner of the Americans at
Gmunden am Traunsee in the summer of 1945. Beside
him in the bottom photo is Walter Lau in England, with
his registration number.

Just before the
capitulation.

Bobby Warmbrunn
in the Darmstadt camp.

SS-Obersturmbannführer
Heinz von Westernhagen,
commanding officer of the
501st SS Panzer Battalion,
was killed on 20 March
1945 near Veszprém,
Hungary.

The grave of the commanding officer of the 501st SS Panzer Battalion,
SS-Obersturmbannführer Heinz von Westernhagen in Veszprém, Hungary.
He died on 20 March 1945.

The grave of Michael Wittmann and his crew in the German military cemetery at La Cambe in Normandy.

The Defensive Battle
in Hungary and Austria

Many—including some on the enemy side—expected that the Sixth SS Panzer Army would be included in the defenses of the Reich capital and moved into the area southeast of Berlin. Generaloberst Guderian, Chief of the Army General Staff, requested the inclusion of this potent army. Adolf Hitler had other plans, however. He was intent on launching a well-prepared offensive aimed at retaining the oil region in the Danube-Drau area for German use and hoped that by doing so he would induce the Soviets to shift their attacks from the Berlin area into that region. Preparations were carried out under conditions of great secrecy. The Cottbus-Guben-Forst area was prepared as the Sixth Panzer Army's probable detraining area. SS-Oberstgruppenführer Sepp Dietrich maintained an imaginary army headquarters in Fürstenwalde. In an effort to further conceal German intentions the soldiers of the front-line units were required to remove their cuff titles and the division emblems on tanks and vehicles were overpainted. The divisions were given new designations: the Leibstandarte became the SS Replacement Echelon Totenkopf, the Hitlerjugend Division the SS Replacement Echelon Wiking, and the Ist SS Panzer Corps was now the SS Sector Headquarters South. The 501st SS Panzer Battalion was redesignated as the Training Battalion Totenkopf.

While the units of the 501st SS Panzer Battalion experienced some of the effects of the Allied bombing attacks in their quartering areas, entraining began in January 1945. The Tiger battalion was complete, apart from the 1st Company.

In the final days of December 1944 the 1st Company had handed its tanks to the other companies in the Ardennes and subsequently left the battalion. On 30 December 1944 it set out in its few vehicles to return to Oerlinghausen. The company was harried by fighter-bombers as it drove back to German territory on the autobahn. The men arrived in Oerlinghausen on 31 December, the place they had left one month earlier. Those who had stayed behind prepared an enthusiastic welcome in the town hotel. Since only a brief stay was planned, the NCOs and men were

337

installed in the foyer of the hotel; the officers were also quartered in the hotel. The men of the battalion spent New Year's Eve there. What would the new year have in store for them?

There were few duties in the following days. The men recovered from their recent trials, wrote letters to relatives—some of who were already fleeing the eastern regions of the Reich which lay in the path of the Soviets—, put their uniforms back in order, and waited for new orders. For amusement tobogganing outings were arranged on the Tönsberg; the snow transformed the men into children and in fact many of them were not long out of childhood. On 6 January 1944 SS-Obersturmführer Wessel led a group of 1st Company personnel to Sennelager, where they took charge of six Tiger IIs. The party included tank commanders SS-Oberscharführer Zahner, Steinwender, Salamon, Bode and Franzl and SS-Unterscharführer Otterbein. The party also included SS-Hauptscharführer Michaelis and SS-Unterscharführer Hartwig, Ahrens and Poerner (gunners), SS-Unterscharführer Belbe (radio operator) and SS-Unterscharführer Bingert (driver) and Dannleitner, as well as other NCOs and men of the combat echelon.

The Senior NCO, SS-Hauptscharführer Lüth, SS-Oberscharführer Quenzer (technical sergeant radio), and SS-Unterscharführer Wölfel (maintenance echelon), Mollenhauer (clerk) and Cosyns (kitchen) also went to Sennelager. This part of the company also took charge of the vehicles that had survived the Ardennes campaign. From that day the 1st Company was divided and henceforth existed in two widely-separated locations. Those of the 1st Company who remained behind in the Oerlinghausen town hotel were tank commanders SS-Untersturmführer Buchner and Henniges, SS-Oberscharführer Fritzsche and Wendt and SS-Standartenjunker Staudegger, as well as SS-Unterscharführer Heß, Przibylla and Hermann (gunners), SS-Unterscharführer Beutel, SS-Rottenführer Koch (driver), SS-Unterscharführer Beuer (weapons and equipment) and SS-Unterscharführer Streubel (uniforms). All the remaining enlisted men of the combat echelon were likewise still with the company. Two days later that part of the company, together with the rest of the men left behind since December 1944, moved to Schloss Holte. Among the latter group were SS-Oberscharführer Bobby Woll and SS-Unterscharführer Bobby Warmbrunn. The 1st Company was now led by SS-Untersturmführer Rolf Henniges, SS-Unterscharführer Kurt Rath became Senior NCO. Now, however, we will turn to the part of the 1st Company which received new tanks in Sennelager.

On 17 January 1945 the understrength company with its six Tigers and other vehicles entrained and was transported to Brilon-Wald, where the train stopped for several days. Fighter-bomber attacks were not long in coming but they inflicted no damage. The train resumed its journey several days later and the company reached Breslau. There it appeared that a request had been made for the unit as reinforcement for Fortress Breslau, for the train sat idle for several days. Afterward, however, the company was sent onward to Hungary. The 2nd Company began entraining in Brüggen, near Cologne, on 24 January 1945; the tanks of the 3rd Company travelled singly to the entraining station in Brühl by way of Euskirchen. The Headquarters and Supply Company assembled in Badorf near Brühl and entrained in Brühl. The two flak platoons of the 4th Company also entrained in Brüggen. The difficult task of loading the Tigers and the numerous vehicles took time and demanded heightened vigilance on the part of the drivers. The entraining took place at night so as not to invite the danger of American air attack. The battalion had no idea where it was being sent; for reasons of secrecy the long transport trains rolled through Central Germany, Saxony, Bohemia and Moravia into the area around Raab in Hungary. The Leibstandarte's transport movements lasted barely three weeks and the deception of the enemy appeared to have been a complete success. The 501st SS Panzer Battalion remained incorporated into the Leibstandarte Panzer Regiment as its IInd Battalion, and Panzergruppe Peiper retained the form with which it had fought in the Ardennes. The platoons detrained in Raab (Györ) and the units drove into their quartering areas on the great sheltering island, the area between the old and new river beds of the Danube. The Leibstandarte was stationed in the area Vének-Enese—railway line to Raab—northern part of Raab. The destination was now known. What situation awaited the Leibstandarte in Hungary?

On 20 August 1944 the Red Army began its offensive from the Jassy area toward Bucharest and from the Tiraspol area in the direction of Bulgaria across the lower course of the Danube between Russe and Varna. Three days later Romania under King Michael I broke with Germany and renounced its alliance with her. All Romanian troops ceased fighting, enabling the Soviets to advance unimpeded toward Bucharest and the Lower Danube. The vital oil region near Ploesti was lost. Hungary, too, broke its word and on 11 October offered the Soviets a ceasefire. Hungary was subsequently declared a war zone by the German Army High Command. Hungary's Reich Administrator Horthy was taken prisoner by one of Skorzeny's special detachments and subsequently withdrew his peace offer to the Soviets. Hungarian troops fought on at the side of the German Wehrmacht, in some cases until the end of the war. In December 1944 the 3rd Ukrainian Front advanced as far as Lake Balaton and occupied the territory between the Danube and the Drais. This move acutely threatened the last oil regions available to Germany. On 24 December the Soviets sur-

rounded the city of Budapest, which was manned by a strong German gar-
rison. The IVth SS Panzer Corps was transferred from the Warsaw area to
Hungary to relieve the city's defenders. Its divisions attacked on 1 January
1945. After promising initial success, high-ranking orders instructed the
corps to cease operations when only twenty kilometers from the city. The
attack appeared to be achieving the desired results and the front-line units
were unable to comprehend the halt order.

OPERATION "SOUTH WIND": THE SMASHING OF THE GRAN
BRIDGEHEAD 17–24 FEBRUARY 1945

The men of the Tiger battalion quickly developed good relationships with
the Hungarian population. With their help the food rations improved considerably. On 1 February 1945 there were twenty-three Tigers operational
with three in repair. The Soviets had been able to establish a bridgehead
west of the Gran in January 1945. On 8 January their spearheads reached
Komorn and Neuhäusel, where they met determined resistance and were
thrown back by the German counterattacks then getting under way. This
prevented a dangerous enlargement of the Gran bridgehead. At the end of
January 1945 the Soviets dug in to defend a front running Karva-Kurt-Bart-
Csata. This bridgehead represented a great threat to the planned German
offensive "Awakening of Spring." If the Soviets advanced south across the
Danube they would drive into the midst of the German buildup. This
potential threat thus had to be eliminated before the start of the German
offensive. Advancing out of the area of Farnad and Für, the Ist SS Panzer
Corps Leibstandarte, the 44th Reichs Grenadier Division Hoch-und
Deutschmeister and the 46th Infantry Division were supposed to break
through between Nem. Szögyen and Bart, cross the Parizsky Canal, advance
toward Nana on both sides of Sárkan (Gywa), and take Parkany.

Movements by the Ist SS Panzer Corps began on 12 February 1945.
The Tiger battalion detrained in Neuhausel. Once again excellent relations were soon established with the local population. The older Hungarians remembered the Austro-Hungarian Empire and told the young
soldiers of that time. The hospitable Hungarians gave the German troops
an extremely warm welcome and the food was outstanding. The Hungarians suspected what lay in store for them if the Soviets should come. On
14 February SS-Untersturmführer Thomas Amselgruber, a platoon leader
in the 501st SS Panzer Battalion's 3rd Company, was awarded the German
Cross in Gold.

Amselgruber had proved an exceptionally brave and willing platoon
and company commander while serving with the assault gun battalion and
the Tiger battalion on the Eastern and Western Fronts. Despite the loss of

four fingers of his left hand in July 1943, the thirty-nine-year-old Bavarian was one of the battalion's veteran officers.

A period of warm weather caused streams to overflow their banks and the roads to deteriorate. On 15 February SS-Brigadeführer and Generalmajor der Waffen-SS Otto Kumm assumed command of the 1st SS Panzer Division Leibstandarte SS Adolf Hitler. Kumm had made a name for himself as commander of the SS Regiment Der Führer in the Das Reich Division and had been decorated with the Knight's Cross and the Knight's Cross with Oak Leaves. He later led the Prinz Eugen Mountain Division in the endless struggle against the Tito partisans in Yugoslavia. In recognition of his efforts there Kumm was awarded the Knight's Cross with Oak Leaves and Swords on 16 March 1945.

The Leibstandarte Panzer Regiment had on strength nineteen operational Tigers and twenty-five Panthers and Panzer IVs. On 10 February thirteen Tiger IIs were delivered to the 501st SS Panzer Battalion. The Wirbelwind anti-aircraft platoon was located near Berecz-Puszta. The attack on the Gran bridgehead began on 17 February 1945. The Tigers crawled forward through the bottomless morass and moved into battle southeast of Farnad, behind the 46th Infantry Division.

SS-Obersturmführer Reiser, platoon commander in the 1st SS Panzer Regiment's 1st (Panther) Company, recalled the first day of the attack: "At dawn it was our time too, and we followed the army infantry division as it set out to break through the Soviet main line of resistance. Road and ground conditions were poor; farm fields and meadows were under water and the panzers leaving the assembly area plowed their way through deep, heavy ground. The 1st Company took the point and subsequently the right wing, providing flanking cover to our attack lane. We were still driving on the road and progress was rapid. Then we drove through the former main line of resistance and halted in a gully. Meanwhile mortar fire had begun but the impacts lay far behind us. The advance resumed after a brief conference on the situation (Peiper-Poetschke-Diefenthal). The battalion formed up to attack. We set off deeply echeloned in inverted wedge formation left of the road leading to Nem. Seldin. Driving with my platoon on the right wing—and somewhat behind—I assumed the flanking cover role. Anti-tank guns opened up from Nem. Seldin; however, as we were supposed to bypass the town, we picked up speed (deep plowed fields!) and escaped the enemy fire by taking advantage of the undulating terrain. We halted behind a hill which lay in front of us and made preparations to attack. There we came under heavy fire from mortars and Stalin Organs. The Ivans must had noticed us gathering in this reverse slope position. As soon as the armored troop carriers of the IIIrd (Armored) Battalion, 2nd

Panzer-Grenadier Regiment and the panzer-grenadiers of the 1st Regiment arrived, the battle group launched the decisive attack on the day's objective, the Parizsky Canal.

Led by the Panthers and Tigers, which were followed by the Panzer IVs and the armored troop carriers, we rolled over the hill and immediately answered the massive fire of the enemy anti-tank guns. Through the combination of our concentric fire and fast-moving attack, we were able to smash the anti-tank barrier and drive the Red Army forces from their positions. The Ivans fled before the force of our attack. Our spearheads reached the canal near Gywa at dusk, however the bridge had been blown!"

SS-Rottenführer Kyriss of the 1st SS Panzer Regiment's 7th Company wrote of this classic panzer attack against the anti-tank position southeast of Nem. Seldin: "Toward noon the armored group prepared to attack in a reverse-slope position. Our task was clear: we had to break through a strong anti-tank front. SS-Standartenführer Peiper took his time; he wanted to play it safe, which later proved the right thing to do. Peiper had five King Tigers drive onto the hill, what a sight! They sat on the crest as on a serving tray and were immediately fired on by the Soviet anti-tank guns. One could clearly see the armor-piercing shells bouncing off the fronts of the Tigers. What a shock that must have been for the Ivans, especially since the Tigers for their part now began picking off the enemy anti-tank guns one after the other. The anti-tank fire lessened, and Peiper immediately gave the order: Panzers forward!' When the battle group drove over the rise en masse there began a fireworks display in the truest sense of the word. Driving at top speed, the tanks and armored troop carriers fired everything they had, and the light trails left by the shells could be seen even better in the failing light; it was an imposing scene. This armored attack, mounted like a cavalry charge, left the Reds only one choice, run away. After overrunning the anti-tank front we halted to regroup. To our surprise the Soviets had taken the greater part of their guns with them under cover of darkness. Kampfgruppe Peiper suffered no losses in this attack."

The infantry group under SS-Obersturmbannführer Max Hansen of the 1st SS Panzer-Grenadier Regiment with attached units of the division established a bridgehead across the Parizsky Canal during the night. The next morning the panzer-grenadiers were able to extend the bridgehead farther south in the face of determined Soviet resistance. Toward midday Panzergruppe Peiper struck out from the bridgehead in a southerly direction. The Tigers destroyed several anti-tank positions and reached Sarkanyfalva. By evening they were northwest of Muszla. Persistent attacks by enemy close-support aircraft had no effect on the Tigers. The neighboring divisions also made good progress that day.

The weather improved on 19 February 1945; sunshine and temperatures as high as six degrees brought road conditions to a bearable state for the armored forces. Soviet close-support aircraft attacked the armored group's assembly area in the morning; this time there were losses among the tanks and wounded personnel. After hearing battle noise from Muszla, the Panthers of the 1st Company, 1st SS Panzer Regiment (SS-Obersturmführer Werner Wolff) attacked Parkany in the direction of the rail station. Tigers and other Panthers followed and joined in the developing tank battle. Three Soviet tanks were destroyed. The tanks were struck by another air attack as they reached the Parkany road and once again there were losses. Tigers and Panthers broke into the northeast section of Parkany at approximately 13.00 hours. The armored troop carriers of SS-Sturmbannführer Diefenthal's IIIrd (Armored) Battalion, 2nd SS Panzer-Grenadier Regiment swung northeast and took Nana.

Other divisions linked up with the Leibstandarte. The enemy in the southern part of the Gran bridgehead between the Parizsky Canal and the Danube had been smashed. The Leibstandarte was deployed in the direction of Kam against the remnants of the bridgehead in the north. While a part of the tanks remained in Parkany to take on fuel and ammunition, the others attacked north during the night of 20 February 1945. The battle group was halted in front of Kam. Darmoty by heavy artillery fire from the east bank of the Gran and nonstop attacks by close-support aircraft. The Hansen group followed up. During the night of 21 February Jochen Peiper's panzers attacked Kam. Darmoty with infantry riding on the tanks, took the village and held it in spite of artillery barrage fire which began in the early morning.

SS-Obersturmführer Reiser of the 1st Company, 1st SS Panzer Regiment furnished a description of this nocturnal attack: "Standartenführer Peiper has decided on a night attack, because by day we are blanketed with massed fire from the enemy artillery positions on the raised east bank of the Gran. The 1st Company has only five operational Panthers left for the action. My tank crew today is quite unusual, for SS-Hauptscharführer Pidun—whose tank is unserviceable—absolutely insists on going along, while no one is willing to step down, so we set out with six men! At high speed we cross the gently-sloping terrain directly below the chain of hills which run west of the road and railway line to Kam. Darmoty. The enemy artillery only lays down harassing fire. Abeam the village we swing east, in order to enter frontally, and now massive Soviet artillery fire begins. A curtain of iron and fire falls before us. Flares and tracing ammunition lights up the night and show us the way to the enemy positions. We hope to drive through this creeping barrage in a rapid advance, and it's 'full steam ahead' into the destructive fire. We clatter over the railway line, then a bang and a flash—they got us! I don't know whether we've been hit by an enemy tank or by an artillery or anti-tank shell. We catch fire immediately. There's no need for the order to get out, however the turret has to be moved first as the gun is blocking the driver's hatch. Finally it is done. My gunner follows me as the last one out of the turret. We land in one of Ivan's trenches; they are just as surprised as we. Armed with nothing but pistols and bare fists we defend ourselves in hand-to-hand combat in the well-built trench system. Under 'cover of the burning tank' and of the exploding ammunition we finish the Soviets."

The Soviet artillery fire and air attacks continued unabated on 22 February 1945. Peiper advanced further north and occupied the fork in the road between Kam. Darmoty and Kemend. The Leibstandarte attacked Kemend from the south on 24 February and ran into a prepared position dominated by an anti-tank barrier consisting of thirty-seven guns. Attacking rapidly, for the greatest danger lay in halting, the Tigers destroyed several anti-tank guns, overran the rest, broke through the anti-tank barrier and reached Kemend. The latter was the scene of house-to-house fighting which raged on into the late afternoon.

The King Tigers were finally able to bring their great firepower to bear against enemy tanks in the battles against the Soviet Gran bridgehead. Exploiting their long-ranging guns, the Tigers destroyed enemy tanks at great range. In contrast to the Ardennes offensive, in Hungary the tanks had sufficient room to operate; employing concentric attacks, accompanied by panzer-grenadiers in armored troop carriers, they were able to drive into the enemy rapidly and gain ground. Nevertheless, a number of Tigers did break down with mechanical trouble on account of the catastrophic road conditions, which were characterized by endless mud.

In addition to its other losses, the Tiger battalion lost SS-Obersturmführer Helmut Dollinger, the commander of the 2nd Company's 1st Platoon. His radio operator, SS-Rottenführer Hubert Heil, recalls: "Our tank got bogged down in a swampy cornfield and was knocked out by a heavy Soviet assault gun. We were able to leave the Tiger by way of the emergency escape hatch. My Obersturmführer Dollinger was with us and we had to work our way back through slush and a hail of shells until we found shelter in the foxholes of our infantry. Enemy anti-tank guns fired at us as like we were rabbits. Dollinger went forward again and in doing so lost his life. The next day the Ivans were beaten back again and we could recover our tank."

The Wirbelwind and Ostwind anti-aircraft tanks, with their quadruple 20 mm and single 37 mm cannon respectively, accompanied the attacks by the Tiger battalion. With their great firepower and maneuverability they provided outstanding support. The flakpanzers also did good work in overcoming the in-depth enemy field positions, taking out anti-tank gun positions, machine-gun nests and mortar sites and pinning down the Soviet infantry. One Wirbelwind was knocked out during the fighting in the Gran bridgehead. SS-Unterscharführer Werner Müller, the commander of the flakpanzer, was badly wounded. Finally a report by SS-Untersturmführer Borchers, platoon commander in the 9th (Pioneer) Company, 1st SS Panzer Regiment: "It was an attack like in our best days. King Tigers, Panthers, armored troop carriers rolled irresistibly toward the positions at high speed. The leading vehicles ran into mines. Under fire from both sides, we cleared the mines and the advance continued. Szögien, Bator-Keszi, Köbelkut, Muszla and other towns were taken. The local population cheered us. They had been forced to suffer greatly under the Soviet occupation troops. They raped women of all ages. They were dragged into the Soviet trenches. We stopped in Ujemet-Szögien and assumed an all-round defensive position."

The capture of Kemend and Bina brought Operation "South Wind" to a successful conclusion; the Soviet Gran bridgehead had been completely destroyed. Nevertheless, it cannot be overlooked that this straightening of the front represented no more than a local success by Army Group South. The enemy had become aware of the presence of the Ist SS Panzer Corps and thus the Sixth SS Panzer Army. Following the first surprise over the appearance of this foe, it was clear to the enemy that a further advance by the Sixth SS Panzer Army could be expected after the conclusion of the fighting at the Gran.

When the Ist SS Panzer Corps was subsequently moved into the area south of the Danube, the Soviet command was able to turn its attention to a planned German offensive from the Stuhlweißenburg area. The Soviets used the time remaining to fortify the expected attack zone and bring up reserves. The concealment of German troop movements, which had been wrought with such care and which had so far been so successful, was rendered irrelevant.

OPERATION "AWAKENING OF SPRING": THE LAKE BALATON OFFENSIVE, 6–14 MARCH 1945

On 25 February 1945 the Leibstandarte transferred into the area north of Komorn. The division had suffered considerable losses in men and materiel in the recent fighting and these could not be entirely made good. The assigned replacements from the Luftwaffe and the navy represented no increase in fighting strength. A status report submitted by the Sixth Panzer

Army on 1 March 1945 puts the 501st SS Panzer Battalion's strength at 970 men. After receiving replacements the Leibstandarte's total strength was raised to 18,871 men.

The objective of the Lake Balaton offensive, which was worked out during Operation "South Wind," was the recapture of the Drau-Danube nook, in order to secure the oil region near Nagy Kamisza and simultaneously win bridgeheads on the Danube as springboards for further operations. The Sixth SS Panzer Army was to attack in a southerly direction between Lake Balaton and the Sárviz Canal and take the high ground at Fünfkirchen. Army Group Balck with the IIIrd Panzer Corps was instructed to advance northeast between Sárviz Canal and Lake Velencze and block the narrows between Lake Velencze and the Danube in the line Adony-Kisvelencze. After infantry forces reached this line, the IIIrd Panzer Corps was to swing south and guard the deep flank of the Sixth SS Panzer Army between Sárviz Canal and the Danube as well as take possession of the crossings over the Danube. Not taken into consideration however were the strong Soviet forces north of Stuhlweißenburg, which might become a threat in the rear of the German offensive.

Shortly before the coming offensive SS-Obersturmbannführer Heinz von Westernhagen, the impression of Soviet bestiality still fresh in his mind, wrote: "It is a difficult time—but I firmly believe that we will do it—for it cannot all have been in vain and the world cannot sink into jewish-bolshevik chaos. It is hard, very hard, and some day when it is all over then we will all probably collapse like empty sausage skins. But we must and will see it through even if we're all hobbling on crutches in the final attack. When one sees and hears how the Ivans ravage it causes shivers to run down one's spine, and hot, unfathomable hate wells up with a desire to destroy this hellish brood. One can never forget that; it is horrible. It is probably the final phase of the war, and the decision is coming. The almighty will grant us the victory for which we have fought so long. We are unspeakably tired and would be grateful for a victorious peace—but there can be no slackening before the victory is ours."

The vehicles of the Leibstandarte began rolling into their assembly area on 1 March 1945. The Tigers were transported by rail via Raab (Györ) to Veszprém. The warm weather submerged the roads and the countryside in melted snow and ice. Tanks, armored troop carriers and other vehicles churned laboriously through the mud. The large-scale troop movements produced traffic jams on the clogged roads, which did not dissipate until dawn on 2 March. Of course this situation did not escape Soviet air reconnaissance. By the evening of 2 March the bulk of the Leibstandarte SS Adolf Hitler had arrived in the area north of Veszprém.

On 3 March 1945 the tank situation was reported as twelve Panzer IVs and nineteen Panthers; SS-Obersturmbannführer von Westernhagen had available four serviceable Tigers. The days until 6 March were spent in preparation for the coming attack; all of the panzer-grenadiers had still not arrived. The Ist SS Panzer Corps, its code name now "Maria Theresia," was still lagging behind and ground its way forward through the mud. With temperatures of five degrees there was sleet, and influenced by the warm weather there was no improvement in road conditions. As a result of the tireless efforts of the Workshop Company the number of serviceable Tigers had risen somewhat; the panzer regiment's strength had also risen, to fourteen Panzer IVs and twenty-six Panthers.

The Leibstandarte's attack began at 04.30 in the morning on 6 March 1945. The armored group set out from Kislány in a southerly direction but after two kilometers it became stuck in the mud west of Hill 149. Progress by the other units was equally slow. The Leibstandarte regrouped during the night; an assault group was formed northeast of Ödon Psz. from tanks and elements of the 1st and 2nd Panzer-Grenadier Regiments. The group attacked on 7 March 1945 and broke through an enemy anti-tank front. West of Káloz the tanks drove through a muddy ravine and reached the town. The enemy fled. The armored group now continued north and attacked Soponya. While elements of the 1st SS Panzer-Grenadier Regiment's IIIrd Battalion attacked the town from the northwest, toward evening the tanks were able to break all resistance, drive into the castle grounds and destroy the enemy after a hard-fought struggle.

On the afternoon of 8 March the Leibstandarte resumed its advance in a southerly direction and together with a battle group of the 2nd SS Panzer Regiment took Nagyhörcsöok psz. The armored group followed and reached the high ground north of the town. On 9 March the armored group and elements of the 2nd Regiment attacked in the direction of Simontornya and, advancing vigorously, reached the hills surrounding János mjr. There the Tigers became involved in a tough fight with a Soviet anti-tank front and were halted by artillery barrage fire from the south bank of the Sió. The armored group was able to continue its advance on Simontornya in the afternoon and went over to the defensive in front of the town. The division's other assault group, which consisted of the 1st SS Panzer-Grenadier Regiment, the 1st SS Anti-tank Battalion and the 1st SS Armored Reconnaissance Battalion, was able to follow by way of Sáregres.

In the muddy terrain the Tigers had more difficulties with final drive breakdowns than with the enemy. On account of the prevailing shortages of chromium and manganese, in 1944/45 German steel had to be tempered with carbon, which caused it to become brittle. As a result the final drives of the Tigers frequently failed in the difficult terrain, but other mechanical problems also led to the breakdown and stranding of tanks. The Tiger proved superior to every Soviet tank in the field. Kills from ranges of two kilometers were commonplace.

The Wirbelwind and Ostwind anti-aircraft tanks of the 4th Company were constantly with the attack spearhead. The Wirbelwind platoon commander, SS-Oberscharführer Kurt Fickert, related: "We drove in open formation behind the Tigers and Panthers to subdue enemy infantry. I was instructed by Peiper to support our infantry in house-to-house fighting. Several Panthers followed us to destroy any enemy tanks that might appear. Two of SS-Obersturmführer Vögler's quadruple flak were also placed under my command. Most of the Tiger IIs were out of action with steering damage on account of the difficult ground. Peiper forbade us to engage enemy aircraft, our infantry were to defend themselves and we were to conserve our ammunition for the ground battle."

The armored spearhead continued to attack on 10 March, however it was forced to fight off repeated Soviet counterattacks. Simontornya was situated in a valley and its defenses had been beefed up by the enemy through the addition of an anti-tank barrier. An unprotected advance to the village across a gently sloping field proved to be impossible. A flanking attack through defiles failed as in each case the point tank was knocked out. Snow and rain again caused the roads to deteriorate. During the night the Ivans reinforced their forces in the Sáregres and Simontornya bridgeheads. There were ten Tigers in action.

On 11 March 1945, a Sunday, the Leibstandarte's attack force stalled in the face of determined Soviet resistance and heavy artillery fire. Close-support aircraft attacked the units in the field. Together with the 26th Regiment detached from the 12th SS Panzer Division Hitlerjugend, the Leibstandarte infantry group successfully stormed the fiercely defended road fork north of Simontornya. Continuing to advance, the grenadiers reached the bank of the Sió between Simontornya and Ozora. From this first bridgehead to be established, Army Group South intended to advance with all available armored forces on the Danube bridges at Dünaföldvar and Dunapentele. On 12 March Leibstandarte infantry elements attacked Simontornya, while Panzergruppe Peiper set out across the high ground north of the town toward the Sió Canal. Advancing rapidly, they were able to break into the west end of the town. No quarter was offered by either side.

SS-Untersturmführer Borchers of the 1st SS Panzer Regiment's 9th (Pioneer) Company recalled: "The Ivans attacked repeatedly with tanks and aircraft. Anti-tank guns fired on us from the flank. We were hit by a Soviet assault gun as we emerged from a defile just short of Simontornya. We got away with our skins intact. The division commander, SS-Brigade-führer Kumm, who was driving several hundred meters behind us, immediately summoned two Panthers by radio which were supposed to destroy the Ivan. Then we were in Simontornya. Here too the Ivans fled. Our infantry went into position.

The enemy had blown the bridge over the Sió. Our pioneers tried to throw up a new one in spite of enemy artillery and mortar fire. We were now taking fire from the right flank. The terrain rose beyond the Sió and there the Ivans were driving their troops away in American trucks. Unfortunately we couldn't interfere. We fell back with the panzers in order to take on ammunition and fuel. The Soviet close-support aircraft were constantly overhead and gave us no rest!"

On 13 March the weather improved; with temperatures of six degrees above zero the roads began to dry out. The struggle to enlarge the bridgeheads went on. Pioneers began constructing a bridge over the Sió Canal. The pioneers' hard work was constantly threatened by artillery fire and air attacks. Nevertheless, by evening the bridge was finished. SS-Oberscharführer Fickert and his flak platoon had been in Simontornya since 11 March: "We were forced to halt at a bridge and clear the road for some Panthers. Then we came under heavy anti-tank fire from the vineyards. The commander of one of the quadruple anti-aircraft guns under my command, an Unterscharführer, was seriously wounded, and as well a Rottenführer was killed. My Unterscharführer Gottlob Braun was also wounded."

On 14 March 1945 the thermometer climbed to thirteen degrees; the sun dried out the terrain further resulting in improved conditions for the armored vehicles. The enemy attacked constantly with air support. In the afternoon a German attack reached Hill 115, two kilometers southeast of Simontornya, further extending the bridgehead. Additional enemy reinforcements were detected opposite IVth SS Panzer Corps's front in the Stuhlweißenburg-Zámoly area. Meanwhile the proportions of a large-scale offensive by the Soviets in the rear of the German front had become abundantly clear to Army Group South. In view of the stalemate at the Sió Canal, a decision had to be made whether to immediately call off the offensive and set out against the impending Soviet offensive with all available forces, in order to possibly resume the attack at the Sió Canal after regrouping. In the face of this serious threat, orders were issued for the removal of the Ist SS Panzer Corps from the Sixth SS Panzer Army in spite of Hitler's refusal to authorize such a move.

TRANSFER NORTH AND BATTLES AGAINST THE SOVIET OFFENSIVE NEAR VESZPRÉM, 15–26 MARCH 1945

On 15 March 1945 the Tiger battalion and the entire panzer regiment were pulled out of Simontornya and transferred into the Deg area. There were eight Tigers in action, twenty-four were under repair. SS-Oberstgruppenführer Sepp Dietrich asked Army Group South to withdraw his Sixth Panzer Army in order to prevent the divisions fighting between Lake Balaton and Lake Velencze from possibly being cut off. During the night orders were sent to the Sixth Panzer Army to make preparations for the imminent withdrawal from the front of the Leibstandarte and Hitlerjugend Divisions by lengthening the fronts of the Ist Cavalry Corps and the 23rd Panzer Division.

On 16 March 1945, a warm late-winter day, the Soviet offensive broke loose between Lake Velencze and Bicske. The Soviet attack spearheads made little headway against the 3rd SS Panzer Division Totenkopf, which bore the brunt of the assault. However the Hungarian 2nd Armored and 1st Cavalry Divisions were unable to hold everywhere and the Soviets neared Komorn. A gap appeared between the 3rd SS Panzer Division and the 2nd Hungarian Panzer Division; Armee Balck had been split. This alarming news caused Generaloberst Guderian to propose sending the Ist SS Panzer Corps north immediately.

The move north by the Tiger battalion with nine serviceable tanks and by Panzergruppe Peiper began on 18 March 1945. The designated target area east of Inóta was reached toward midday over clogged roads. At that point the Leibstandarte put its combat strength at: 140 officers, 666 NCOs and 3,408 enlisted men. SS-Obersturmbannführer Peiper set up his command post in Inóta. The enemy situation was completely uncertain. Inóta first had to be cleared by the armored troop carrier battalion; fighting in the town was fierce and casualties were heavy. The arriving panzers took up covering positions during the night.

On 20 March 1945, a sunny spring day, the Soviet 4th Army and the 6th Guards Tank Army attacked the Leibstandarte in its line of security east of Inóta-Bakonykuti. Panzergruppe Peiper attacked toward the hills northeast of Inóta in the morning but soon became bogged down in the face of enemy defensive fire. The Soviets now took the offensive and in heavy fighting forced the panzers back toward Inóta. SS-Oberscharführer Fickert was sent toward the line of hills near Várpalota with four anti-aircraft tanks, two Wirbelwind and two Ostwind, to cover the withdrawal by the grenadiers against pursuing enemy elements. Hungarian units went over to the Soviets. The situation became confused.

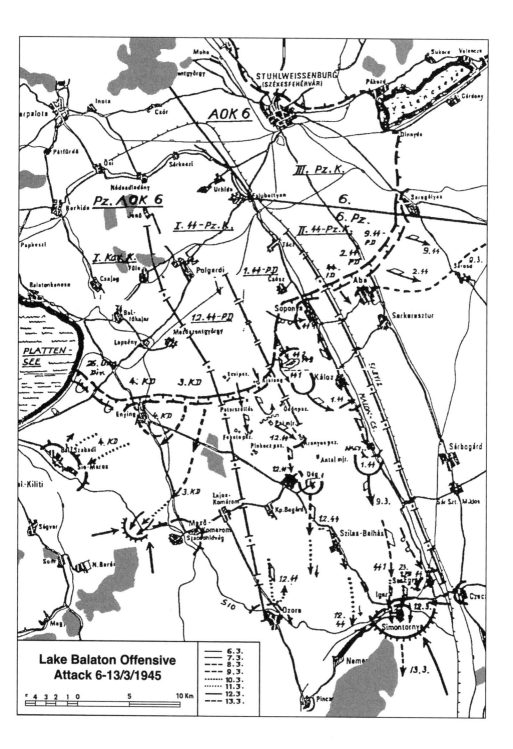

Lake Balaton Offensive
Attack 6-13/3/1945

———	6.3.
———	7.3.
———	8.3.
– – –	9.3.
·········	10.3.
··········	11.3.
– · – · –	12.3.
– – – –	13.3.

4 3 2 1 0   5   10 Km

The commander of the Leibstandarte, SS-Brigadeführer Kumm, who was in his command post west of Inóta, about 100 meters north of the Inóta-Várpalota road, recalled the part played in this action by a Tiger: "The commander of the rocket battalion, Hauptsturmführer Menzel, who had gone into position with his battalion west of the division command post, reported enemy tanks behind his position driving north-south in the direction of the Stuhlweißenburg-Várpalota road. I summoned the last Tiger from the front and briefed its commander. The Tiger drove down the road in the direction of Várpalota, came upon the tanks crossing the road and destroyed fifteen. I pulled a battalion battle group under the command of Standartenführer Hansen out of the front line and with it combed the wood south of the road-another fifteen enemy tanks were destroyed. Meanwhile the enemy attacked the main line of resistance from the east with tanks, infantry and strong artillery support. By evening the front had to be pulled back toward the east end of Várpalota."

Panzergruppe Peiper was attacked by strong infantry forces supported by approximately forty tanks. Bitter fighting raged on both sides of the Stuhlweißenburg-Onóta road and north of the railway line near Réti psz. Close-support aircraft attacked the tanks and bombed Inóta. Réti psz fell. Soviet infantry infiltrated through the very thinly manned defense line at dusk and threatened the panzer regiment's command post in Inóta. Two Tigers under SS-Obersturmführer Wessel of the 1st Company, 501st SS Panzer Battalion fought alongside the Panzer IVs of the 6th (now renamed the 3rd) Company, 1st SS Panzer Regiment under SS-Obersturmführer Sternebeck:

"3rd Panzer Company (six Panzer IVs) and two King Tigers (Obersturmführer Wessel) were instructed to establish a defensive position east of Inóta and prevent the enemy from advancing down the Stuhlweißenburg-Várpalota-Veszprém road. We were at first able to delay and temporarily halt the advance on both sides of the road. In the late afternoon we realized that we were being outflanked—north of the road, on the south face of the Bakony Mountains, by strong armored forces, and in the south, along a ravine, by infantry forces. We were tied down frontally; there was no radio contact with the battalion or the regiment and withdrawing without orders was out of the question. After dark we saw fires in Inóta and heard the sound of battle. In the late evening our artillery and rocket batteries fired into the town. Now it was clear: Inóta had been occupied by the enemy."

On this day of sustained fighting the serviceable Tigers and the armored vehicles of the 4th Company were in action almost nonstop resisting the masses of Soviet tanks and repeated charges by waves of infantry. A number of enemy tanks were destroyed, nevertheless the enemy continued to attack, oblivious to the heavy losses taken by his infantry. SS-Obersturmbannführer von Westernhagen received a surprise order to leave his Tiger battalion and join the officer reserve. With a heavy heart he was forced to hand over the battalion to SS-Sturmbannführer Heinz Kling. There was bitterness and disbelief in the battalion staff over this decision. The first commander of the Tiger company was back at the front, but what was left of the battalion!

After handing over the battalion Heinz von Westernhagen drove to the command post of the Ist SS Panzer Corps to give notice of his departure. His Schwimmwagen, which was being driven by SS-Rottenführer Haupt, reached the farmhouse in which the command post was situated. SS-Obersturmbannführer von Westernhagen got out and had almost reached the house when a small bomb fell right in front of him. A fragment pierced the scar of his old head wound and killed him instantly. Soon afterward an eye witness, who was good friends with von Westernhagen, wrote to his wife, who at that time was in the advanced stages of pregnancy: "I have often experienced the death of comrades, but never so suddenly and unexpectedly as with my dear Heinz. We were expecting him at the division command post in a farmhouse by the road. He drove up. I knew that it must be Heinz and went to the door.

At that instant a small bomb from a lone Soviet aircraft fell near the house. When I stepped outside my Heinz lay on the doorstep, fatally hit; hit so suddenly that he couldn't have felt a thing." The fatal bomb was dropped by a Soviet Po-2 observation aircraft; the German troops called these obsolete biplanes "sewing machines." Why von Westernhagen failed to see or hear the aircraft and take cover is unknown. A possible explanation is the Soviet tactic of throttling back the engine and approaching the target in a near silent glide. At any rate, with the engine of the Schwimmwagen running the approaching enemy aircraft would have been all but inaudible. SS-Brigadeführer Kumm, who witnessed von Westernhagen's unfortunate death, wrote: "Unfortunately I scarcely knew our comrade Heinz von Westernhagen—I am sorry that he was on his way to see me when it happened. He wasn't just on his way to the corps command post, but already at the front door, when the aerial bomb struck—he was killed instantly. Sepp Dietrich, Hermann Prieß, Jochen Peiper and I were all present."

The officers present were shaken by the tragic incident. There was nothing left for SS-Rottenführer Haupt to do but lay his dead commanding officer in the back seat of his car and take him back to the battalion command post. News of the commander's death caused great dismay in the battalion. Heinz von Westernhagen had been much loved and respected by his men. The burial took place soon afterward at Veszprém cemetery. The panzer regiment formed an honor guard commanded by SS-Oberscharführer Siptrott, a member of the 7th Company and a wearer of the German Cross in Gold. A number of members of the 501st SS Panzer Battalion and the panzer regiment gathered at the grave.

An officer spoke the eulogy and, accompanied by the cracking salvoes of the honor salute, and with an eerie background of the distant thunder of guns, the coffin was lowered into the ground. The men remained silent during this final salute to their fallen commanding officer. Many battle-tested soldiers of the Tiger battalion had tears in their eyes. Heinz von Westernhagen was one of their own and now they had to leave him in foreign soil in the midst of the heaviest fighting. The old song of allegiance, which they sang in farewell to their respected CO, made a powerful impression.

In the evening, the Tigers under SS-Obersturmführer Wessel were isolated with Sternebeck's tanks at the outskirts of Inóta, out of contact with Panzergruppe Peiper. SS-Obersturmführer Sternebeck related: "Before midnight of the 21st of March we decided to break out through Inóta. Order: one King Tiger, then six Panzer IVs and bringing up the rear a King Tiger. Taking advantage of the darkness and another barrage we reached the east end of the village. First mistaken by the Soviets as their own troops, but then recognized as the enemy, we were saved by the darkness and the crooked street.

We raced through the village at full throttle. Almost at the west end of the village our 'point Tiger' had to knock out several T-34s so that we could leave Inóta notwithstanding. Things almost took a tragic turn when we reached Várpalota, where we encountered the rest of the regiment. Our elements in Várpalota assumed the enemy from an easterly direction, not us. Only our signal flares saved us from being fired on by comrades. Poetschke confirmed to me during the night that they had given up on the rest of the 3rd Panzer Company and the two King Tigers, after there was no more radio contact and Inóta had been taken by the enemy. Once again luck was on our side at the last second."

Heavy fighting raged in Várpalota on 21 March 1945. SS-Untersturmführer Borchers of the 9th (Pioneer) Company, 1st SS Panzer Regiment wrote in his diary: "I received orders from Standartenführer Peiper to reconnoiter north of the highway to the east in my car. Just beyond Várpalota I was fired on by tanks from the southeast. I drove through a Luftwaffe flak position. They hadn't seen anything yet, so I continued on. After about a thousand meters I was fired on from behind. Our flak was firing at me. A signal flare sufficed. But then there was Ivan with his tanks, about twenty.

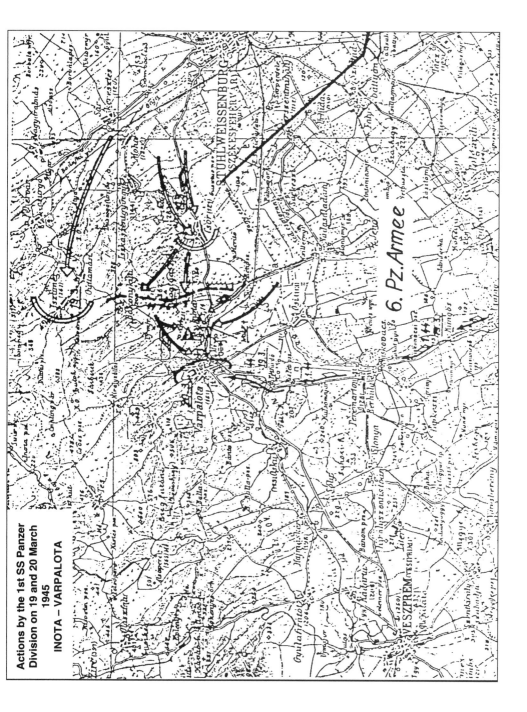

Actions by the 1st SS Panzer
Division on 19 and 20 March
1945

INOTA – VARPALOTA

SS-Hauptsturmführer Malkomes, a wearer of the Knight's Cross, followed me. Thirteen T-34s were knocked out; he himself was shot in the head and killed. We had to fall back again. The enemy broke through with tanks again south of the highway. My other eye has now become inflamed, I can scarcely still see."

Borchers had already been hit in the face and one eye by splinters on the previous day. SS-Untersturmführer Walter Brauer, commander of the Tiger battalion's pioneer platoon, took over Borcher's armored troop carrier. Most of his own troop carriers had been put out of action in the recent fighting as had those of the reconnaissance platoon. The enemy's advance was stopped in the industrial area of Várpalota through the destruction of three of his tanks. The Ivans were finally halted in the southern part of the city after tank-versus-tank fighting; seven Soviet tanks were destroyed for the loss of three German. To the southwest of Várpalota, in Hajmáskér, the enemy broke through toward the highway. SS-Hauptsturmführer Birnschein and several Tigers of his 3rd Company waged a defensive battle there against a far-superior enemy. SS-Untersturmführer Heubeck of the 1st SS Panzer Regiment's 1st Company was sent to Birnschein's aid with two Panthers. Birnschein transmitted the following report by radio: "Enemy tank column driving down the parallel-running Öskü-Hajmáskér road in the direction of Veszprém—am engaging."

The Tigers and Panthers destroyed seventeen Soviet tanks in the ensuing engagement, and the Soviets were prevented from breaking through to the highway. Vérpalota had to be abandoned after extremely fierce house-to-house and close-quarters fighting. The few panzers assumed covering positions in the area of the railway line northwest of Petfürdo-Öskü during the night. The fierce Soviet attacks made a concentrated counterattack by the Ist SS Panzer Corps impossible. Every unit was engaged in desperate defensive fighting. The defenders were only just able to halt the onrushing masses of bolshevik infantry, which were effectively supported by close-support aircraft. Casualties were heavy. The losses suffered by the Leibstandarte were irreplaceable. The panzer-grenadiers clung to the Tigers and other tanks during the defensive battles, for by counterattacking the panzers often forced the waves of Soviet tanks to halt and enabled the infantry to fall back to a new position. The achievements of the tank crews were admirable. Steadfast and unperturbed, they stood in the heaviest fire and covered the withdrawals of their grenadiers.

On 22 March 1945 tanks and elements of the 1st SS Panzer-Grenadier Regiment barricaded the Várpalota-Veszprém road east of Öskü. Another battle group consisting of elements of the 2nd SS Panzer-Grenadier Regiment, the Ist SS Flak Battalion and the Ist SS Anti-tank Battalion held west of Tés. The force of the attack by the Soviet 6th Guards Tank Army split the two battle groups. The group surrounded near Öskü was able to fight its way out and reach Hajmásker. All the divisions of the Sixth SS Panzer Army fought desperately to avoid the looming threat of encirclement. General Balck, however, denounced the divisions of the Waffen-SS, which were fighting for their lives to the point of self-sacrifice, to Army Group South and mocked their ". . . at times clumsy command, poor system of reporting and lack of discipline behind the front . . .", as General Wöhler, Commander in Chief of Army Group South, related. These malicious aspersions also reached Hitler by way of Guderian.

The 22nd of March found the Leibstandarte fighting in two groups cut off from each other; the group on the left maintained contact with the Hitlerjugend Division. The group on the right, which included the Tigers, was engaged further to the south around Veszprém, which had to be abandoned after bitter fighting against the masses of Soviet tanks and infantry. During a briefing in Veszprém, a group of tank commanders standingaround SS-Sturmbannführer Poetschke was shelled by Soviet artillery. Poetschke and the other commanders were severely wounded, none was capable of continuing his duties. This was another serious blow to the Leibstandarte Panzer Regiment, following as it did the deaths of the veteran commanders of the 1st and 2nd Companies, Werner Wolff and Hans Malkomes, both wearers of the Knight's Cross. Oak Leaves' wearer SS-Sturmbannführer Werner Poetschke died of his injuries on 24 March 1945.

The Leibstandarte withdrew toward Márko. The heavy and costly fighting for Veszprém had further minimized the strength of the division. The regiments and battalions were mere remnants of their former selves. The Sixth SS Panzer Army with its six battered divisions was facing four Soviet armies. In spite of repeated inquiries by the Sixth SS Panzer Army, General Balck refused to release the Leibstandarte's southern group. Nonstop attacks by the Soviets further increased the gap between the two elements of the division on 24 March. The 2nd Company had two serviceable Tigers, commanders were Knight's Cross wearer SS-Standartenjunker Franz Staudegger and SS-Unterscharführer Eduard Stadler. Both destroyed numerous enemy tanks and repeatedly halted Soviet armored spearheads that had broken through. Stadler was decorated with the Iron Cross, First Class by SS-Sturmbannführer Kling and was promoted to SS-Oberscharführer. There was warm spring weather on 25 March; massed enemy forces assaulted the Leibstandarte's positions, for some time little more than a series of strongpoints. SS-Hauptsturmführer Birnschein was caught in an air attack and was wounded in the face and hands by bomb fragments. The southern group was engaged in the line Kislöd-Ajka-Urkút. The following note concerning the Leibstandarte appears in Army Group South's war diary: "Led by the division commander, the battle group of the 1st SS Panzer Division stands with the Sixth Army, already awash in the enemy, like a bridge pier in the raging river."

There was no rest for the battle-weary units of the 1st SS Panzer Division Leibstandarte SS Adolf Hitler in the days that followed. Waves of T 34s with mounted infantry broke through the gaps and tried to encircle and destroy the strongpoints which still held out. Again and again the Tigers sallied forth against the enemy, destroying tanks and assault guns and thereby creating breathing room for the hard-pressed panzer-grenadiers. But the respites were brief, for the enemy soon attacked again and broke through the main line of resistance somewhere else. The Tigers then raced toward the new point of penetration to halt the enemy there.

The panzer-grenadiers and tanks were forced to endure constant air attacks by Soviet close-support aircraft. During a nocturnal raid on Köbeskut psz.—there was a full moon and it was almost light as day—SS-Sturmbannführer Kling was hit in the head by two bomb fragments. It was the eleventh time he had been wounded. The Administrative Officer, SS-Hauptsturmführer Veller, took a fragment in the shin and had to be hospitalized. The Soviet aircraft, one of the so-called "sewing machines," had switched off its engine, consequently the attack was a complete surprise. The bombs caused several Panzerfaust rounds to explode, leading Kling to suppose that the command post was being attacked by Soviet tanks. A young sentry was buried; he was dead by the time he was dug out.

On 26 March 1945 the Leibstandarte fell back toward the Marczal Canal; a 1st SS Panzer-Grenadier Regiment battle group was surrounded and had to fight its way west out of the encirclement. In the previous weeks General Balck had sent a series of falsified and biased reports to the Army High Command concerning the alleged conduct in battle of the Waffen-SS. On 26 March 1945 an application to withdraw the IInd SS Panzer Corps beyond the Marczal Canal led to an explosion in the Führer Headquarters. A bitter Adolf Hitler ordered the SS divisions of the Sixth SS Panzer Army to take down their cuff titles. The 1st General Staff Officer of the Sixth SS Panzer Army, SS-Obersturmbannführer Georg Maier, described the announcement of the order:

"In the early morning hours of 27 March 1945, between 05.00 and 06.00, the duty operations officer of the Ia-Section handed me a priority telex from the Führer Headquarters. Of course after such a long time I cannot recall the precise wording and the exact time it was received. The gist of the contents of the telex was that, on order of the Führer and Supreme Commander of the Armed Forces, all divisions of the Sixth SS

Panzer Army were declared disentitled to the cuff bands they had once been awarded, on account of failure to fulfil their soldierly duties and a lack of bravery, and were therefore to take them off. The telex was signed with: 'signed Heinrich Himmler'. . .

I couldn't believe my eyes. Filled with anger and indignation, I was on the verge of losing my self-control. I was considering waking the Chief of Staff, Generalmajor der Waffen-SS Kraemer, and calling the Commander in Chief's personal adjutant, Sturmbannführer der Waffen-SS Weiser, when the door opened and Sepp Dietrich came in. I made my report, read out the morning situation report and then handed him the disgraceful telex. He looked at me speculatively, probably because my 'state of mind' had not escaped him; but he said nothing and began to read. He turned away slowly and leaned over the map table, on which he supported himself with both hands, so that I could no longer see his face. He was deeply shaken and moved, and he needed quite a long time before he recovered his composure.

Then, after a long pause, still bent over the map table, he said in an unusually soft, almost brittle voice, which rang with the deepest disappointment and bitterness: 'That's our thanks for everything!' Finally he stood up, looked at me with moist eyes, pointed to his cuff title and said tersely, 'It stays on.' He shook his head repeatedly, as if he couldn't believe it all. After a while, now in complete control of himself, he asked me: 'What do you suggest?'

Although I later realized the senselessness of my words, I spontaneously said something like: 'I suggest that we inquire of Führer Headquarters whether the cuff titles should also be removed from the thousands of brave Waffen-SS soldiers who fell between Lake Balaton and the Danube.' Sepp Dietrich looked at me sympathetically, gestured to the telex lying on the map table and ordered: 'You will not pass that telex on to corps; let Kraemer know about it later; we'll talk about it when I get back.' Then he gave me his hand, a rare gesture on his part. I accompanied him outside. Shaking his head, he got into his car and drove off to the front, to his soldiers."

Sepp Dietrich subsequently informed only the commanding general of the corps, who likewise did not pass on the order. By acting in the way that he did, Sepp Dietrich once again proved the extent of his humanity and prevented a loss of trust among the combat troops that could never have been made good. Such an unjustified disciplinary action would have had incalculable consequences for the morale of the sorely-tested divisions. Thus the 501st SS Panzer Battalion also remained unaware of the order. In any case, for reasons of secrecy its personnel had removed their cuff titles prior to entraining for Hungary.

THE SOVIET BREAKTHROUGH: RETREAT THROUGH WESTERN HUNGARY TO THE REICH DEFENSE POSITION, 27 MARCH–1 APRIL 1945

The Leibstandarte was forced to fall back toward the Raab on 27 March 1945. In some cases the Soviets got there first. Near Niczk several tanks and the remnants of the armored troop carrier battalion battled the pursuing Soviets. SS-Brigadeführer Kumm wrote: "Since this morning the enemy attacked the fiercely-resisting battle groups of the 1st SS Pz.Div. in the line west of Celldömölk-Kenye and in the afternoon threw them back toward the Raab River line. However, in several places the enemy crossed the Raab before the division. The commander of the IIIrd Battalion, 2nd Regiment, SS-Sturmbannführer Diefenthal, was badly wounded during a briefing on the west bank of the Raab by the division commander prior to a counterattack. A defense of the Raab with these weak forces is out of the question—only five or six tanks—little artillery ammunition. The enemy is marching past us everywhere."

On 29 March 1945 the battle groups of the 1st and 2nd SS Panzer-Grenadier Regiments were able to repulse a frontal attack by the enemy near Lócs, north of Bük and Felsösag. In the evening the order came from Führer Headquarters that the units should move into the Reich Defense Position. The Soviets had already set foot on German territory north of Grüns. The nonstop defensive fighting claimed heavy casualties among all the German units. The men were hard put to find the time to give their comrades a simple burial. The hate-filled enemy rolled flat all the graves in the areas they controlled. More frequently it proved impossible to bury the dead at all. This bothered the men a great deal, for it was an unwritten law in the Waffen-SS that the fallen did not remain in no-man's-land.

The 31st of March saw the battle groups of the Leibstandarte engaged in Nikitsch and Sopronkövesd in bitter defensive fighting against masses of enemy infantry strongly supported by tanks. The Soviets had launched an attack on Wiener-Neustadt from Oberpullendorf-Kirchschlag and had reached Erlau. There they were halted by the officer cadet battalion of the Wiener Neustadt Military Academy.

However, the Reich Defense Position had already been breached. The division commander reported: "We passed the Reich Defense Position long after the enemy—here too again much too late—so there was no 'moving into position!' The division withdrew in the direction of Wiener Neustadt. On the airfield, already abandoned by the Luftwaffe, sat a large number of Me 262s, the world's first jet fighter—completely intact! We shot them up with machine-guns to prevent them falling into enemy hands. Also at the airfield was a goods train with gasoline tank cars—at last the last vehicles and tanks were able to fill their tanks again." The Tiger battalion's 2nd Company, which still had three Tigers, reached German soil near Deutschkreuz.

TOWARD THE END: FINAL BATTLES IN THE REICH
1 APRIL–8 MAY 1945

On 1 April 1945 the Leibstandarte's armored group picked up ten new tanks at the freight depot in Wiener Neustadt. From that day on SS-Hauptsturmführer Birnschein formally took over the remnants of the Ist (Mixed) Battalion, 1st SS Panzer Regiment; however, he continued to lead the Tiger battalion's 3rd Company and the few Panthers of the panzer regiment simultaneously.

The Ostwind platoon commander, SS-Oberscharführer Kastelik, an Austrian, had been missing since the withdrawal to his homeland. During the night of 2 April the battle groups of the Leibstandarte withdrew to the west and occupied the mountain entrances to Piestig Valley (Piestigtal). Positions were occupied east of Fischau and Wöllerdorf. Deployed south of Wiener Neustadt, Panzergruppe Peiper fought its way back through the enemy-occupied city and in the afternoon reached the road at the Piestig Valley. The enemy kept up a rapid pursuit. SS-Unterscharführer Ludwig Esser, a tank commander in the 2nd Company, was killed that day near Neudörfl on the Leitha.

On 3 April the armored group, which also included the Tigers, was forced back into Piestigtal. After further fighting, which included local counterattacks, on 5 April 1945 the panzer regiment transferred via Buchriegel and Berndorf to Pottenstein. As soon as it got there it was forced to repulse Soviet attacks from the west and north. There was persistent fighting for Pottenstein and Berndorf in the days that followed. The Soviets repeatedly tried to enter both towns by outflanking the German positions. All enemy attacks were repulsed and some were beaten back by counterattacks. On 9 April 1945 the situation in the Berndorf-Pottenstein area relaxed somewhat for a brief period. The 501st SS Panzer Battalion began preparations for the formation of infantry battle groups. Those crews without tanks, who represented the vast majority of the men, were combined with the train and prepared for employment in the infantry role. The Workshop Company under SS-Hauptsturmführer Klein also formed an infantry battle group, for in any case there was little left for the men to repair. SS-Obersturmführer Vogt formed another battle group from his Headquarters and Supply Company and sixty men assigned from the military police.

Some members of the Tiger battalion were also transferred to the Leibstandarte's panzer regiment, SS-Oberscharführer Fickert and SS-

Standartenoberjunker Hartmann, for example. The 4th Company was particularly affected by this move. SS-Hauptsturmführer Möbius returned many of the men to the battalion. It was the beginning of the end for the 501st SS Panzer Battalion. The Supply Company's fuel transport column underthe command of SS-Unterscharführer Arthur Görtz went missing in the Wiener Neustadt area. The 3rd Company moved to Wilhelmsburg, south of St. Pölten. SS-Standartenoberjunker Waldemar Warnecke, who had fought as an Unterscharführer and tank commander in Normandy, returned to the 3rd Company after attending the military academy in Königsbrück. On 9 April 1945 he led an infantry battle group of the 3rd Company in its first action in Wilhelmsburg.

On 10 April the enemy attacked St. Pölten but was soon brought to a halt. Due to the threat to the Ist SS Panzer Corps' flank from the north, the corps headquarters demanded that the divisions form infantry units from the free men of the heavy weapons and also mobilize the replacement units based in Germany ("Godfather" movement). Using a Panzerfaust, the Senior NCO of the 4th Company, SS-Hauptscharführer Fritz Müller, destroyed three Soviet tanks from an armored attack near St. Pölten. From the remnants of the 1st SS Panzer Regiment, the 501st SS Panzer Battalion and the infantry elements of the Hitlerjugend Division was formed Einsatzgruppe (Task Force) Peiper. SS-Sturmbannführer Heinz Kling combined the remaining Tigers and those crews without tanks into a battle group which bore his name and assembled it in Rotheau, south of Wilhelmsburg. It was Task Force Peiper's mission to protect the Traisen Valley near Wilhelmsburg against Soviet attacks from St. Pölten, and the corps' deep flank in the Gölsen Valley, in the line Hainfeld-Wilhelmsburg, against enemy advances from the north through the Michelbach Valley, and to harass the enemy movements.

Battle Group Kling was assigned the Wilhelmsburg blocking position. Peiper took charge of covering the flank north of the Golsen Valley with several Panthers and an infantry group made up of tank crews on foot, reinforced by men of the supply units and the train. A panzer IV group under SS-Obersturmführer Sternebeck remained in action in the Triesting Valley. After joining the division, on 13 April 1945 the 1st SS Panzer Regiment's IInd (Mixed) Battalion commanded by SS-Sturmbannführer Gühl intervened in the fighting and recaptured Pöllau, but was unable to take Steinhof against fierce Soviet resistance. The battalion had come from Germany without tanks and had then been incorporated as an infantry battle group. The unit completely lacked heavy weapons.

Battle Group Kling was committed against Soviet forces attacking south in the Traisen Valley. The tankless crews and a few Tigers took St. Georgen and drove the Soviets back to the north. On 16 April 1945 all elements of the Peiper group were engaged in the defensive struggle. The Tiger battalion group faced the Soviets storming St. Georgen. Though the men put up determined resistance, the Soviets poured in reinforcements and took St. Georgen before continuing to advance on Wilhelmsburg. There the enemy was stopped after two tanks were destroyed. An armored attack from Ochsenburg against Wilhelmsburg was also repulsed and two tanks were knocked out. In the evening the Red Army attacked from St. Georgen again. They came in regiment strength as far as the northern outskirts of Wilhelmsburg, where hand-to-hand fighting broke out. The men of the Tiger battalion succeeded in gaining the upper hand. The enemy was beaten back with heavy losses.

Kling did not have his entire battle group in action with him; SS-Untersturmführer Brauer of the 4th Company's pioneer platoon fought further east at the Schöpfl. The fighting in the mountains and forests continued unabated on 17 April. Battle Group Kling tried with all available means to hold Wilhelmsburg against the Soviets. Now they were fighting for German soil, German people. They hoped to spare the civilian population the fate of being left at the mercy of the Soviets. Memories from Hungary and the acts of cruelty they had seen committed against wounded comrades and the Hungarian populace by the Red Army were imbedded deep in every man. In the morning the men of the Tiger battalion attacked enemy troops which had infiltrated into the northern part of Wilhelmsburg and drove them out of the city in heavy fighting. Eleven enemy tanks were destroyed. The Soviets attacked again after nightfall. Dense masses of infantry and groups of tanks rolled toward Wilhelmsburg. Battle Group Kling was able to halt the enemy in the ensuing night action, which was fought out at close quarters. Nevertheless, the situation was becoming increasingly difficult.

On 18 April 1945, the Soviets launched a surprise attack from the forest northwest of Wilhelmsburg, drove past Wilhelmsburg to the east and captured Schwarzenbach; the town was subsequently retaken in a counterattack, however. In Wilhelmsburg the soldiers of the Tiger battalion battled the Soviets who had renewed their efforts to take the town. When the Red Army realized that it had run into a brick wall there and their costly attacks gained them nothing, they went around the town and swung south. Their objective was to advance to the main St. Veit-Altenmarkt road, cut off the Ist SS Panzer Corps from its supplies, and bring about the collapse of the corps' main line of resistance which extended east in a wide arc from Buchberg to Hainfeld.

The Tiger battalion's trains assembled in St. Veit. SS-Oberscharführer Kurt Fickert, commander of the battalion's quadruple flak platoon, related:

"During the fighting for Wilhelmsburg I had to give up two flakpanzers (Wirbelwind) to SS-Hauptscharführer Schröter (10th Flak/1st SS Pz.Rgt.) on Peiper's order. During the retreat from Wilhelmsburg a bridge collapsed beneath the Tiger of SS-Standartenjunker Staudegger. I was forced to blow up a flakpanzer. Luckily one had crossed the bridge ahead of Staudegger. The Tiger then proved too heavy for the bridge. With Staudegger, his crew and my men, we made our way to our own lines during the night. We were met by SS-Obersturmführer Vogt, who was also in command of a battle group."

Fickert, Staudegger and their crews rejoined the battalion in Lilienfeld. On 19 April the southward attack by the Soviets on both sides of Wilhelmsburg reached the Rotheau area. Waiting there were elements of Einsatzgruppe Peiper, which were able to beat back the enemy. SS-Standartenoberjunker Warnecke and his group from the 3rd Company saw action in front of Hill 621 near Plambach. On 20 April 1945 the panzer regiment's medical officer, SS-Hauptsturmführer Dr. Knoll, was able to treat the wounded of Battle Group Möbius, who were in Rohrbach on the Gölsen, and evacuate them with a tank. On 20 April Battle Group Warnecke was also on Hill 621. Warnecke was promoted to the rank of SS-Untersturmführer that day, as was the Technical Officer Ordnance, SS-Standartenoberjunker Hubert Hartmann.

On 21 April 1945 Battle Group Kling attacked Eschenau from Rotheau and in a vigorously-executed attack was able to drive the Soviets from the town. SS-Standartenführer Peiper's task force barricaded the Traisen Valley road north of Rotheau. On that day SS-Obersturmführer Oskar Glaeser of the Workshop Company was killed near Türnitz. The fighting continued undiminished on 22 April. The battle groups conducted a fighting withdrawal toward the south. SS-Untersturmführer Warnecke's group held on near Plambach until 23 April. The next day it reached Kleinzell and was immediately forced to intervene against the pursuing Soviets. In those days a former acquaintance from the old 13th Tiger Company turned up at SS-Sturmbannführer Kling's command post: SS-Untersturmführer Rolf Schamp ("My dream was always the German Cross in Gold"). He related: "I reported directly to Kling in some village in April 1945 and he immediately took me on as his operations officer: 'We only have a few tanks.' There wasn't much left to do as operations officer. There was one transaction with Peiper, who welcomed me briefly—on the Kalte Kuchl—and, just before the surrender, notification of the individual command posts on the execution of the disengagement from the enemy, in the course of which I almost landed by mistake in the middle of the Red Army in the dark on my motorcycle-sidecar."

Kling's adjutant, SS-Untersturmführer Kalinowsky, had already been taking part in infantry actions since the previous day. The 20th, 22nd and 27th of April were recognized as combat days for him and others. The remaining days passed in positional warfare and mutual firefights. In spite of the hopeless situation discipline held up everywhere in the Tiger battalion. The men had long since ceased to have any illusions, nevertheless they felt bound by their oath to the flag and with their comrades saw through those difficult weeks. The tank crews also proved themselves as grenadiers in the infantry actions. 2nd Company runner Hans Schmidt was decorated with the Iron Cross, First Class and promoted to the rank of SS-Unterscharführer.

The battalion was spared any manifestations of disintegration. The solidarity that bound them together was too deep-seated. The only suspected cases of desertion involved two Austrians, both members of the 2nd Company, who left together in Hainfeld. Warnecke's group battled the Soviets, who advanced assault-team style, in Kleinzell, Kalte Kuchl and Kirchberg. On 28 April it made its way to St. Anton on the Geßnitz and on 29 April to Neubruck, Scheibbs and Grafenmühl. SS-Rotteqnführer Blumberg, formerly the commander of a Wirbelwind anti-aircraft tank, was wounded near Maria Zell and was subsequently reported missing. On 1 May 1945 the battle group of the Leibstandarte SS Adolf Hitler received news of the death of the Führer. This news matched the mood of the men, which in any case had reached its nadir.

Everyone was lost in his own thoughts in the general depression of those days. The question of what to do now occupied everyone's mind. Eastern Germany was occupied by the Red Army, in places as far as the Elbe, the Americans were on German soil in the west and south. Everyone knew that the end of the war was at hand. Concern for relatives in the homeland, especially those in the east where Stalin's hordes were, was great. The men did not wish to die in those final days. Fear of falling into Soviet hands shortly before the end of the war was oppressive. In those days the very latest development of the Tiger II, the Jagdtiger, joined the battalion. With its 128 mm gun and twenty-millimeter-thick frontal armor, this unusual derivative of the Tiger II was nearly invincible. A total of only seventy vehicles of this type were built.

SS-Sturmmann Ernst Kufner of the 3rd Company served as radio operator in one of the Jagdtigers, which had a crew of six: "In Traisen/Lilienfeld the battle group was loaded into trucks and transported to a new area of action in the mountains of the Kalten Kuchel. At the end of April I was relieved with two tank crews, each of six men. On 1 May we were driven by truck through Amstetten to St. Valentin on the Enns. Our job was to prepare Jagdtigers built in the Hermann-Göring Werken for action. We had to lend a helping hand and install the machine-guns, radios and other components ourselves. Two Jagdtigers were in running order and ready for action on 4 May. In the morning hours of 5 May 1944 we drove to Reichsstraße 8 (Linz-St. Pölten-Vienna). There we received the order: 'Off to meet the Soviets.' By then the Amis had already advanced to within twenty kilometers north of our position."

The 501st SS Panzer Battalion received a total of six Jagdtigers. Decorations were awarded on 6 May 1945. SS-Untersturmführer Walter Hahn of the 2nd Company received the Wound Badge in Gold as well as the Close Combat Clasp in Bronze for infantry actions in which he had taken part. SS-Standartenführer Peiper assembled all the elements of his armored group he could reach and gave the men a brief speech. SS-Untersturmführer Schamp recalled that Peiper warned against the possibility of suicide, reminding the men that Germany needed them alive not dead.

On the morning of 8 May 1945 all units of the Leibstandarte were ordered by radio to move at once into the Steyr area. The surrender was announced. Ernst Kufner recalled: "On 7 May we reached the division command post in Scheibbs. Rumors were going around that the war was to be ended. Negotiations were being held with the Americans, but as it was still unclear whether all members of the division were allowed to cross the demarcation line at the Enns, we were sent ahead with the Jagdtigers and several Panzer IVs in order to force a crossing of the Enns if need be. We stopped in Waidhofen on the Ybbs during the night of 8–9 May.

Now our orders changed: cover the retreat against the Soviets! A stone bridge in Waidhofen was the undoing of a Jagdtiger. It was too narrow. The tank shed a track while backing up. We subsequently blew it up with a Panzerfaust and pulled it away from the bridge with our Jagdtiger. There was great agitation among the fleeing soldiers because we blocked their avenue of retreat for some time. We moved to the exit from Waidhofen, to the road to Weyer-Markt on the Enns. We waited there impatiently until the morning hours of 9 May 1945. Soldiers of every branch of the service streamed past us, including the regimental commander, SS-Standartenführer Peiper. He saluted and wished us all the best. In order to ensure ourselves transportation we seized a civilian truck, one powered by wood gas, with a French driver, and positioned it about 200 meters behind our tank. We planned to use it to drive home.

We stowed our belongings inside. Toward midday the last soldiers and civilians, some on horses, arrived. They were all extremely agitated and told us that behind them Soviet tanks with mounted infantry had already reached Waidhofen. However my tank commander kept his nerve. He had our tankdrive onto the road and the Panzer IVs into the meadow beside us. We blew up all the tanks. A tree-lined stream ran along the other side of the road. This could not be crossed by tanks. We ran to the parked truck and drove off, but our journey ended after only about five-hundred meters. The road was clogged with vehicles. The Soviets got as far as our tanks but no farther. The Ivans fired several shells after us in farewell. We rounded up some army horses running around in a field and headed across the mountains. In the evening hours of 9 May 1945 we—four members of the crew—reached the Enns in Großraming and crossed the stone bridge without seeing an American. The circumspect behavior of my tank commander had spared many soldiers from Soviet captivity. On 15 May we surrendered voluntarily to the Americans near Kirchdorf on the Krems. From there we were transported to Mauerkirchen, where we were reunited with our company comrades. Further stations of captivity were Altheim, Ebensee, Großraming, and Wegscheid near Linz, to name only several."

THE 1ST COMPANY AND THE REMAINING ELEMENTS OF THE BATTALION IN SCHLOSS HOLTE AND THE END OF THE WAR, APRIL–MAY 1945

A remnant of the battalion remained behind in Schloss Holte in December 1944, from then on forming "Support Base Schloß Holte." On 6 January 1945 the 1st Company with the crews and supply elements took charge of six Tiger. Its and transferred to Hungary; two days later the remaining part of the battalion moved from Oerlinghausen to Schloß Holte. The ranking NCO of that part of the 1st Company not sent to Hungary was SS-Unterscharführer Kurt Rath. The remaining men of the 1st Company and personnel of the other companies who had been left behind, which included Knight's Cross wearer SS-Oberscharführer Woll and SS-Standartenjunker Staudegger, among others, formed a training platoon in which gunners and tank commanders were trained. Training was carried out on a single King Tiger, the tank which SS-Unterscharführer Salamon had brought back from France in September 1944, the only 1st Company Tiger to return.

The following tank commanders were in Schloß Holte in February 1945: SS-Untersturmführer Rolf Henniges and Heinz Buchner, SS-Hauptscharführer Benno Poetschlak and Hans Höflinger, SS-Oberscharführer Bobby Woll, Heinz Mengele and Werner Wendt, SS-Standartenjunker Franz Staudegger and SS-Unterscharführer Bobby Warmbrunn. Also there was driver SS-Unterscharführer Franz Elmer. On 3 February 1945 there was a unit party in the Hölle Inn at the railway station in Oerlinghausen and another rag newspaper was put out for the occasion. On

8 February 1945 another officer, SS-Untersturmführer Hahneberg, joined the company. SS-Hauptsturmführer Dr. Rabe, who was actually the battalion medical officer, combined all the battalion personnel in Schloß Holte into a new 1st Company. It was organized into three platoons commanded by SS-Untersturmführer Buchner, Henniges and Hahneberg. Suddenly things began moving very quickly; the company received fourteen new Tiger IIs in Sennelager on 10 February 1945 and once again found itself at full strength. The Tigers entrained in pouring rain in Sennelager on 9 and 10 March and were then sent to Dresden. Due to the maelstrom of fast-happening events and the catastrophic war situation the shipment never reached the battalion in Hungary and was instead sent back to Sennelager. Worst of all, however, the company arrived there without tanks!

In the beginning it was supposed to be assigned to the 506th Army Panzer Battalion in Höhr-Grenzhausen, but then it was found that this only applied to the Tigers. On 30 March 1945 the 506th Panzer Battalion took charge of thirteen Tiger IIs. The 1st Company was once again without tanks. SS- Hauptsturmführer Dr. Rabe, SS-Standartenjunker Staudegger, SS-Hauptscharführer Höflinger, SS-Standartenjunker Fiedler and others made their way to Hungary and there took part in the battalion's final battles. The men were back in Schloß Holte on 12 March; two days later a part moved to Oerlinghausen. The Americans were not far away in the last days of March. On 30 March the men of the battalion gathered in Schloß Holte. Warmbrunn was instructed to guard the town with a tank-killing squad. He and his men, who were armed with Panzerfaust anti-tank weapons, took up position near Senne II in anticipation of the enemy's arrival. On 31 March Warmbrunn alerted the company that the enemy was approaching and withdrew to the Senne-Ebinghausen crossroads. On the morning of 1 April the company was placed on alert, for American tanks had been reported approaching Bielefeld. At first the men couldn't believe the news. Orders were issued for the formation of a combat unit in order to oppose the Americans.

A crew was chosen for the lone Tiger, which was placed under the command of SS-Untersturmführer Rolf Henniges. Others were to escort the tank, some sitting on the tank others following the Tiger on bicycles, many were armed with Panzerfaust weapons. And that's how the 1st Company went into action—Tiger commanders on bicycles. The group neared Senne II. Near the Krack Station, a few meters from the Kaufmann property, a Panzerfaust round struck the turret of the Tiger. The entire crew was killed: SS-Rottenführer Lorenz Mähner, SS-Panzerschützen Walter Moor, Gerhard Kröber and Swietek, and SS-Untersturmführer Rolf Henniges. There was great bitterness among the men over their deaths. Rolf Henniges' wife, who was in the advanced stages of pregnancy, was not told of her husband's tragic death until later.

The fatal shot was fired by a lone army soldier, Walter Barking, who in his nervousness must have mistaken the Tiger for an American tank. Members of the company took Barking to see the dead in front of the Freitag house. Later Barking was to lose his own life. Once the Tiger had been made drivable again SS-Untersturmführer Buchner assumed command and set out with the entire outfit. Five-hundred meters from the fork in the road east of the Elbrecht farm the Tiger was hit by American tanks which were on the autobahn and began to burn. Buchner was the only one to escape the blazing tank. There were several more exchanges of fire with the Americans, during which SS-Oberscharführer Wendt destroyed a US tank with a Panzerfaust. SS-Rottenführer Ewald Pelludat and Emil Layer of the 1st Company, together with SS-Panzerschutzen Heinz van Rossum and Albert Habenicht of the Headquarters Company, were reported missing in action. The company personnel were subsequently taken away in trucks and then travelled by train via Magdeburg to Austria, where they reached the 501st SS Panzer Battalion.

With few exceptions the men of the 501st SS Panzer Battalion were taken prisoner by the Americans and ended up in the large camps in Austria. The CO of the 4th Company, SS-Hauptsturmführer Spitz, managed to escape in Ebensee. Later, after spending time in camps in Altheim, Ebensee, Wegscheid and Heid, the men were taken to Germany. Several were questioned during the Malmedy Trial held in Dachau: SS-Hauptsturmführer Birnschein and SS-Untersturmführer Buchner, but also enlisted men as well. No members of the battalion were included in the proceedings of this political show trial.

Since the Americans released the German prisoners from captivity and sentenced them to internment, they avoided the supervision of the International Red Cross. The last members of the battalion were released in 1948. Some were lucky and were able to make their way home after the war ended, subsequently being interned for a brief period. Those who were handed over to the French had it worse. A typical case involved SS-Rottenführer Kurt Koch, a tank driver of the 1st Company. He was captured near Braunau am Inn on 17 May 1945 and was later taken to Luneville by way of Auerbach, Tuttlingen and Epinal. The guard consisted of French and Polish troops, who beat the prisoners with rifle butts and sticks. Koch languished in the work camp at Luneville, where food and conditions were poor, until 5 May 1946. The worst off were undoubtedly those who fell into the hands of the Soviets. SS-Hauptscharführer Rolf von Westernhagen, the brother of the commanding officer, was kept a prisoner by the Soviets for ten years.

In closing, SS-Rottenführer Siegfried Walther of the 3rd Company: "On 31 December 1944 I had a motorcycle accident in the Eiffel and broke my left leg. From then on I wandered from hospital to hospital, until at the beginning of May 1945 I came to Oeswitz hospital in Vogtland and after some time to Gera. The Russians came after the Americans left. Then I went home again. I arrived there on Friday evening and on Saturday morning the communists took me away. I was taken via Breslau and Moscow to Baku, where for five years I had to toil in Azerbaijan for much hunger and no pay. I was released in the west in January 1950."

Epilogue

This documentation comprises the wartime experiences of the Tiger units of the Leibstandarte SS Adolf Hitler and their sacrificial battles on all fronts. They achieved tremendous success, suffered bitter defeats at the hands of a superior foe and on 8 May 1945 experienced unconditional surrender.

In their ranks lived, commanded and fought the fearless, exemplary and most successful tank commander of the second World War, Michael Wittmann, whose person and outstanding achievements receive their due recognition in this book. The men of then 13th (Heavy) Company, 1st SS Panzer Regiment Leibstandarte SS Adolf Hitler and of the 501st SS Panzer Battalion were volunteers from the first to the last hour of the war. They all fought for the existence of the German Reich and to this cause committed all the strength of their youth, just as naturally as did almost a million of their comrades of the Waffen-SS from almost every European nation.

They were forced to bury their ideals following the collapse of the Reich under a crushing superiority and the end of all their hopes for a favorable outcome to the war. They, the elite of the front, once heroes, were now outcasts. The men of the 501st SS Panzer Battalion did not give up, however. Following their release from captivity and internment they rebuilt their Fatherland—in West and Central Germany—which had been destroyed and partitioned by their "liberators," and in the years that followed they were committed volunteers in their work for their home, for family, people and Fatherland.

Many wounds have healed in the past fifty years, some of them only externally, for many never heal. The solidarity that developed back then in hours of bitter distress and under the greatest danger still exists today. This front-line comradeship is greater and stronger than any distress, than the intervening decades, than any such infamous slander. The men of the 501st SS Panzer Battalion meet once a year. On those days the atmosphere is such as if they had never been separated from each other. The elderly men get along as they did when they were young lads of eighteen to twenty years. This getting along needs no explanation, the survivors know that they can always depend on their comrades. And that marked them for life. There is therefore no need to speak of this unique front-line comradeship, it requires no renewal, it is never lost.

The dead are spoken of at all these reunions, they return and are present, as if they had not been killed on the battlefield. The survivors know that each of them could have fallen in their place and that their survival is no credit to them, but an unfathomable chance. Gratitude to their fallen comrades and their bond with them is an indelible component of the former soldiers, for—Their Honor is Loyalty!

Index

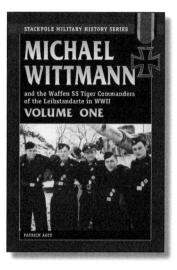

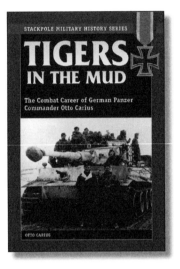

Stackpole Military History Series

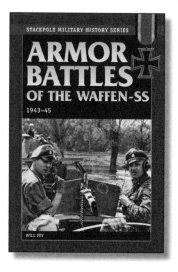

ARMOR BATTLES
OF THE WAFFEN-SS
1943–45

Will Fey, translated by Henri Henschler

The Waffen-SS were considered the elite of the
German armed forces in the Second World War and
were involved in almost continuous combat. From
the sweeping tank battle of Kursk on the Russian
front to the bitter fighting among the hedgerows
of Normandy and the offensive in the Ardennes,
these men and their tanks made history.

$19.95 • Paperback • 6 x 9 • 384 pages
32 photos • 15 drawings • 4 maps

WWW.STACKPOLEBOOKS.COM
1-800-732-3669

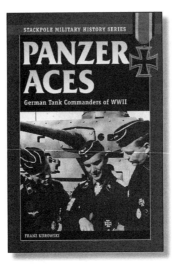

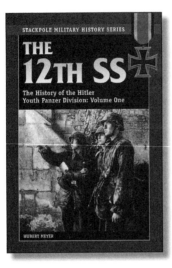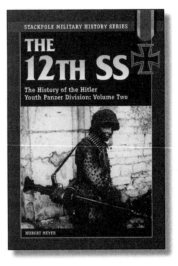

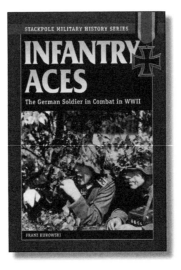

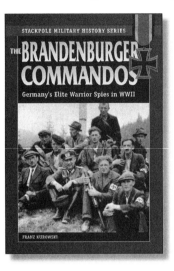

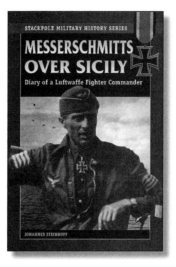